COURAGE

STORIES OF 100 PEOPLE WHO CHANGED THE WORLD

To Morgan

Best wishes for all
that is good in life.
May these stories of Courage
add to your own courage —

Roy Russell

ROY RUSSELL

Plain Sight Publishing
An Imprint of Cedar Fort, Inc.
Springville, Utah

For Pat and Kerwin and Darrin

ISBN 13: 978-1-4621-1909-7

Published by Plain Sight Publishing, an imprint of Cedar Fort, Inc.
2373 W. 700 S., Springville, UT 84663
Distributed by Cedar Fort, Inc., www.cedarfort.com

LIBRARY OF CONGRESS CATALOGING-IN-PUBLICATION DATA

Names: Russell, Roy, 1931- author.
Title: Courage : stories of 100 people who changed the world / Roy Russell.
Description: [Springville, Utah] : Plain Sight Publishing An imprint of Cedar
    Fort, Inc., [2016] | ©2016 | Includes bibliographical references and index.
Identifiers: LCCN 2016009436 (print) | LCCN 2016012263 (ebook) | ISBN
    9781462119097 (perfect bound : alk. paper) | ISBN 9781462126880 (epub,
    pdf, mobi)
Subjects: LCSH: Courage--Biography. | Soldiers--Biography. |
    Heroes--Biography. | Conduct of life.
Classification: LCC BF575.C8 R87 2016 (print) | LCC BF575.C8 (ebook) | DDC
    179/.6--dc23
LC record available at http://lccn.loc.gov/2016009436

Cover design by Kinsey Beckett
Cover design © 2016 by Cedar Fort, Inc.
Edited and typeset by Chelsea Holdaway

Printed in the United States of America

10 9 8 7 6 5 4 3 2 1

Printed on acid-free paper

CONTENTS

CONTENTS

CONTENTS

CONTENTS

PREFACE

Nearly a half century ago, my very good friend Robert B. Fox wrote a book titled *Courage to Live*. It's a priceless little book. I have quoted the complimentary copy that he sent to me countless times over the years. We can probably never have enough books dealing with courage and bravery available to us. With that in mind, I have compiled one hundred stories of courageous people who have inspired and uplifted me.

What is the common thread by which we define courage? We can express it as an attitude of or a response to facing and dealing with anything recognized as difficult, painful, or dangerous, instead of withdrawing. We can define it as a quality of being fearless or brave or having valor or doing what is right in the face of criticism or ridicule. Sometimes, it means living up to one's own beliefs or acting in accordance with those values we have chosen to live by.

Yes, it's doing the right thing when the wrong thing seems the easy way out. It's getting past limited self-wants and achieving a better life for mankind. Courage is doing what you were born to do, regardless of the obstacles and setbacks. For some, it simply means taking that first step. A brave young journalist, Dan Eldon, who was stoned to death in Somalia, probably put it as simply as possible: It's recognizing that the journey is the destination. As John Wayne said, "Courage is being scared to death and saddling up anyway."

One of my favorite writers and philosophers is Ralph Waldo Emerson who said, "Our greatest glory is not in never falling, but in rising up every time we fall."[1]

Yet the emphasis here is primarily with those who faced physical danger and possible death. In fact, some of the courageous people you will meet did sacrifice their lives—and always for others. In my freshman English class in college, we studied Aristotle's *Ethics*. He said that lack of courage—cowardice—is a deficiency. To the one hundred people in this book, cowardice is not a word in their dictionary. They are fearless, intrepid, spirited, brave, valiant, heroic, undaunted, and bold. Certainly, they possess courage as a virtue. They are people who, like Beowulf, are heroic figures who insist on doing the right thing even in the face of certain defeat without promise of reward or even salvation. Courage is often bargaining your life when others will not act. Sometimes, it takes one person to stand up for the whole community—an Erin Brockovich or a Gary Cooper who meets the adversary at *High Noon*.

All of us enjoy freedom—bought by the sacrifice and lives of thousands of soldiers, sailors, marines, and airmen who were willing to defend our country. These men and women were, and are, willing to put their lives on the line for us. Few receive the Medal of Honor, and many more should than do. In the War in Iraq, Michael Murphy—just one of those many—fought off the enemy to save the lives of his fellow soldiers. In doing this, he lost his own.

Courage is at its best when people step up to save others in harm's way. Out of Nazi Germany and the war years came stories of courageous people—of resistance fighters who dared and did. Many of them paid the ultimate price for their bravery. The firefighters entering the Twin Towers only to have the buildings collapse about them is an event we should never forget. The signers of the Declaration of Independence faced possible execution, but they went forward even facing the threat of death. Two older Scouts went back three times on a stormy lake to save their younger friends but in the end lost their lives when the winds swept them away.

I'm a great fan of William Shakespeare. His definition of courage probably says it all: "Cowards die many times before their deaths. The valiant never taste death but once."[2]

You can find the reason for this book on the Internet: dozens of worried citizens lament the decline of stories about heroes and courageous people in our society. Others point out that new generations believe that movie celebrities are heroes. They miss the real heroes who are left in the shadows and those who really personify bravery and valor. I hope that what you read here will give you a renewed picture of courageous people.

If you still believe in valor, integrity, and courage as virtues, you will find the stories here of value to you. If you believe that success and sacrifice are worthy assets to the human soul, you'll find support for your belief.

Much of the inspiration for this book was found in a series of readers for young people. The stories were unique and inspiring. They inspired me to adapt some of their basic story lines, coupled with additional research, for a general audience, especially those who are being denied the kinds of stories that inspired me as a youth. Here a reader can renew his or her kinship with heroes.

From the websites that I visited, I have gleaned basic knowledge, research, and insights that have become invaluable. Nearly all website owners and blog writers were gracious in granting permission to use their material. I certainly must thank them because I have taken liberal advantage of their generosity.

One of my sources involved Cody McCasland, who was born without useable legs but met life and his loss with great courage. I received emails from his mother, Tina, thanking me for including Cody's story in the book. I included eight-year-old Alexandra, who had incurable cancer, because she faced her impending death with resolute courage to the point of being heroic.

Certainly I have a strong feeling for what I have accumulated—it's taken me eight years. Half of that time was devoted to obtaining permissions for copyright sources. Writing for magazines is a little different than writing a book. Careful attention to sources and honoring copyright is a primary concern with a book, and I have agonized over that these past eight years.

How do you thank the dozens who helped? One thing I need to make clear at this point, for those who gave permission to use their material, is that I found many instances where a single piece of work was claimed by various owners—the same piece of writing was copyrighted by different persons. Additionally, some persons claimed copyright to material that is obviously in the public domain, but, to the hundreds who shared so graciously, I cannot thank you enough.

To you readers, have a brave, exciting, heroic, and courageous time.

NOTES

1. *Gems of Literature, Liberty and Patriotism,* arr. Paul DeVere (A. Flanagan Co. 1900), 83.
2. *Julius Caesar* Act 2 Scene 2.

SAVING OLD GLORY

My eleven-year-old son Darrin and I were sitting along third baseline at the Dodgers versus Cubs game in Los Angeles on April 25, 1976. The weather was clear with some light cirrus clouds high overhead. The temperature was about seventy degrees. Playing center field for the Cubs was Rick Monday.

This thirty-year-old native of Batesville, Arkansas—born in 1945, two days before Thanksgiving and two months after the end of WWII—would compile a .264 batting average with 241 home runs and 775 RBIs over the course of his career. The league selected him as All Star in the years 1968 and 1978. He played for the Kansas City/Oakland Athletics, the Chicago Cubs, and the Los Angeles Dodgers. It was while he played for the Cubs in this game against the Dodgers in 1976 that he performed one of two memorable feats in his life.

The Vietnam War had just ended, but people didn't need a war to protest something. Thousands of young people had been protesting the war for years. During the game, a man and a boy ran to the shallow left corner of Dodger field, the older man carrying something under his arm. At first, neither the fans nor Rick could make out what it was. The guy pulled the cloth from under his arm. Rick could see it now. It was an American flag.

The man laid the flag on the ground and pulled a shiny object from his pocket. "Having gone to college, I figured two and two is four," Rick said later of the incident. "They were dousing the flag with lighter fluid." The man lit a match, but the light breeze wafting across the playing field blew it out. He tried a second time. It flared briefly and died. By now Rick was in full stride, running toward them. "To this day, I don't know what I was thinking," Rick said. "I wanted to bowl them over." He did not break stride as he dashed passed, swooped down, and grabbed the flag up in his arms. He trotted off the field toward third baseline and handed the flag off to Dodgers pitcher Doug Rau. His actions moved the crowd to hysteria. Baseball fans are some of the most patriotic people walking. We yelled, screamed, cheered, whistled, stomped our feet, and nearly shook the stadium down. All twenty-six thousand of us broke into spontaneous singing of "God Bless America." The scoreboard lit up with the message: "Rick Monday, you made a great play."

When Rick came to bat, Dodgers fans stood again. We clapped and screamed and stomped our praise for several minutes. It just so happened that America was celebrating its two hundredth year as a nation. Rick's action in saving Old Glory was a catalyst that brought America together again, at a time when we needed it badly. Rick later said, "If you're going to burn the flag, don't do it around me. I've been to too many veterans' hospitals and seen too many broken bodies of guys who tried to save it." It turned out that the protestors were a father and his son.

Rick said, "What those guys [were] doing was wrong. It was wrong then, and it's wrong now." Wherever he played that season, all across the nation, he received a hero's welcome and standing ovations. His moment represents our nation's history, sacrifice, and freedom. So many have lost their lives in battle to save Old Glory. Part of Rick's patriotism is the result of six years served in the Marine Reserves. Later, League officials presented the flag to him. After all these years—and after many offers to buy it—he still displays it.

Rick's actions had incredible meaning for the twenty-six thousand who watched. Quite simply, he changed lives. Americans owe much to the men who sacrificed for our freedom—to the patriots throughout history, to those who put their lives on the line and often sacrifice them for flag and country. On this balmy Sunday, Rick Monday became a hero and a patriot much like them.

NOTES

1. "Bicentennial Rick, Old Glory, And Dodger Stadium," *Captain's Quarters*, http://captainsquartersblog.com/mt/archives/004815.php. (Ed Morrissey.)

2. "Monday's act heroic after 30 years," Ben Platt, *MLB*, last modified April 25, 2006, http://m.mlb.com/news/article/1415977.

3. "Rick Monday celebrates flag-saving moment 40 years ago in Dodger Stadium outfield," Bill Shaikin, *Los Angeles Times*, last modified April 25, 2016, http://www.latimes.com/sports/dodgers/la-sp-dodgers-report-20160426-story.html.

ANGEL OF MERCY

An angel of mercy appeared on the frozen slopes of Marye's Heights on December 14, 1862, more than a year into the Civil War. Union general Ambrose Burnside had ordered five unsuccessful assaults against the Confederate forces, which were protected by a stone wall at the top of the Heights. Burnside's objective was unknown; the Heights were of no military value. His orders stated, "Push a column of a division or more along the Plank and Telegraph roads, with a view to seizing the Heights in the rear of the town." The Union soldiers were ground down by Confederate fire like grain in a gristmill.

The town was Fredericksburg, Virginia. The five assaults had resulted in deaths and wounded of more than eight thousand Union soldiers. A freezing wind cut across the battlefield, turning the damp air to ice crystals. Earlier, Union general Edwin Summer's soldiers had attached their bayonets and, with a Yankee war cry, charged up the hill. In the same time that it takes to breathe, the Confederate artillery and rifle fire rained death down on the struggling troops. All were mowed down like wheat before the harvest scythe.

With the odds against them, the Union troops kept charging from the protection of a canal ditch. The slope was open: no place to take cover. Each wave of Union soldiers was cut down as the men tried to advance. All attempts to breach the Confederate line behind the stone wall failed. Not one Union soldier made it over the wall that day.

Night came on, leaving the slope littered with thousands of dead and dying. Under the protection of darkness, the Union soldiers ventured out to gather as many of their wounded as they could find. Darkness could not cover the suffering—ghostly, unearthly, terrible-to-hear sounds. The cries and moans and shrieks of the wounded filled the freezing night air. The cold winter wind drove the temperature to zero.

Dawn came. With it came more cries from the dying. As their lives drained from their bodies, they cried out in thirst: "Water! Water!" No one from either side dared venture onto the no-man's-land. They knew as surely as death that they would be a target for enemy fire. Yet the slope between the Confederates and the Unions was bridged with the dead and dying. Their cries became unbearable for nineteen-year-old Richard Kirkland, sergeant in the Confederate Second South Carolina Volunteer Infantry.

With an expression of pain and remorse, he approached his commanding officer. "General, I can't stand this anymore." He waited for the general to reply. "What is it, Sergeant?"

Richard said, "All night and all day I have heard the cries for water from those poor people, and I can't stand it no longer. I come to ask permission to go and give them water."

The general regarded Kirkland for a moment with feelings of profound admiration and said, "Kirkland, don't you know that you might get a bullet through your head the moment you step over the wall?" He replied, "Yes sir, I know that, but if you will let me, I am willing to try."

General Kershaw hesitated, then said, "Kirkland, I ought not to allow you to run the risk, but the sentiment which actuates you is so noble that I will not refuse your request, trusting that God will protect you." He put a nervous hand to his brow.

The sergeant's eyes lit up with pleasure. He said, "Thank you, sir," and ran rapidly downstairs. The general had set up a command post in an abandoned house at the top of the Heights. He heard the sergeant pause for a moment, then come bounding back up, two steps at a time. He thought, *The sergeant's heart has failed him—he has changed his mind.* He was mistaken. Richard was breathless and excited as he appeared, but he abruptly stopped at the door and asked, "General, can I show a white handkerchief?" General Kershaw slowly shook his head and said, "No Kirkland, you can't do that."

The sergeant responded as cheerfully as the prince he was, "All right, I'll take my chances." He turned and bounded back down the stairs, a broad grin on his handsome face.

With profound regret, the general watched Kirkland gather canteens from as many of his fellow soldiers as he could carry. Once he'd filled the canteens with fresh water, Kirkland leaped over the stone wall as light as a gazelle and ran to the nearest wounded man.

The Union soldiers, thinking he was there to loot and rob the Union dead, opened fire. Their bullets crashed into the very ground on which Kirkland stood. Gently, he lifted the man's head in his arms, rested him on his own breast, and poured the precious water down the fever-scorched throat. This done, he placed his own knapsack on the ground and tenderly lowered the man's head onto it. He traded the man's empty canteen with a full one. By now the Federals realized what he was doing. Silence fell upon the battlefield, the air as still as the dead who lay about him. Then both sides sent up a cheer, as loud as any cannon roar ever was.

Sergeant Kirkland hurried from one wounded soldier to another, gently tending to each. He leaped over the wall, returned again and again to the battlefield until he had attended every wounded man scattered on the slope. This continued for nearly two hours. Finally, he returned to his post, unharmed. No bullet had even grazed his skin.

Sergeant Kirkland's act not only showed compassion, it was an attempt at reconciliation—a friendly gesture by a Confederate soldier willing to risk his own life to comfort a dying Union man. Would you, if in similar circumstances, be willing to do what Richard Kirkland did? Could you risk your life to comfort an enemy?

Richard Kirkland went on to fight in several other Civil War battles. He paid the full price when he was killed at the Battle of Chickamauga. To those around him at the moment, he said, "Tell my pa I died right." Perhaps, we should tell everyone that he lived courageously.

NOTES

1. *Civil War Trust*, accessed May 20, 2016 http:/civilwar.org/education/history /primarysources/richard.kirkland.

2. "Civil War History–General Discussion," *Civil War Talk*, civilwartalk.com/forums. (Mike Kendra, Forum Director.)

3. "Civil War Trust," *Civil War Trust*, accessed May 20, 2016, http://www.civilwar.org. (Gary Adelman, Director.)

4. Editors of Life, "Samaritan at Fredericksburg" in *Great Battles of the Civil War* (Time Inc., 1961), 16.

5. Joseph B. Kershaw, *Richard Kirkland, The Humane Hero at Fredericksburg* (Richmond: Southern Historical Society Papers, 1880)

6. Nathan Greene, "Nathan Greene Studio," http://www.nathangreenestudio.com /category/sgt-richard-kirkland.

PIONEER OF THE AIR

She knew it was a miracle that the plane was still in the sky. The young woman at the controls felt a pang of fear crawl over her. She watched as the engine spit tongues of flame over the wing of her single-engine Lockheed Vega. She thought she might not be able to finish what she had begun, but she was beyond turning back. As she watched the engine and the flames, she knew her flight to Paris, France, would be danger all the way. Her fear grew, but she throttled the plane ahead.

Earlier, when a company offered a big money reward for the first woman to fly solo across the Atlantic, she could not turn down the invitation. She joined two other aviators on the transatlantic flight. So in 1932, when aviation was in its infancy, she guided her plane through the blackness and rain, lightning crackling about her. The plane continued to stall and then sputter back to life.

Waves rose up from below and almost splashed over the wheels of her small craft. She was tired, her eyes were red-hot coals, and lines of fatigue crossed her boyish face. The engine began to cough hoarsely like a sick child; it was failing seriously. Her heart pounded until she could feel it against her flight jacket. Then dawn appeared like a thousand searchlights on the horizon ahead of her. She felt her heart leap, and she smiled when she saw the Irish coastline that lay like a green carpet atop chalky cliffs. The plane continued to cough as she brought it down in a grassy field. Startled sheep bolted, not knowing which way to run.

An amazed sheepherder ran to greet her as she climbed out. "I'm from America," she said. "My name is Amelia Earhart." She had beaten the

10

other aviators to become the first woman to solo a flight across the ocean to Europe. It would become a moment in history, and the world would learn that she had also broken the record—making the trip in a little over thirty hours.

Amelia was flying at a time when prejudice met her at every attempt. Men doubted that a woman had the strength to make a stunt flight with such heavy demands. Many had told her not to try. They were wrong. It was a shock to them to discover that this gal really knew her stuff. Amelia had developed courage and strength as a child.

At an early age she climbed trees with the boys, belly-slammed her sled to start downhill, and hunted rats with a .22 rifle—all activities that girls weren't supposed to do. Amelia's beliefs were strong. They went against prejudice and money obstacles.

At age ten, Amelia saw her first airplane at a state fair. "It was a thing of rusty wire and wood and not at all interesting," she wrote in her diary. Ten years later she went to a stunt flying show. She and a friend were standing in a clearing when a pilot saw them and dove at them. "I'm sure he said to himself, 'Watch me make 'em scamper.'"

When the plane made its swoop passed them, she felt both fear and pleasure, but she stood her ground. "I did not understand at the time," she said, "but I believe that little red plane said something to me as it swooshed by." Her first ride in an airplane changed her life.

"By the time I got two feet off the ground, I knew I had to fly."

In the heyday of early flight, she had repaired engines, made parachute jumps from airplanes, and explored the ocean floor in a regular diving suit. With her successful flight across the Atlantic, her fame exploded overnight. The world loved her.

When Amelia returned from France, she was honored with staged tickertape parades in New York. President Hoover presented the National Geographic Society's Special Medal. Following her success in flying across the Atlantic, Amelia flew a plane from Hawaii to California. Before her flight, ten pilots had attempted this same feat and all had died trying. Amelia made her successful crossing in 1935.

Amelia opened the new field of flying to women. With her courageous flights to Europe and from Hawaii, she became the only woman to fly solo anywhere in the Pacific. She was also the first woman to fly solo across both the Atlantic and the Pacific. Later, she joined the faculty of Purdue University as a woman career consultant. Although financial help was hard to come by, enough friends believed in her dream to give her money for a new plane. After flying across the Atlantic and the Pacific, she had a new dream. This time she would fly around the earth.

"I have a feeling that there is just about one more good flight left in my system," she said. "I hope this trip is it. Anyway, when I have finished this job of circling the globe, I mean to give up long distance stunt flying." Her words were more prophetic than she realized. She planned to fly west with a stop in Hawaii. In attempting to take off, a tire blew out and the Lockheed Electra crashed. She shipped the plane to California, the airplane center of America, for repairs.

On June 1, 1937, the plane was ready to go. Amelia and navigator Fred Noonan climbed in, eased the plane onto the runway, and took off, headed east. They had reversed their flight plans because of bad weather. They left Miami, Florida, and flew to San Juan, Puerto Rico. From there they skirted the northwest edge of South America and then flew to Africa and the Red Sea. The flight from Karachi was another first. No man had flown nonstop from the Red Sea to India before. From here, Amelia flew her Electra to Calcutta, India, arriving June 17. So far she had not met with any trouble. Next came Yangon, Bangkok, Singapore, and Bandung.

Monsoon weather set in. The rain was as thick as soup. With the flight delayed, Amelia made some minor repairs to the long distance instruments. At Darwin, Australia, she had the direction finder repaired, as it had been cutting out. She should have given it more careful attention. She and Noonan also packed their parachutes and sent them home. They thought the chutes were of no use over water: another fatal error.

At every stop, Amelia cabled her progress. Eagerly, the world waited for each message.

When she arrived at Lae in New Guinea on June 23, she had flown twenty-two thousand miles. She had seven thousand more to go. At this stop, she cabled her last commissioned report to the *Herald Tribune*. Photos showed her looking very tired. She had one more fuel stop to make at Howland Island in the South Pacific. At the time, the atoll was claimed by the United States. American engineers had built a landing strip on the island just so that Amelia could make the stopover.

Before she could get to Honolulu and return to California, she would have to find that tiny dot on the equator that rose all of twenty feet above sea level and was shaped like a flattened hot dog. The world held its collective breath, following her every move. Everyone was with Amelia in her daring attempt to circle the globe. She battled a head wind that was slowing her flight. The thousand gallons of gas might not be enough.

She radioed her position. She said she was on course about twenty miles southwest of the island and northwest of Australia, flying at twelve thousand feet. Forty minutes later she sent her last message. Those aboard the *Itasca*—a boat waiting just offshore—didn't know if she was really on course; no one saw her plane or heard anything. They did receive several very short radio transmissions but could not get a fix on Amelia. They didn't know where she was. They waited and hoped for better contact.

A message crackled from the Electra. "KHAQQ calling *Itasca*. We must be on you but cannot see you . . . Cannot see island . . . Circling . . . Gas is running low . . ." It was 8:14 p.m. when the *Itasca*, waiting off the island, received this last message. The Electra disappeared July 12, 1937. What did Amelia feel at this moment? Did she think about dying? Like so many, did she think about all the things she hadn't done? Did she land on a Japanese stronghold only to be taken prisoner? Did she feel fear, or did she remain true to her belief in herself?

The navy made an extensive search but failed to find any trace of the plane, co-captain Noonan, or the courageous pioneer of the air, Amelia Earhart. To this day, no trace of her has ever been found, but what she did will live forever.

NOTES

1. "Biography," *Amelia Earhart the Official Website*, accessed May 23, 2016, http://www.ameliaearhart.com/about/bio.html. (Mark Roesler, Esq.)
2. Richard A. Boning, *Getting the Facts: Book B* (Barnell Loft Books, 1997).
3. "Amelia Earhart," Keri Rumerman, *U.S. Centennial of Flight Commission*, accessed May 23, 2016, http://www.centennialofflight.net/essay/Explorers_Record_Setters_and_Daredevils/earhart/EX29.htm.

LIBRARIES FOR KIDS

For Brandon Keefe, life really began when he was eight. Until that time, everything had revolved around his Game Boy and the mod, the slightly cropped, spiked hairstyle that every eight-year-old boy sported in America in 1993. He said, "I woke up one morning with a case of sniffles. It turned out to be one of the best things that happened to me. I went with my mother to one of her meetings at Hollygrove. It was a school for orphans. There she was to speak. I sat in a corner playing my Game Boy. I wasn't really paying attention to what the board members were talking about. I heard them mention the need for books."

As irony would have it, the next day his third grade teacher assigned a service project. What could they do for the community? Yesterday's boring day came racing back. Hollygrove had a problem that needed to be solved. Within seconds he had an idea. He remembered that his mother had never failed to supply him with books to read. He had a room full of them, most of them, ones he had outgrown. For that matter, so did his friends. Say! What if he and his friends gave all their unused books to the school?

"I raised my hand, gave my idea, and the class decided that collecting books would be our community service project." In a short time, Brandon had collected nearly one thousand books. He spread them out over his bedroom floor. To get around his room was like playing hopscotch. "I knew a few of the kids at Hollygrove, and I knew that the books would be going to a good place." A group of retired librarians came forward to catalogue the books. The Rotary Club, a local business organization, donated shelves, tables, and chairs. Brandon and his friends were happy to watch the hundreds of books fill the empty room of the children's school. Every orphan now had a book or two.

The service didn't stop there. When Brandon entered seventh grade, he suggested that the class have another book drive as a service project. At first, only his friends helped. They passed out fliers tied to paper bags that people could fill with books. In only one week, Brandon and his friends had collected five thousand books. He sent these to Limerick Elementary—the library shelves had been filled with pinecones and paper airplanes instead of books.

One day a photographer showed up at Brandon's school and called him out of class. Brandon was featured in the *Los Angeles Times*. He was given several community service awards. Oprah, the most popular talk show host in America at the time, asked him to appear on her show, followed by more guest appearances on television. From the book drives, Brandon created the organization BookEnds, a nonprofit organization that collects books. These projects are the work of student volunteers collecting books for kids who need them. As Brandon said, "Many kids have books at home that they no longer read or that they have outgrown. They are not willing to throw them away. BookEnds is a simple way to recycle books and instill the spirit of community service in kids." By 2001, more than forty thousand Los Angeles school children had benefitted with forty-six libraries, and thirty-two more in the works—the efforts of Brandon and sixty thousand student volunteers.

Brandon is modest about his fame. He said, "I am with these other kids who have done awesome things. One kid organized a huge anti-tobacco campaign. Another kid took a bullet for a friend. One has met almost every major world leader and written a book by age eighteen. How did I get in this group? I just collected books. I feel really humbled." He added, "I used to hate reading, but when I see the faces of people when we give them books, they go nuts, like we were giving them ice cream." Brandon concluded, "I read a lot now."

NOTES

1. Vic Magary, "Brandon Keefe," *My UBBT 10 Living Heroes (In No ParticularOrder)*, http://10livingheroes.blogspot.com. (Vic Magary.)
2. Brandon Keefe, interview by Yoonhee Ha, "Interview with Brandon Keefe, amazing-kids.org, http://www.amazing-kids.org/old/ezine_03/interview.html.
3. Accessed May 23, 2016, http://www.bookends.org. (Robin Keefe.)
4. "Digital Learning—Good News and Bad," in *The Read-Aloud Handbook*, 7th ed. (Penguin, 2013). http://www.trelease-on-reading.com/rah-ch7.html. (Jim Trelease.)

PATRIOT SPY

Disguised as a Dutch schoolmaster, handsome twenty-one-year-old Nathan Hale set out on his mission on Thursday, September 12, 1776, a little more than two months after the colonists had declared their independence. He had changed his Continental army uniform for a plain brown suit and a round, broad-brimmed hat, common wear of most citizens. He also removed the silver buckles from his shoes, thinking that they would not match his disguise. He did keep his college diploma, as an introduction to his assumed calling. After checking the location of the main British forces, he planned to retrace his course back to Huntington and across the Sound. There he would relay to Washington what he had learned. As it turned out, the British were gone.

The young spy crossed over into New York to take notes on British camps and make sketches of fortifications. As Washington had had no contact with Hale, when the young man did not return, he thought that Hale had deserted. This assumption would bring about terrible consequences.

The previous year, five of Nathan's brothers fought the British at Lexington and Concord in Massachusetts on April 9, 1775. Nathan joined them on July 6, just one month after his twentieth birthday. Through his bravery and devotion to the fight for freedom, he rose quickly to the rank of captain. He fought with General Washington in New York, where British General Howe had begun a military buildup on Long Island. At the battle of Harlem Heights, General Washington, facing Howe in battle yet again, needed information about British strength and battle plans. To obtain his information, he would have to send spies. He got a volunteer—only one. On September 8, 1776, young Nathan Hale became that one spy for the Continental army, with no knowledge about spying.

He hoped to move about unnoticed, but his good looks drew unwanted attention to him. His eyes were deep pools of azure, his hair as flaxen as morning sun, his skin the complexion of alabaster. He stood six feet, sturdy as stone with muscles toned by intense play in wrestling and football. His skills in sports endeared him to the townspeople; they kept stakes pounded in the ground marking his broad jump records. He was highly educated—a Yale grad at eighteen, in a time when very few went to college. All his classmates had envied his ability to acquire knowledge and call it forth when needed. What he didn't have was training in spy work.

On the night when the moon was in its first quarter, Nathan was ferried across the river and set afoot behind British lines. He hid himself in reeds along the river's bank south of Flushing Bay. Much of the vegetation had been ripped away by a hurricane that had passed along the eastern coast a few days before. The cold mud seeped into his shoes. Nathan might have been afraid, had he shared the common belief that night air was bad.

For a week Nathan gathered information. He planned to recross the river where a schooner waited to sail him back to New York.

The night of September 21, Nathan noticed that the moon was now in its half stage. A thermometer on the tavern wall stood at sixty degrees. For whatever reason, he decided to enter, perhaps to get out of the chill. Sitting at a far corner drinking with friends was Nathan's cousin, Samuel Hale. He was a loyalist to the core. He was actually engaged in work for them. He did not identify himself to Nathan. Into the tavern walked Major Robert Rogers of the Queen's Rangers. He was wearing deerskins. He sat near Samuel, who quickly arose and went to the major's table to whisper to him that Nathan was sitting not more than a few feet from them.

Rogers arose and sat at the table with Nathan. "And how be ye, my good friend," he said. "The weather is getting colder, is it not?" With a very warm and friendly smile, which hid his intentions, he asked, "And what business be ye on? Personally, I'm on the business of spying out the motion of the British troops." He was lying through his teeth.

Nathan responded. "I, too, am on a secret mission for General Washington. I am to learn of their strength and what they plan to do." He leaned back in his chair with a satisfied grin.

The major said, "My good friend, why don't you join me at my quarters for supper? We can continue our talk there, and maybe work together." Nathan was flattered at the offer.

Very shortly, Nathan and his new friend were about to sit down to dinner when a squad of British soldiers surrounded the major's house. On order from Rogers, the troops stormed the house and took Nathan captive. They brought him before British Commander Sir William Howe. They found the secret notes folded and hidden in Nathan's shoes. Since Nathan had been president of the Latin club at Yale, he logically wrote his findings in that language. The British could still make out his drawings of their locations and fortifications.

On this same night, a catastrophic fire swept through New York City, starting at Whitehall, reducing Trinity Church to rubble, and burning itself out in the empty lots north of St. Paul's Chapel. The British, who had just occupied the city after Washington's retreat, were certain the loss of a quarter of the city's dwellings was due to arson by the American rebels. In fact, Major Rogers thought that Nathan might be involved, a good reason to bring him in for questioning.

When interrogated, Nathan gave damaging information about himself. "I am Nathan Hale. I am a captain in the Continental army. I volunteered for this mission. I am to find out the strength of British troops and what fortifications are in place."

The British commander did not waste any time deciding what to do with Nathan. Without any form of a trial and in keeping with the practices of the time, General Howe said, "You are out of uniform, Captain Hale. You are an illegal combatant. You are a spy. We have no time for spies. I order you to be hanged tomorrow."

Nathan was placed in custody of the provost marshal. The man was large with a dark complexion and hairy arms. Despite having arrived as an immigrant and enduring the suffering of refugees, the marshal was without pity. He had no sympathy for others who suffered the same hardship. When Nathan asked for a clergyman to be with him, the man said no. A request for a Bible was refused.

On the following morning, Nathan was taken from the British headquarters in Beckman House in a rural part of Manhattan. He was marched along the Post Road to the Artillery Park, which sat next to Dove Tavern. He walked quietly but bravely. An officer asked that Hale be allowed to sit in his marquee, a large tent with open sides, while the provost made the necessary preparations. Nathan entered and sat. Considering the fact that he was about to be hanged, he remained calm and bore himself with gentle dignity.

The officer gave him paper and quill; he wrote a letter to his mother and another to a fellow officer. The provost and a thirteen-year-old loyalist and former slave stood by as hangmen. They threw a rope over a branch of a nearby tree and tied the noose around Nathan's neck. Before they lifted him from the ground, Nathan said in a strong, clear voice, "I only regret that I have but one life to lose for my country."

NOTES

1. "A Time for Heroes: The Story of Nathan Hale," Circian, *Archiving Early America*, accessed May 23, 2016, http://www.earlyamerica.com/early-america-review/volume-5/a -time-for-heroes-the-story-of-nathan-hale/. (Don Vitale.)

2. "Nathan Hale Revisited," James Hutson, *Library of Congress*, accessed May 23, 2016, https://www.loc.gov/loc/lcib/0307-8/hale.html.

3. "Revolutionary War", *Central Intelligence Agency*, last modified April 15, 2007, https:// www.cia.gov/kids-page/6-12th-grade/operation-history/revolutionary-war .html#.

4. *Central Intelligence Agency*, accessed May 23, 2016, https://www.cia.gov/library /center-for-the-study-of-intelligence-csi/vol.%20117.

5. *Forgotten Delights*, accessed May 23, 2016, http://www.forgottendelights.com /NYCsculpture/salute/SaluteSeptember.htm.

6. "Nathan Hale: One Life to Give," Christian, *Home of the Brave: the American Story*, published January 9, 2009, https://homeofthebravejournal.wordpress.com/2009/01/09 /nathan-hale-one-life-to-give/.

7. Jean Christie Root, *Nathan Hale* (Cleveland: Macmillan Company, 1929), https:// www.gutenberg.org/files/31650/31650-h/31650-h.htm.

8. Fremont P. Wirth, *The Development of America* (American Book Company, 1946).

SAVING THE TRAIN

When walking in the rain in Iowa, it's like walking underwater. Thick, ebony clouds come down to earth. Giant sparks of lightning crash through the sky. The light all but disappears. These summer storms often visit Boone County, which is just northwest of Des Moines. On one of these summer nights in 1881, Kate Shelley was tucked safely in bed—safe but awake—in the family's small, cramped house near the Honey Creek. The house sat very near to the train tracks that crossed the Honey Creek Bridge.

Kate's father had worked for the railroad and was killed in an accident. Her older brother, Michael, drowned while swimming in the Des Moines River. Her mother's health failed because of the stress, and at fifteen, Kate became head of the house. She always watched the trains passing by, waving to the familiar engineers. With their close ties to the railroad, on this night the family kept a wary eye on the storm. Strong winds blew through the valley. The creek was at its crest already, about to run over its banks.

About 11:00 p.m. they heard the No. 12 engine chugging along the rain-soaked tracks. Given the poor conditions, Kate worried that something terrible might happen. She heard the bell toll twice, a horrible crash, and fierce hissing of steam. She clamored out of bed and grabbed her father's old lantern. Running to the Honey Creek Bridge, she saw that it was down. The bridge had been smashed by floating logs, and the engine had plunged into the raging water.

Below, two men were hanging onto the submerged engine. They looked like half-drowned puppies. She realized that she could not get to them. "Hang on!" she screamed above the roar of the water. "I'll get help!"

Despite the shock of the accident, Kate had another thought. *The Express will be coming soon. It has to be stopped. If it goes into the river, many people will be killed.* Like a drum, her heart pounded until she could hear it. What could she do? "The catwalk," she said to herself. Crossing the narrow catwalk over the Des Moines in clear weather and daylight was dangerous enough. Now, at midnight, with blinding rain and fierce winds, the danger increased. She discovered that the railroad owners had removed some of the flooring to discourage kids from playing on the trestle. Kate's first steps proved how dangerous it really was. Hopping across the open gaps, she nearly fell. There was only one way to cross—on hands and knees. Track spikes ripped her skirt and the log ties shoved thin splinters into her hands and knees. The wind blew out the lantern light. Still, she groped her way across. Once in a while, lightning lit up the bridge. Finally, she felt solid ground. Her heart almost skipped a beat. The tenseness drained from her. Running down the track, she came to the Moingona station. Just before she fainted, she heard someone say, "The girl is crazy." When Kate came to, she saw the stationmaster getting a rescue squad together. Others doubted the need for the rescue party. "The Express is coming, and it has to be stopped," she cried. Only then did the doubters understand.

Kate insisted that she go with them. They had to recross the Des Moines and get back to the washed-out bridge. The lights of the Express became visible in the distance. Kate ran along the tracks waving a lantern and red light. The train screamed to a stop just short of the Honey Creek washout. Fifteen-year-old Kate Shelley had saved the Express from going into the river.

Kate guided the men from the rescue squad to the west bank on Honey Creek where the survivors of old No. 12 still clung to the half-submerged engine. The rescue squad tossed a rope down and pulled the men up.

Soon after Kate's brave actions, owner's built a new bridge, this time made of steel. They named it the Kate Shelley Bridge. Not many trains cross the river anymore, but those people who do often think of the brave young girl who saved the train on that stormy night.

NOTES

1. Richard A. Boning, *Getting the Facts: Book D* (Barnell Loft Books, 1997).

2. "Kate Shelley—Heroine of Iowa," *Irish in Iowa*, accessed May 23, 2016, http://www.celticcousins.net/irishiniowa/kateshelley.htm. (Jean Kearney.)

3. Tina Keister, "IAGenWeb Project," accessed May 23, 2016, http://iagenweb.org/boone/historical/society. (Tina Keister.)

4. "Kate Shelley Saves the Train," S. E. Schlosser, *American Folklore*, accessed May 23, 2016, http://americanfolklore.net/folklore/2010/07/kate_shelley_saves_the_train.html.

5. Joe Trnka, *Building the Kate Shelley Bridge* (Union Pacific Railroad, 2010).

6. "The Story of Kate Shelley," *Union Pacific*, accessed May 23, 2016, https://www.uprr.com/newsinfo/attachments/media_kit/regional/northern/kate_shelley/kate_shelley.pdf. (Union Pacific—Building America.)

HE HAD THE STRENGTH OF GIANTS

People who make history in their time do not realize that what they do will interest people of the future. As a result, they often do not keep records to prove what they did. A man, born in 1863, in Quebec, Canada, was one of those people. He did not know that he would become known as the Strongest Man Who Ever Lived. The records that do exist contain little data.

His parents named him Noe Cyr, but everyone called him Louis. He weighed eighteen pounds at birth and was the second of seventeen children. It is believed that he got his unusual strength from his mother who was six feet one inch tall and 265 pounds. At age six, when a calf would not come home, Louis carried it all the way from the pasture. At school one time, fourteen boys were bullying him like wild dogs after a stray sheep. Louis became angry and succeeded in knocking down all fourteen of his tormentors. Only then were teachers able to calm him.

Louis received public attention when he was seventeen. While walking near his home, he came across a farmer whose wagon was stuck in deep mud. No matter how the horses pulled, they could not pull it free. The owner was upset and about to give up in despair. Louis said that he would help. He placed himself under the wagon and pressed his back against the wagon bed. He lifted it as if it were lightweight balsa wood. The horses were then able to pull it out.

He spent much of his youth working in the forests around Quebec. He came across a lumberjack with a broken leg. The man asked Louis to walk the seven miles to the man's village and bring help. Instead, Louis lifted the man onto his own shoulders as if he were a sack of flour and carried him the entire distance to medical care. This act of mercy proved to be of great benefit to Louis. The man became a lifelong friend and backed Louis with needed money. For the rest of his life he was a benefactor who helped Louis in his new career of putting on exhibitions of strength. Louis admired the local blacksmith, who performed acts of strength as entertainment. Louis learned many stunts from his idol and used these stunts in his weight-lifting acts around the world. As Louis grew older, he grew stronger. Although he was only five feet eight inches tall, his huge chest was 60 inches around. It looked like a barrel had popped out of his 300-pound body. His legs and biceps were enormous. He went on to a life of performing weight-lifting stunts, amazing audiences in Canada, the United States, and many European countries.

In 1891, at Sohmer Park in Montreal, Canada, Louis performed a stunt never before done. It is probably his most dramatic act. While he stood before a crowd of ten thousand people, helpers fitted him with a special harness. Horse wranglers lined up four powerful horses with a pair on his left and a pair on his right. Workers wrapped heavy leather straps around his body like a gladiator ready for the arena. They attached strong hooks at the ends of the straps to whiffletree crossbars fitted to the harnesses on the four horses.

The strong man stood with his feet planted wide apart, his legs like two solid tree trunks in the ground. He placed his arms over his chest. Regulations ruled out any sudden jerk. Everyone agreed that if the horses could dislodge the arms of Louis Cyr, or if he lost his footing, he would lose the contest. Louis gave the signal, and the horse trainers urged their steeds to pull. The animals pulled as if their lives and honor depended on winning this contest of strength. The trainers whipped their horses and urged them in every way they knew to pull harder and harder.

The animals snorted and strained. Their muscles quivered and steam shot from their nostrils with every breath they exhaled. Legs nearly buckled and hooves would only slip and slide on the hard ground. Louis remained solid as if planted in concrete. After a few minutes of tugging, everyone conceded that Louis was stronger than the horses. Louis could lift a barrel full of cement with one hand. Another feat that set him apart as the strongest man who ever lived was his ability to lift five hundred pounds off the floor with one finger. His unmatched physical feats included an unbroken record of lifting more than four thousand pounds of dead weight. With a special harness strapped to his body, he lifted 3,439 pounds in a stunt he called the Pig Iron Shoulder Lift.

During a trip to England, Louis aroused much interest and curiosity. At his appearance in London at the Royal Aquarium, five thousand people packed the theater to watch his act. He pressed a 273.5-pound dumbbell as an open challenge to members of the audience, inviting them to do the same. Years later the same dumbbell was loaned to a gym. During the time that it was housed there, more than 500 men tried but failed to lift the weight.

Louis went on a tour of the United States. His promoter was Richard Fox, sports organizer of the *Police Gazette*. As a result, Louis's fame was spread even more. His acts impressed everyone. Each feat of strength built upon the last until Louis was performing acts of strength that remain unequaled today. Strongmen have always been of interest for people, from biblical Samson to modern day weight-lifting champion Arnold Schwarzenegger, the former California governor.

One of Louis's greatest stunts was pushing a train car. He pushed the car on regular railroad tracks uphill. Very little is recorded about this feat. We do not know the weight of the car nor how far he moved it. We do know that other strongmen have pulled train cars.

Mark Kirsch, who also performed as a strongman, pulled a train car that weighed 76,250 pounds or over 38 tons. We can guess that the following story is much the same as what Louis did. Kirsch made a film of a strongman pulling such a car. The strongman wore a body harness. It had two nylon ropes attached that were connected to the front of the car. A rope attached to a stationary pole opposite him was stretched from the pole and attached to the harness. For two or three minutes, the man stood in place and thought only about what he was going to do. He braced himself all the while pulling on the rope, which tended to counteract the dead weight of the train car. He moved the car twenty-five feet.

Louis stunned audiences when he lifted a horse completely off the ground. One of his final acts took place at the end of a tour. In Boston, in 1885, he asked eighteen large men to sit on a platform. Louis kneeled on a small stool that was about fourteen inches in diameter. He got under the platform and raised his back. Up went the eighteen men and the platform—all 4,300 pounds of it.

Through the years, there have been several strongmen who claimed to have unrivaled strength. Whether or not that is true, none compare to Louis. Louis Cyr was no myth. He was not a legend. He was real. He was the Canadian Sampson, the Canadian Hercules. He out-lifted all strongmen who tried to beat him. The list of his deeds reads one after the other, each overcoming the one before it. Even the strongest animals in the world could not lift as much as Louis. From his lifting eighteen men on a platform to out-pulling two teams of horses, Louis Cyr was truly the strongest man who ever lived.

NOTES

1. Richard A. Boning, *Getting the Facts: Book D* (Barnell Loft Books, 1997).
2. Josh Buck, "Louis Cyr and Charles Sampson: Archetypes of Vaudevillian Strongmen," *Iron Game History*, vol. 5, no. 3, (1998): 18–28, http://library.la84.org /SportsLibrary/IGH/IGH0503/IGH0503h.pdf.
3. "Louis Cyr: World Strongest Man," Yvon L. Cyr, *Acadian.org*, accessed May 23, 2016, http://www.acadian.org/louiscyr.html. (Dan Cyr.)
4. "Cyprien Noe Cyr—World's Strongest Man," Dennis Mitchell, *USAWA*, published January 23, 2010, http://usawa.com/?s=cyprien+noe+cyr.
5. David Norwood, "The Legend of Louis Cyr," *Iron Game History*, vol. 1, no. 2, (1990): 4–5, http://library.la84.org/SportsLibrary/IGH/IGH0102/IGH0102d.pdf.

CRASH OF FLIGHT 93

ayday! Mayday! Mayday!" came the cry of a crewman in the cockpit of Flight 93 over the radio amidst sounds of violence. A Cleveland air traffic controller responded, "Somebody call Cleveland?" but received no reply. Seconds later another transmission was made from United Airlines Flight 93. "Mayday! Get out of here! Get out of here!" Islamic terrorists had assaulted the cockpit after moving passengers to the rear of the plane.

Among the passengers was thirty-two-year-old Todd Beamer, former high school athlete, now a loving husband and doting father with two very young sons. He was an account manager for Oracle Corporation in Cranbury, New Jersey. At the moment, he was traveling to California for a business meeting and planned to return on a red-eye flight that night.

From his position in row thirty-two, Todd phoned the GTE Customer Center in Illinois. He was connected to the supervisor. Calmly he explained, "The flight has been hijacked, and the pilots are on the floor dead or dying. One of the hijackers has a red belt strapped to his waist. He claims that it's a bomb." Todd and another passenger, Tom Burnett, began to doubt that. They learned of the attacks on the World Trade Center towers. They heard talk from the hijackers. "They're talking about crashing the plane. It's a suicide mission!" Todd reported details to the GTE supervisor: how many hijackers, how many knives, that one passenger had been knifed. For a moment he lost his composure. "I don't believe that I'm going to make it out of this alive," then he said, "We're going to try to regain control."

"Are you sure that's what you want to do?"

"It's what we have to do," Todd replied.

Islamic terrorists had been killing people around the world for years, blowing up passenger trains, setting off bombs in crowded restaurants and buildings, attacking embassies and military bases, and blowing airplanes out of the sky. "We're going to jump the hijackers. I'm going out on faith." It wasn't directly his job to fight terrorists. This chore had been thrust upon him and his fellow passengers. He began to recite the Lord's Prayer; the GTE supervisor joined him.

"Our Father which art in heaven, Hallowed be thy Name. Thy Kingdom come, Thy will be done . . . Jesus help me," Todd said when they finished.

Since Todd relied as much on his faith as he relied on his own abilities, he and the other thirty-six passengers decided that they could use all the help that they could get. So, in unison, they recited another prayer—the prayer David scripted so many centuries ago. David had written the prayer in a time of great lament. It seemed appropriate for the thirty-seven passengers of Flight 93. Their voices were like the hum of the great engines of the 757, yet they rose above the drone, strong and united and courageous:

> The Lord is my shepherd; I shall not want.
> He maketh me to lie down in green pastures;
> He leadeth me beside the still waters.
> He restoreth my soul . . .

"I will dwell in the house of the Lord forever." Todd said, "Are you guys ready? Let's roll!" Todd Beamer led the charge up the aisle and the assault against the cockpit door. They poured their full strength against it. They hurled food trays and dishes against the walls. A passenger screamed. They raised their voices against the threats of the hijackers.

Once inside the cockpit, they tried to get to the controls. The terrorist pilot rocked the plane and rolled the craft over onto its back like a giant beached whale. They crashed against the roof of the plane in a tangle of bodies. The huge passenger jet plunged into the ground. It exploded and nearly vaporized. Todd may have been afraid. They all may have been afraid. They didn't want to die. With no alternative, they went down fighting, and by giving up their lives, saved countless others. They became heroes. Perhaps we should call them patriots.

NOTES

1. "Did Heroes Force Flight 93 Down?" Don Branum, accessed May 23, 2016, http://www.flight93crash.com/flight93_heroes.html.

2. "United Airlines Flight 93," *Fact-Index*, accessed May 23, 2016, http://www.fact-index.com/u/un/united_airlines_flight_93.html.

3. "Flight 93," *National Park Service*, accessed May 23, 2016, https://www.nps.gov/flni/learn/historyculture/index.htm.

4. "The Heroes on Flight 93," Jeff Head, *Attack on America!* accessed May 23, 2016, http://jeffhead.com/attack/heroes.htm.

5. *Schriever Air Force Base*, accessed May 23, 2016, http://www.schriever.af.mil/news/story_print.asp.

VICTORY AT HILL 617

Following the bombing of Pearl Harbor, the American government reacted by moving all Japanese away from the Pacific Coast. Among them was George Sakato, whose family voluntarily moved to Arizona to avoid being herded into an internment camp. George opted to join the military rather than go with his family. He was assigned to a segregated unit, the 442nd Regimental Combat Team. It was made up of second generation Japanese Americans. It became the most decorated unit in American military history and was known for its extraordinary bravery. Its motto was "Go for Broke." George believed this motto and followed it while he was a member of the 442nd.

In battle after battle, the 442nd fought and died.

In October of 1944, George and his unit were sent to find the Lost Battalion. They nearly destroyed two enemy defense lines near Biffontaine, France. During the action, George was able to eliminate five enemy soldiers and capture another half dozen. Suddenly, everything changed, and George found himself pinned down by heavy enemy fire. Paying no attention to this deadly rain of bullets, George made a one-man rush against the German forces. His charge gave encouragement to the platoon to join him.

The Germans came at the Americans. They came in large numbers with heavy weapon fire. They put up an assault with bullets as solid as a wall. The 442nd platoon needed to regroup. With enemy fire whizzing past him, George rushed headlong into battle. His actions again inspired the rest of his combat team. At this point, the squad leader was killed by enemy fire. Not missing a step, George took command. He continued his relentless tactics of rushing and firing his rifle and rushing again. He thought about basic training, just eight weeks of shooting a rifle and learning about different guns. Back then, he couldn't even hit the target.

George thought, *I couldn't even hit the side of a barn with this .45-caliber pistol.* He was so glad that his aim was better now. The battle moved into a forest. The bushes were shoulder high, and the trees dense and dark as night. He couldn't even see his hand right in front of him. Suddenly, light came down through the trees. *There's an abandoned tank that's been blown up,* he thought to himself, *That's it! I can have more firepower.* With the gun from the tank, George could merely point the weapon in a general direction and probably hit something.

He was sent with his squad on patrol up Hill 617. The unit was searching for German positions. An enemy soldier spotted them. "He's yelling some instructions to another German soldier," George called to his buddies. What happened next was like a blur; the enemy soldier fired his Luger pistol and hit the man standing beside George. George in turn shot the German in the leg, but the wounded German was still able to command his men. More Germans opened fire. The Americans decided that the better part of valor at the moment was a quick retreat down the hill.

George became separated from his unit. He continued to fight up the hill. The Germans kept shooting, and George kept shooting. He took shelter behind a huge fallen tree that lay across his path. From across the log he fired his rifle. Lo and behold! On the other side, a German lieutenant and a private threw down their weapons and put up their hands. They surrendered, and George merely pointed them back to the American lines.

By continuing to ignore enemy fire and by his courage and fighting spirit, George Sakato turned almost sure defeat into victory. He helped his platoon complete its mission. He went beyond the limits of ordinary valor and the measure of military heroics. His bravery is a credit to himself, his outfit, and the honor of the United States Army.

Back home after the war, American feelings toward the Japanese were not good. Resentments still boiled because of Pearl Harbor. Time does heal all wounds, and George was awarded his Medal of Honor on October 29, 2000, some fifty-six years after he earned it.

NOTES

1. *Nikkei Veterans Honor Roll*, accessed May 23, 2016, http://www.ajawarvets.org/campaigns/campaign_07_lost_battalion.cfm.

2. "Veteran 'went for broke' to serve country," Renita Foster, *Weihsien*, accessed May 23, 2016, http://www.weihsien-paintings.org/The7Magnificent/TadNagaki/Story4.htm.

3. "Presidential Unit Cations (Army) awarded to: 100th Battalion & the 442d Regimental Combat Team," *US Army Center of Military History*, last modified November 19, 2010, http://www.history.army.mil/html/topics/apam/puc.html.

THREE TIMES INTO
THE JAWS OF DEATH

The first American military advisors left for Vietnam in August 1954. The first Americans were killed in 1959. The first combat-ready troops arrived there in 1962. Five years later, on November 8, 1967, thirty-year-old Lieutenant James Taylor, executive officer of B Troop, Third Brigade First Cavalry Division, was shuffling some papers at his base camp when he received news that his commanding officer had been wounded and was being flown from the battle zone. Command ordered Taylor to replace the wounded man and make ready for a search and destroy mission the next day. He arrived at the combat area to learn that Command had decided to consolidate the troop. The combined units would attack at dawn.

Before the mission began, Taylor was ordered back to base to resume his duties as executive officer. He was to get the wounded to safety, direct troop support, and provide supplies.

Two days into the firefight in the la Drang Valley at Khe Sanh, as the troop's armored personnel carriers lumbered forward, they were attacked by the Viet Cong (a Vietnamese political organization) with recoilless rifles, mortar, and automatic weapons from an enemy stronghold directly in front of them. Taylor thought the weapons chattered like the keys of his typewriter. He and his sergeant realized they had walked right into a force the size of a regiment. When the Third Brigade found itself surrounded and unable to take cover, the men became sitting ducks for the enemy fire, which swept the earth like a fire that devours the grassland of the plains. The armchair generals had greatly underestimated the strength of the enemy. The seventy-seven-day siege of Khe Sanh had begun.

The injured men in the burning carrier were trapped. Taylor dashed recklessly into the enemy fire to save the wounded before the vehicle exploded. With great disregard for his own life, he pulled wounded men from the wreckage. He returned every time until he had removed all the wounded, and each time he faced the danger that the ammunition would catch fire. Like a Chuck Norris movie scene, after pulling the last of the wounded to safety, the damaged personnel carrier exploded in a ball of fire and black smoke. Taylor had escaped injury this time.

Only minutes later, a second carrier was hit, injuring the men inside. Again, they were unable to lift themselves out. Taylor, daring the machine-gun fire that sprayed the area like gravel blasted from a mountainside by a hydraulic hose, darted toward the burning wreckage. Again, he lifted each man from the vehicle and dragged each to cover behind a mound of dirt. By now the air was thick with red dust blown up by enemy mortars that had exploded around the Americans. For the second time, as if on cue, the ammunition in the burning wreckage exploded into a massive ball of flame.

This time the force of the blast from an exploding mortar shell ripped through Taylor's body, knocking him to the ground, yet he shielded the man he had dragged from the burning wreckage. He paid no attention to his own wounds and did not seek medical aid. He managed to crawl to his command vehicle and lift himself into it. With bleeding wounds and in unspeakable pain, Lieutenant Taylor was determined to move the evacuation-landing zone closer to the wounded men on the front line. As he was moving his own vehicle, he came under machine-gun fire from a hidden enemy position about half a football field away. He returned fire and wiped out the three-man Viet Cong crew manning the deadly weapon. As he came on the evacuation site, he saw yet another assault vehicle explode into flames.

For the third time, Lieutenant Taylor ran to rescue the wounded. He pulled them from the smoldering wreckage and loaded them into his transport. He was able to move them to the safety zone where helicopter medics flew them to nearby hospitals.

Three times Lieutenant James Taylor had rushed into the jaws of death. Later in November 1968, with tears in his eyes, President Lyndon B. Johnson draped the Medal of Honor around Taylor's neck.

NOTES

1. "Medal of Honor: James A. Taylor," *NBC News*, published October 3, 2007, http://dailynightly.nbcnews.com/_news/2007/10/03/4373215-medal-of-honor-james-a-taylor.
2. "Vietnam War Medal of Honor Recipients: James Allen Taylor," *U.S. Army Center of Military History*, last modified May 7, 2015, http://www.history.army.mil/moh/vietnam-m-z.html#top.
3. "Medal of Honor Recipient James Taylor Interview," interview by Ed Tracy, *Pritzker Military*, online interview, March 23, 2009, http://www.pritzkermilitary.org/whats_on/medal-honor/medal-honor-recipient-james-taylor-interview/.

VOLCANO IN A CORNFIELD

On a late afternoon in February 1943, Dionisio Pulido went to his cornfield to burn some cut branches. He noticed that a crack had opened on one of the knolls of his farm. The crack, or fissure, had a depth of about half a meter. He tried to ignite the branches but failed because he was too nervous. He tried again but heard something like thunder. The trees trembled as he turned to speak to his wife. He could not see her! What had happened to her?

In the hole he saw the ground swell and raise itself two or three meters high. Smoke and fine ashes rose up from the fissure. More smoke rose with a loud, continuous whistle. He smelled the odor of sulfur, like rotten eggs.

Dionisio was greatly frightened. He tried to unyoke one of the ox teams. He was so stunned, he hardly knew what to do. He was frightened because he could not find his wife or son, or the other animals. Maybe they took the animals to the spring for water. When he arrived there himself, he found the spring dry! It was gone! With one leap, he climbed upon his horse and urged the animal to a gallop toward town. To his relief, he found his family and friends. They said, "We thought that you were dead." Dionisio laughed weakly.

He and some of the townspeople mustered as much courage as they could. They knew that they had to return to the cornfield to better see what was happening. When he came back with the other men, he found a strange sight. There, where he had seen the crack in the earth with the smoke pouring out, stood a pile of black, smoking rocks as tall as a tree. "It looks like a chimney," Dionisio commented to the others. From the opening in the ground, rocks shot high into the air. The earth kept bouncing and exploding. By the next morning, the pile was fifty feet.

Within twenty-four hours the eruption had generated a fifty-meter scoria cone. Scoria, Dionisio noticed, was dark-colored basalt rock that formed as the lava cooled and hardened. He noticed that it looked like a hardened piece of sea sponge, full of bubble holes. On the following day, he harnessed his oxen and led them to the fields to graze before walking the short distance to his farm to see what had happened. He arrived at about 8:00 a.m. to find a hill about ten meters high. Smoke rose from it, and rocks hurled up with great violence.

By the week's end, the volcano had grown to a height of one hundred meters. The cone was mostly made of scoria (a low-density lava rock) and finer fragments or pieces of ash. The farm was quickly buried by the volcanic eruptions. The volcano blasted these same bombs and ash great distances. They rained down on the village of Parícutin. Loud explosions that sounded like great cannons continued for many months.

Lava flows advanced toward the surrounding villages so that the people had to leave them. By August of 1944, most of Parícutin and San Juan were buried under many feet of lava and ash. Finally, the lava covered everything but two church towers that stood like frozen statues above the sea of bubble-holed lava.

In less than a year, the volcano had built a cone three hundred meters tall. For nine more years it kept smoking and exploding. By the time the volcano began to cease its growth, it was almost 460 meters—as tall as a skyscraper. It became known as Dionisio's volcano. He was terrified and feared the volcano at first. He never went very close to it, but after a while he could stand his ground against it. He was like a warrior who met an enemy in battle and beat him. Also, he became accustomed to its changing moods and size.

He no longer has to fear it. His volcano is no longer active, but for nine years he watched it grow. Now it's 2,272 meters tall. His farm is buried under it.

NOTES

1. Richard A. Boning, *Getting the Facts: Book F* (Barnell Loft Books, 1997).

2. "Eruption of Paricutin," *Dartmouth College*, accessed May 23, 2016, https://www
.dartmouth.edu/~volcano/Se17p19.html.

3. "Paricutin, the volcano that grew out of a cornfield," *Mexonline.com*, accessed May 23,
2016, http://www.mexonline.com/paricutinvolcano.htm.

4. "Volcan Paricutin and Pico Tancitaro National Park," Bruce Whipperman, *Planeta
.com*, accessed May 23, 2016, http://old.planeta.com/planeta/98/0898paricutin.html.

THE LADY WITH
THE LAMP

As she prowled the dark, dirty halls of the army hospital, Florence Nightingale carried a lamp with her. The lamp was the only available light. At the time, hospitals were neglected, filthy barracks where the wounded were housed. Women who served as nurses were not allowed to perform nursing duties, but worked as cleaners. Because the doctors lorded their authority over the nurses, no one was allowed to question their opinions or orders. If a nurse were to pose a question, the doctor would often snap back, "You are wasting my time!" Prior to this time, businesses separated work as male and female tasks and the army did not allow women in their hospitals at all.

Because of her family's status in society, Florence had friends who were in a position to help her work in the hospital. Her associates extended to Britain's secretary of war who was in charge of the army hospitals. In 1854, Great Britain and other countries declared war on Russia. Florence thought she was in the exact position that God had planned for her. Army hospitals were really places where the wounded were kept until they died. Reports from Crimea about inhumane, cruel, and brutal treatment, or lack of care for the wounded upset the country. The people raised money to buy supplies for the hospital. The secretary of war wanted Florence to take responsibility to change conditions, to go to Crimea herself. With the secretary of war's blessing and authority to change things, Florence and thirty-eight female nurses traveled to the army hospital at Scutari in Turkey. She found it to be a disgusting rat hole. The floor moved like a swelling sea as cockroaches scurried about. She discovered dozens of injured soldiers who were not receiving even basic care for their injuries. They lay in bed linens unwashed for weeks and encrusted with filth. Hygiene was nonexistent. The men were not even bathed, and the injured were often denied sufficient food. A sewer ran under the building, causing the whole place to reek and smell of putrid human waste. Chances of surviving the hospital were less than on the battlefield.

For a while, despite the authority vested in Florence and the great need throughout the hospital, the male army doctors refused to allow the nurses to help at all. Shortly, at the battle of Balaklava (a town in Crimea) scores of men were killed or wounded. The hospital was overrun with seriously injured soldiers. The army doctors could not even begin to provide first aid for the numbers of men brought in. They could no longer claim that nurses did not have a place or significant role in the army facility.

Florence and her female nurses immediately set about scrubbing and cleaning the filth from the place. They made it as healthful and sanitary as possible. She ordered clean bedding and bandages for the patients. The nurses gave the injured and dying compassion. They gave this at a desperate time in the lives of the soldiers. Even then, the male doctors still restricted what Florence and her medical crew was allowed to do.

She wrote a letter home, and the secretary of war learned of the miserable conditions in the hospital in the war zone. The situation was so dire that the male army doctors grudgingly gave into the needs of the injured. The government gave Florence the power to make the hospital livable— and she did. She knew that infection was caused by dirt, poor air, and neglect. The wounded still lay in their filthy combat uniforms. She got clean clothes for them. She even got workers to rebuild one shabby, collapsing wing of the hospital.

It was at this time that Florence became known as the Lady with the Lamp, because she regularly checked *all* parts of the hospital day and night. While doing this, she needed light, so she carried a lamp. Although she had to fight the stubborn, ignorant bias of the time to bring about needed change, the Lady with the Lamp was truly a woman of conviction and courage.

NOTES

1. "Florence Nightingale (1820–1910), Marjie Bloy, *The Victorian Web*, last modified January 3, 2012, http://www.victorianweb.org/history/crimea/florrie.html.

2. "Florence Nightingale," John Simkin, *Spartacus Educational*, accessed May 23, 2016, http://spartacus-educational.com/REnightingale.htm.

3. John Simkin, http://www.spartacus.schoolnet.co.uk/nightengale. (John Simkin.)

4. Lois A. Monteiro, "Florence Nightingale on Public Health Nursing," *American Journal of Public Health*, vol. 75, no. 2 (1985), http://www.ncbi.nlm.nih.gov/pmc/articles /PMC1645993/pdf/amjph00278-0075.pdf.

5. Sir Zachary Cope, "Miss Florence Nightingale and the Doctors," *Proceedings of the Royal Society of Medicine* (1956), http://www.ncbi.nlm.nih.gov/pmc/articles /PMC1889251/pdf/procrsmed00377-0063.pdf.

6. Thomas T. Mackie, "The Life of Florence Nightingale," *Am J Public Health Nations Health*, vol. 32, no. 11 (1942), http://www.ncbi.nlm.nih.gov/pmc/articles/PMC1527343 /?page=1297.

ONE-MAN ARMY

After the Third Infantry Division had liberated Sicily, the unit landed at Salerno as part of the mainland invasion. As a member of the Third, Corporal Audie Murphy was sent out as leader of a night patrol. In the dark, they ran into a German ambush but were able to fight their way out. They found safety in a rock quarry and fought off an enemy squad sent to eliminate them. The Americans countered with intense machine gun and rifle fire. Some of the Germans were killed and the rest taken captive.

Audie Murphy was from Texas. As one of twelve children and the son of poor sharecroppers, he had to leave high school after his father abandoned the family. Audie picked cotton and plowed fields for a dollar a day. In any spare time he had, he practiced with a rifle. He hunted small game to help feed the family. His friend Dial commented, "Audie, you never miss anything that you shoot at." Audie replied, "Well, Dial, if I don't hit what I shoot at, my family won't eat tonight." This statement would also prove true later in battle. If he didn't hit his mark, the men might not live to come home to eat that night.

Following the attack at Pearl Harbor on December 7, 1941, Audie went to the nearest recruitment office to enlist. Since he was underage, he was rejected. Only after his sister doctored his birth records was he able to enter the military at age sixteen. He tried for the marines and paratroopers, but his small stature of five feet five inches kept him out. He eventually got into the army. Even then, his company commander tried to have him assigned as the cook because of his baby-faced, youthful appearance.

Audie insisted on being a combat soldier; his wish became reality, and after basic training, he found himself in the Italian campaign.

His heroics at Salerno earned Audie another rank stripe, and he was promoted to sergeant. In battles that followed at Volturno River and the bloody Anzio Beachhead, Audie charged into the thick of battle fighting like a one-man army. In Italy, climbing the rugged mountains in the drenching cold rain, he again used his rifle skills to defeat the enemy. His actions earned him promotions and decorations for valor.

During World War II, military units were not allowed to rest on their laurels, or their past achievements. Their success in one fight merely ensured them another. The Third Division went from battle to battle leaving their mark. It was this routine that brought the Third into the invasion of France. Audie and his close friend, Lattice Tipton, found themselves exchanging rifle and machine gun fire with enemy soldiers. The Germans were protected by the dirt walls of a foxhole. One of the enemy soldiers raised his rifle over his head in an act of surrender. When Tipton stood up to take them captive, the German bought his rifle down and fired several shots. Tipton died.

Audie was enraged. Screaming at the cowardly soldier, he charged at the machine gun nest. By himself, he wiped out the crew that had used treachery to kill his friend. He took the enemy weapon, and like a whirlwind sweeping across a desert landscape, he rushed a machine gun emplacement nearby. Similar to the best traditions of Hollywood, Audie swung the machine gun from his hip and sprayed deadly fire across the battlefield. He threw hand grenades to destroy the enemy positions. He avenged the death of his friend and received the Distinguished Service Cross. His luck continued to hold in his many encounters with the enemy; 4,500 members of his unit did not share in his luck.

As the Third Division moved across France, Audie continued to be put in the most dangerous positions. By now he was platoon sergeant. In fight after fight, he gave no thought to his own safety, but only to the safety of his men. For his heroic actions he received two Silver Stars. Eventually, the army gave him a battlefield promotion to second lieutenant. A German sniper, hidden in the woods where his unit was camped, wounded Audie only twelve days later. The healing of the wound took ten weeks. With bandages still wrapped about his body, he returned to his unit. Army brass promptly made him company commander on January 25, 1945. While carrying out his duties, he was again wounded

43

by a mortar round that landed in the compound. The explosion killed two other men standing near him. The next day the battle of Holtzwihr began. Temperatures stood at fourteen degrees. Two feet of snow blanketed the ground like a great white carpet. The company's manpower was down to 19 of the original 128.

Audie knew that they were outnumbered. Always putting the safety of his men ahead of his own, he ordered them to the rear. During the move back he took pot shots at the enemy. Pot shots are easy or random shots, fired at close range. They are sometimes haphazard shots. His men withdrew to set up strategic positions in the woods. From his post, Audie continued to give directions by telephone to the artillery in the rear of the front lines.

Behind him, to his right, one of the army tank destroyers took a direct hit from an enemy mortar. The explosion looked like a fireworks display as smoke and flaming parts leaped into the air. The vehicle began to burn. The crew climbed out of the disabled vehicle and ran for cover in the woods. With the German tanks abreast of his position, Audie climbed onto the burning tank destroyer. He knew when the flames reached the shells still inside the destroyer, it would explode.

Wounded, alone, and surrounded on three sides by enemy soldiers, he stayed at his chosen post. With the machine gun cradled in his arms, his deadly fire stopped dozens of Germans where they stood. This caused the enemy infantry to waver in their attack.

Still determined to overrun the Americans, the Germans tried for an hour, using everything they had, to eliminate Second Lieutenant Audie Murphy, yet he continued to hold his position. His Texas farm-boy skill with a rifle proved useful now with the heavy machine gun. He wiped out an enemy squad trying to sneak up on his right flank. Enemy soldiers came within ten yards, only to be mowed down by Audie's fire.

Audie did not escape unharmed. A German bullet found its mark and lodged itself in his leg. Still, he ignored it, thinking it little more than a wasp sting, and continued his lone fight against greater numbers until his ammo ran out. He jumped from the flaming destroyer only seconds before it erupted like a fiery volcano. He made his way to his company, refused medical aid, reorganized his men, and rallied them into a force to drive the Germans into retreat. His refusal neither to give in to superior numbers, nor to give an inch of ground, saved his company from being destroyed. They held the woods, which had been the enemy's objective all along.

By the end of the war Audie was a legend in the Third Division. He is credited with destroying six enemy tanks. Coupled with his bravery throughout his battles with the Third Division and his courageous action at Holtzwihr, Audie won the Medal of Honor. He also received the Legion of Merit, and in addition to his two Silver Stars and his Distinguished Service Cross, he received two Bronze stars, three Purple Hearts, and two Presidential Citations. The French government bestowed its highest award on Audie—the Legion of Honor with the grade of Chevalier, and two Croix de Guerre medals.

By the end of the war, Audie had earned thirty-three combat medals, enough to cover his entire chest, which made him the most decorated soldier in United States history. He was overseas twenty-nine months, twenty-four of them spent in actual combat. All this before he was twenty-one. In June 1945, he returned to the United States to a hero's welcome. The people showered him with parades, banquets, and speeches of praise. He represents the finest in American spirit and loyalty. As the one-man army that he was, he is one of the people who changed the world.

NOTES

1. "Audie Leon Murphy," *Arlington National Cemetery Website*, accessed May 23, 2016, http://www.arlingtoncemetery.net/audielmu.htm.

2. "Audie Leon Murphy," *Texas State Cemetery*, accessed May 23, 2016, http://www.cemetery.state.tx.us/pub/user_form822.asp?pers_id=11255.

3. "Audie Murphy," *Find A Grave*, published January 1, 2001, http://www.findagrave.com/cgi-bin/fg.cgi?page=gr&GRid=75.

4. "World War II Medal of Honor Recipients: Audie L. Murphy," *U.S. Army Center of Military History*, last modified April 13, 2016, http://www.history.army.mil/moh/wwII-m-s.html#top.

WATANYA CICILLA

In our country a little more than two hundred years ago, shooting was a national pastime, and people shot guns like they play golf today. Shooting guns was also part of the daily occupation of our forefathers. Both countrymen and city folk were devoted to this practice. No town was without a shooting range, and all offered facilities for tests of marksmanship. No gathering, either of business, political, or religious ever ended without a shooting match. Part of our heritage is marksmanship with guns.

Some of the most outstanding shooters were women. Annie Oakley, born in 1860, was one of the best sharpshooters of the time. Almost everyone attended shooting contests. Once, a contest was set up between a famous sharpshooter named Frank Butler and petite fifteen-year-old Annie. She was just five feet tall and weighed one hundred pounds. She looked like a large doll in fancy dress. Both of them hit twenty-four birds in a row. (A bird is a small, round clay disc called a "pigeon" that is thrown into the air for shooting practice.) Frank missed his last shot. Annie bested him by hitting her twenty-fifth bird. She won the match. She also won Frank Butler's heart.

She and Frank formed their own traveling Wild West show. Frank took star billing, but he soon realized that Annie was the better shot and a better show person. He gave her top billing and became her manager. By 1861, they were married. In 1885, they were ending a traveling season in New Orleans. Buffalo Bill Cody just happened to be in town with his own renowned "Wild West Show." They hoped to join Cody's show, but he turned them down. Later, when a ship sank with Cody's sharpshooters, he agreed to give them a try.

What a show Annie put on for the crowd. Decked out in a buckskin dress with fringe, she rushed to the table on the field and picked up a gun. An assistant tossed two glass balls into the air. Annie was without emotion: cool, calm, and steady. Her years of practice made her sure and self-confident.

The guns, almost at hip level, and seemingly without taking aim, she blasted both glass balls into bits. The crowd was pleasantly surprised. The assistant tossed six glass balls. Again, with her steady aim, she hit all of them while they were still in the air. Fragments flew from the shattered glass. More amazing, she did it with two guns! She did it so quickly that some only saw the shattering of the glass. Most of the crowd, its collective mind not thinking that a woman could do what had just happened, missed it.

Others in the stands clapped loud and long. Some jumped up to roar their approval. To perform a more daring trick, she turned her back to the glass balls as they were thrown into the air. She used a mirror to shot over her shoulder. She hit her target every time. At ninety feet, Annie shot a dime tossed into the air. One day, using a .22 rifle, she shot 4,472 of 5,000 glass balls in midair. A playing card was mounted with the thin edge toward her, and at nearly one hundred feet, Annie split the card and shot it five times as it settled to the ground. Shooting the ashes off a cigarette held in Frank's mouth sent the crowd into hysteria.

Annie and Frank went to Europe. While touring the Continent, they were asked by Wilhelm, Crown Prince of Germany, to shoot a cigarette held in his lips. Annie had him change it to his hand and shot it away effortlessly. Queen Victoria invited Annie and another female sharpshooter in the touring company to perform before her court. Competition was fierce. On this day, the other woman shot badly while Annie shot well.

Unfortunately, Annie suffered spinal injury in a train wreck and became partly paralyzed, but she recovered enough to continue her show, although she toured less often.

Because she shot so well, Chief Sitting Bull, a member of Buffalo Bill's company, gave Annie the name Watanya Cicilla—Little Sure Shot. Annie's legacy, as a little sure shot, lives on.

NOTES

1. "Letter to President William McKinley from Annie Oakley," *National Archives*, accessed May 23, 2016, http://www.archives.gov/research/recover/example-02.html.

2. Richard A. Boning, *Getting the Facts: Book D* (Barnell Loft Books, 1997).

3. "Cavalcade of America: Annie Oakley," *Homeschool Commons*, accessed May 23, 2016, http://homeschoolcommons.com/2012/07/cavalcade-of-america-annie-oakley/.

4. "Annie Oakley—Crack Shot in Petticoats," Mike Dewine, *Local Legacies*, accessed May 23, 2016, http://memory.loc.gov/diglib/legacies/loc.afc.afc-legacies.200003446 /default.html.

THE MAN WHO LOST IT ALL

On the morning of January 24, 1848, temperatures stood at thirty-five degrees along the south fork of the American River at Coloma. The river flowed at about 750 feet above sea level. Thirty-four-year-old James Marshall was looking at the bottom of the channel below the John Sutter Saw Mill. Earlier, he had built the mill for Sutter, who had emigrated from Switzerland in 1834 and who was still the *alcalde,* or governor of the area, because California was still part of Mexico's claims. It would not become an American territory for another few days.

Marshall noticed some shiny flecks in the riverbed. He picked up some to examine them more closely. He had a general knowledge of metals and decided that these resembled sulphuret of iron—very bright and heavy, and gold, very gold! Malleable—easily reshaped. He pounded the flecks between two rocks and found that he could beat them into very thin shapes, but they would not break. He picked up a few more pieces and took them to Sutter's office.

Breathless with excitement, Marshall said, "I have found it!"

"Found what?"

Marshall cautioned Sutter, "No one must hear about this." He closed the door. He put the pieces of metal on the desk. "Gold! I know it to be gold. I know it to be nothing else."

Sutter examined the specimens and made some simple tests to determine if the specks were what Marshall claimed. He boiled the flecks in a lye solution and hammered the pieces to test for malleability; would it reshape without breaking? They passed the test.

Sutter looked at Marshall. "You're right. You've discovered gold. We must keep it a secret." Thoughts of getting back the land and possessions he had lost earlier raced through Marshall's mind. He was pleased that he might no longer have to labor as a carpenter. He would be rich.

Marshall and Sutter were unable to realize their hope of keeping the gold discovery a secret.

Others began to find the yellow specks. News of the find spread around the world. "Gold! Gold's been discovered in California!" went the cry. Like swarms of locusts, thousands rushed to California. They came from all over America and even some from Europe. Sailors went AWOL (absent without leave) from their ships. Farmers left their fields untilled and headed for the goldfields instead. Store owners nailed shop doors shut and put up signs: "Gone to California." Sutter closed his sawmill when all the able-bodied workers abandoned their labor. They flocked like hordes of birds into the rivers and streams to search for the golden metal.

Many who had never been to the goldfields repeated wild stories. People cried, "Gold is everywhere! It can be found in the fields, under bushes, even in the streets. There's so much gold, the rivers give off a yellow glow. The river bottoms are beds of gold!" (This may still be true; in very recent times a man found a large nugget of gold when he pulled up a bush in the Lancaster, California area.) No matter how wild and crazy the stories, people believed they could get rich quick. Hordes of men arrived every day to wade in the cold streams to search for gold.

They soon learned that digging all day for gold was plain, hard work. Standing in cold water that turned their legs blue wasn't much fun. Sifting the sand from the bottoms of rivers meant bending over for hours. Their backs ached as if someone had beaten them with a two-by-four. For their efforts, they gained very little. The gold they found was mostly tiny flakes. Discouraged, they packed up their possessions and headed back to their homes. Not only did they not find gold, they arrived home to discover that they had lost their original property.

Surely, the gold on Sutter's land should have been his, but fate did not deal him a fair hand. Gold seekers, strangers from unknown places, had stormed onto his land. They trampled his crops and took what they wanted without paying. They stole his cattle and used them for food. They took the wood from his mill to build shelters for themselves.

Without the use of his land and mill, Sutter was without income and about to lose everything. The Russians who owned the lease on Sutter's holdings threatened foreclosure (to take back the property for nonpayment). Sutter sent for his son, a trained accountant, who came to rescue his father from bankruptcy. Sutter transferred the ownership of the property to his son. This kept the Russians off his back for a while. Young Sutter planned and laid out the city of Sacramento and sold lots from his father's land. He was able to make enough money to pay off the Russian debt. His efforts only brought temporary relief.

At age twenty-one, young Sutter was not a good businessman. Unscrupulous men took advantage of his trusting nature and often paid far below market value for the lots. Elder Sutter regained control of his lands and sold them and moved east. Like Marshall, his dreams of becoming rich from the gold discovery were trampled on by the gold seekers of 1849.

Marshall contributed to the growth of California through his efforts, but it was Sutter who truly stands out. He was more than a pioneer. He was one of the true leaders of California. When the state constitution was signed in 1850, he was the keynote speaker at the convention. He even became a candidate for governor. Among his peers, he was highly respected. Of him, General William T. Sherman said, "Sutter was the man most responsible for California's becoming a part of the United States." Navy officer Joseph Revere said, "Men have been deified, been given God-like status by others, for lesser deeds than those accomplished by Sutter."

He was part of the gold discovery that changed the world. He had begun successfully and in 1841, had received a grant of forty-eight thousand acres along the Sacramento River. His was one of the first *rancheros* in the Central Valley of California. He was the first non-Indian person in Northern California. His partnership with James Marshall, to build a sawmill and furnish lumber to the area, helped build the state. The mill provided jobs and income. Enterprise grew. The vision that Sutter had was solid, like the adobe he built a few miles back from the river.

What became of James Marshall? He must have done better, but alas, he suffered a sadder fate. He never struck it rich. He never did find the mother lode or enough gold in one place to make him rich. He mined for gold in many places. While he searched for the elusive fortune, a dispute arose between the peaceful Nisenans of the area and some aggressive gold miners from Oregon. The dispute became ugly. Marshall did his best to defend his friends, the Nisenans, but the Nisenans were murdered, and Marshall was forced to flee for his life.

Years later, after the incident was almost forgotten, Marshall returned to California where he had hoped to become wealthy. By now the gold-fields were empty, the miners have left penniless and broken. By 1855, the rich Lotus gold was largely gone. By 1864, California's gold rush had ended. Unable to find gold or make a living, Marshall settled in a small, crude, ramshackle cabin perched on a steep, dry, powdery hillside buried under decades of pine needles.

In the beginning, as his empire expanded, Sutter moved into the foot-hills to find more suitable lumber. He hired Marshall, who had moved with the frontier. Of course, their fate changed with the discovery of gold. As it turned out, others did not share their vision, and Marshall died pen-niless not far from where he had found gold. He became the man who lost it all.

NOTES

1. Richard A. Boning, *Getting the Facts: Book E* (Barnell Loft Books, 1997).
2. "The Forty Niners," *American Memory*, accessed May 23, 2016, http://memory.loc.gov /ammem/cbhtml/cbforty.html.
3. "The Discovery of Gold," *American Memory*, accessed May 23, 2016, http://memory .loc.gov/ammem/cbhtml/cbgold.html.
4. "Gold Discovery History," Alan Beilharz, *Coloma California*, accessed May 23, 2016, http://www.coloma.com/california-gold-discovery/history/.

FIRST PROTESTANT MISSIONARY TO KOREA

Some 225 years ago, Korea was known as the Hermit Kingdom. The people had no contact with the outside world, nor did they want anyone coming there. A few Catholic priests had arrived in Korea in 1785 and had converted many people to their religion. The rulers of Korea did not favor Christianity and did not like what the priests were doing. To show their power, in 1863 they massacred more than eight thousand Christian converts.

It was against this background that Robert Jermain Thomas sailed to Korea. He had learned of the cruel actions of the rulers from Korean traders. He also learned that the converts had only crosses and rosaries but no Bibles. He said that he would take some, but to be able to do so, he had to become an agent for the National Bible Society of Scotland so that the Society would pay his travel expenses. On September 4, 1865, Thomas sailed for Korea.

He went secretly, his identity hidden. The Bibles that he carried were hidden as part of his luggage. He knew that anyone in possession of a Bible risked having his head cut off. He could suffer the same fate if he were caught selling the books. He was able to sneak in.

Learning the language was simple for him. He already knew a dozen other languages. Moving about secretly, always in a disguise that hid his religious connections, he was able to meet the people. He learned early that they were hostile to foreigners. Little by little, chatting with them in their own language, he could persuade some of them to accept a book. Thomas carried out his secret activities for four months before he had to make his way back to China. No sooner had he returned to the mainland than a serious uprising took place in Korea. Rulers killed hundreds of Christian converts; some priests were executed. Thomas quickly returned to Korea.

He obtained employment as a translator on an armed American schooner called the *General Sherman*. They sailed up the river to Pyongyang, which is now the capital of North Korea. The rulers warned the Americans to leave, but the captain opened fire with his cannons. The shells burst like a canopy of brightly colored streamers. Thomas was horrified. The chief of police came aboard the schooner but was taken prisoner. The captain said, "The chief will be released only after I talk with the governor." He continued to sail up the river.

Angry crowds lined the riverbanks shouting and cursing. The captain, not aware that the river depth became shallower with the change of tide, ran his vessel onto a sandbar. The Koreans brought their army into action, firing on the ship. They also set barges afire and floated them down the river toward the disabled schooner. Like a man about to meet his maker, Thomas ripped open his cases of Bibles and began throwing them to the crowds on shore. He hoped only that someone would pick them up and read them.

The flaming barges bumped against the ship, which caught fire and began to burn fiercely. The flames leaped along the sides of the ship and up the canvas sails. Thomas was caught in the fire. With his remaining Bibles and clothes aflame, he leaped into the slowly moving, muddy water.

Like a drowning puppy, haplessly cast into a lake, Thomas splashed to the bank and frantically gave out all but one of his Bibles. He was quickly taken prisoner and given a very brief, mock trial. All twenty-four crew members and the captain were quickly executed. Although Thomas had nothing to do with the captain's aggressive actions, he would pay with his life.

After meekly dropping to his knees, he urged the executioner to accept the last Bible that he held in trembling hands. As useless as the gesture was, Thomas was still hopeful that the man might be converted. He closed his eyes, prayed, and stiffened his body in anticipation of the executioner's blade. The man hesitated, as if not wanting to carry out his orders, but knew that he must obey or suffer the penalty himself. He swung the heavy blade and ended Robert's life, but Robert Jermain Thomas had courageously lived his belief right up to the very horrific end.

NOTES

1. "North and South Korea The First Protestant Missionary to Korea," *Revival and the Great Commission,*" accessed May 23, 2016, http://www.byfaith.co.uk/paulkorea.htm.

2. "The Hermit Kingdom and the General Sherman Incident," *Home of Heroes*, accessed May 23, 2016, http://www.homeofheroes.com/wallofhonor/korea1871/2_hermit.html. (Doug Sterner.)

3. "Korea and Great Britain," William Haines, *Tparents.org*, published February 16, 2010, http://www.tparents.org/Library/Unification/Talks1/Haines/Haines-100216 .htm.

FIREFIGHT AT BAGDAD AIRPORT

Without any enemy fire along the route, the company arrived at Bagdad Airport. Sergeant Paul Smith was concerned. The men had been on the road two weeks; they were homesick, welted with mosquito bites, dripping with sweat, and covered in dirt. They could smell the acrid stench of exploding shells in the distance and hear the occasional gunfire that peppered the hot air. Still, the absence of enemy soldiers worried him.

"Too quiet. It's kind of eerie," said Lieutenant Brian Borkowski. He and Paul had served together in the Gulf War twelve years before. On this mission at the Baghdad Airport, their objective was to set up a roadblock on a highway to the airport. With high adobe walls blocking their view on both sides, and the ease with which they had arrived at the airport, they were uneasy.

While Brian left on a scouting patrol, Paul called for a bulldozer to plow through the adobe wall. The machine arrived and punched a hole through the adobe. The wall crumbled like a dry cracker. On the other side was a courtyard with a few scraggly trees. Smith received a call from the command center: build a prisoner of war (POW) holding yard. The courtyard was the ideal arrangement. On the far side of the yard was a thick wooden gate. He needed to know what was on the other side. He called for a personnel carrier that crashed through the gate like a fist would punch through a paper bag. He, and his sixteen men, found what he had feared: a nest of militant Iraqis. At first, the Americans thought that they could handle the situation. He relayed the details to the company commander who remained unconcerned.

Paul deployed his men around the area. As the enemy, numbering over one hundred by now, advanced, he tossed a hand grenade over the wall. He phoned for a Bradley, an armored vehicle styled after the half-track of World War II. It arrived and sprayed machine-gun fire into the Iraqis. Paul thought he was in control now. To the surprise of everyone, the Bradley turned and drove away. "What the . . . what are they doing?" cried Corporal Daniel Medrano. All the men felt as if they had been abandoned, and they had been. They were alone now without armored support.

The fighting got worse. The personnel carrier that had rammed through the gate was hit by a rocket-propelled grenade. The three men inside were wounded, unable to escape. The Iraqis had taken over a tower that overlooked the courtyard. With the advantage of high ground they had the Americans in a murderous crossfire. Not only did they have the advantage of the tower, but they were also harassing Paul and his men outside the smashed gate. What had begun as a minor engagement was now a major Iraqi strike against the American forces, who thought that once they occupied the airport, the war would be over.

At this point, the fighting was at its fiercest. Paul knew that every action counted. He also knew that if his men could not hold the position, they would be trampled by the Iraqi troops who would be able to push all the way to the nearby command center, and overrun the base. Wounded men in the nearby building were also hurting, as were all the men in his command. He had the damaged personnel carrier placed so that he could control the tower and the enemy trenches outside. Corporal Medrano was lifting one of the wounded from the damaged vehicle. He looked up to discover his sergeant exposed to enemy fire, manning the gun atop the carrier. They made eye contact. Paul waved him off. "Take care of the men," he was saying. He emptied three hundred to four hundred rounds at the enemy and succeeded in halting the enemy attack—at the cost of his own life.

Earlier, in an email to his parents, he wrote, "There are two ways to come home: stepping off the plane or being carried off. It doesn't matter how I come home; I'm prepared to give all that I am to ensure that all my boys make it home." All his boys survived the firefight at Bagdad Airport and they all came home. Only Paul was killed, but he had earned his nation's highest award—the Medal of Honor.

NOTES

1. "Baghdad Airport, April 4, 2003," *Army.mil*, accessed May 23, 2016, https://www.army.mil/medalofhonor/smith/citation/printable.html.

2. "Sergeant First Class Paul Ray Smith," *Army.mil*, accessed May 23, 2016, https://www.army.mil/medalofhonor/smith/profile/index.html.

3. "Iraq War Medal of Honor Recipients: Sergeant First Class Paul R. Smith," *U.S. Army Center of Military History*, last modified May 7, 2015 http://www.history.army.mil/moh/wwII-m-s.html#top.

4. "A Sergeant and His Men," *The Christian Science Monitor* (2005). (Ed Blomquist.)

AN AMERICAN BEAUTY

Of legal knowledge I acquired such a grip
That they took me into the partnership,
And that junior partnership I ween,
Was the only ship I ever had seen.
But that kind of ship so suited me,
That now I am the ruler of the Queen's navee!

These were some of the very first words that eighteen-year-old Lillian Russell heard when she joined the chorus of Gilbert and Sullivan's play, *H. M. S. Pinafore.* Acting in one of their musical nonsense shows assured actors and singers of an income. She had dreamed of being an opera singer but had settled on a career on the popular musical stage.

She could also meet people, which led to her marriage to the orchestra leader two weeks later. In November, she left the show. She got a chance to appear on Broadway. Tony Pastor, known as the Father of Vaudeville, had given many actors and singers their first chance. He offered Lillian that chance. She jumped at it and sparkled as a ballad singer in a special sketch in one of his variety shows. She was an instant success.

She had been at Tony Pastor's a month when a humorous event took place. Since her mother was too busy with her own life and the women's movement, she did not know that her daughter had a new life on stage. One evening at dinner, a newspaperman appeared. He spoke to Lillian's mother. "Mrs. Leonard, do you know that there is a girl named Lillian Russell who sings at Tony Pastor's Theater, who looks enough like your little Nellie to be her sister?" Nor did her mother know that her daughter had dropped her given name of Helen Leonard and adopted a stage name.

The man told her mother that Tony Pastor's Theater was a respectable place. Very nice people go there. Lillian's mother accepted the man's invitation to see the show.

When the show ended, after recognizing her daughter, Mrs. Leonard clapped louder than anyone in the theater. Lillian, with her beauty, bell-tone voice, and hourglass figure, packed the house every night with devoted fans. She became the first prima donna of modern American musical theater.

Lillian made appearances at the Bijou Opera House on Broadway and in various Gilbert and Sullivan comic operettas. She was the star in *Patience* and was Aline in *The Sorcerer*. Traveling abroad, she starred in *Polly* and in Solomon and Grundy's *Pocahontas*. Returning to America, she toured two years with Solomon's comic opera company, yet she always returned to her first love, Gilbert and Sullivan. Because of her natural beauty and glamorous role in Tony Pastor's musical review, *An American Beauty,* Lillian became known as an American beauty. This title would go with her the rest of her life.

Fellow actress and eventual motion picture star, Marie Dressler, said of Lillian, "I can still recall the rush of pure awe that marked her entrance on the stage. And then the thunderous applause that swept from the orchestra to the gallery, to the very roof."

When Alexander Graham Bell, inventor of the telephone, introduced long distance service in 1890, the first voice heard over the line was Lillian Russell's. From New York City, Russell sang "Sabre Song" to eager crowds in Washington, DC, and Boston. Audiences who could not attend her shows in New York got a firsthand experience listening to her on the telephone.

In 1902 she was to star in *Twirly Whirly.* The songwriter who wrote several songs for her earlier held off giving Lillian her solo. "It's not ready," he said. A few days later he committed suicide.

The music was found in his pocket. "Come Down, Ma Evenin' Star" was to be Lillian's showpiece. It became her signature song. It was the only song she ever recorded. The musical stage successes that Lillian performed were as numerous as the flowers of a garden. When her voice gave out, she switched to comedy. She finally retired in 1919.

NOTES

1. Gerald Bordman and Thomas S. Hischak, "Russell, Lillian," in *The Oxford Companion to American Theatre* (New York City: Oxford University Press, 2004), 542–43.

2. William Gilbert and Arthur Sullivan, *H.M.S. Pinafore* (1893).

3. Mike B., "December 4: Lillian Russell, Master of the Comic Opera," *Great Lives in History*, http://greatlivesinhistory.blogspot.com/search/label/Lillian%20Russell.

4. "Today in History: November 22 An American Beauty," *The Library of Congress*, last modified November 5, 2010, https://memory.loc.gov/ammem/today/nov22.html.

5. W. S. Gilbert, *The Story of H.M.S. Pinafore*, performed by Noel Badrian, 2012, ebook, https://librivox.org/the-story-of-the-h-m-s-pinafore-by-w-s-gilbert/.

6. "Musical Theater: Lillian Russell (1861–1922), *Spotlight: Biography*, accessed May 23, 2016, http://www.smithsonianeducation.org/spotlight/musical.html. (Tad Bennicoff.)

THE SWAMP FOX

During the early period of America, when the colonists were fighting the Native Americans for control of the new land, the Native Americans used a hit-and-run military tactic that worked well for them. It was also a tactic that regular armies did not use. Their gentlemen's fighting style of marching in solid lines was a fatal tradition. The result was that the regular armies suffered many casualties. When the Revolutionary War began in America, the British continued to use the solid line formation. This worked to the advantage of Francis Marion, who led troops from South Carolina against them. Marion adopted the Native American way of fighting.

In 1780, the British captured the city of Charleston, forcing the Americans to withdraw from the area. Francis Marion did not move with them. He organized his own band of revolutionaries, men who had revolted against British rule. They had little in the way of weapons, but Marion trained them in guerrilla warfare. His method made up for what they lacked in equipment. The little band lived off the land, found food wherever they could, upset British communications, broke supply lines, rescued Americans who had been taken prisoner, and captured enemy soldiers. Following each raid, Marion melted into the South Carolina swamps. The British were not familiar with the swamps. They didn't know how to cope with them, so they were unable to follow him. The general in charge of British troops complained, "We cannot catch this Marion. He attacks and runs. He hides in the swamps. He's like a fox—a wily old fox of the swamps." It was true. Marion was a master of strategy.

He was never caught, could not be followed, yet was always *there* just when he was needed by the Americans.

When the British armies were ordered to burn and destroy "all that will not submit," Marion was angry. Acting on orders from American forces, he took his men to destroy all craft on the Santee River. This would prevent the British Lord Cornwallis from escaping. When Marion and his men came upon the British forces, they discovered that the British had stacked their rifles and coats in a careless manner. The Americans dashed into the British camp and quickly overran them.

While these raids were always successful, Marion did have one bit of a problem: his men were all volunteers and came and went as they pleased. They went about working their farms one day and fighting the British the next. He was never sure that he would have enough men to mount a successful raid, but somehow, he always did. Without risking open battle, he zeroed in on British troops like a swarm of hornets then flitted into the forests.

Even though his men were all volunteers and came with their own rifles, clothing, and food, Marion was still able to build a fierce loyalty in them. The men were fighting on their homeland and had a strong desire to protect it, to make it free of British tyranny.

Hiding in the Blue Savannah, an area surrounded by a tangle of stunted pine and scrub oak, the little band waited for the British to appear. They waited only minutes before the British came marching in their usual solid column. Marion's men attacked, rushing at the British like phantoms from the woods. The British fled into the swamps, but Marion did not follow. He knew the British could not survive, since malaria mosquitoes and poisonous snakes would take care of any who did not suffocate in the quicksand.

He was placed in charge of an outpost at Sheldon. Marion's little band, now about fifty men, were ordered to watch the movement of a British unit. They were to prevent the British from obtaining supplies from the Carolina side of the Savannah River. Not only did Marion and his little band succeed, they contributed much to the winning of the Revolutionary War.

A marble monument now stands at Belle Island in memory of Francis Marion. He was a loyal citizen soldier of the revolution who lived without fear. His courage changed the world.

ROY RUSSELL

NOTES

1. http://www.fofweb.com.
2. Fremont P. Wirth, *The Development of America* (American Book Company, 1946).

CREATURE FROM THE EONS

Sometime in 1938, the captain of a small trawler working at the mouth of the Chalumna River pulled up his nets and returned to the harbor at East London, Africa. As usual, he telephoned his good friend, Marjorie Latimer, curator of the small museum there. "Do you want to look over today's catch?" he asked. "I'll be right there," she answered. She always inspected the captain's catch, looking for anything interesting. While inspecting the contents, Marjorie noticed a bright blue fin among the hundreds of other gray fish. The captain pulled the fish into full view. Marjorie examined the find. "It's the most beautiful fish I've ever seen! What can it be?" She examined it more closely, marveling at its appearance.

The fish was more than five feet long and bright blue with iridescent markings. Marjorie noticed its fins. "They're like legs." After the other fish died, this beautiful creature continued to live for several hours, snapping at everyone with its razor-like teeth. When she could not find a description of the creature in any book, she tried to contact her friend, Professor L. J. B. Smith, who was an expert on sea life, but he was on a Christmas vacation, so she made drawings. With no way to preserve the fish, she did the next best thing; she sent it to a taxidermist who mounted it. She also sent the drawings to Smith.

When he opened the letter, Smith gasped aloud. Could the drawings be what he thought they were? It wasn't possible, yet he could not really disbelieve what he saw. The drawings were a likeness of a coelacanth (pronounced "see-luh-kanth"). Scientists only knew the fish from fossils.

Smith knew that this fish had been alive when dinosaurs roamed the earth. The idea of a coelacanth swimming in the ocean today wasn't possible. Records showed that the fish had been extinct for more than fifty million years. He ended his examination with a firm resolve. He knew his friend Marjorie would not play tricks on him, but he had to find out. He had to make certain.

Even with his resolve to find out if the fish were really a coelacanth, he could not at this time. The specimen had been stuffed, the gills and skeleton removed; therefore he could not prove that it really was the same species. He began a hunt for a second specimen. "If one coelacanth had been found, there must be another," Smith reasoned.

He prepared a poster offering a reward of one hundred British pounds—a year's income to the average South African fisherman in 1938. The posters were handed out among the fishermen. If another fish were caught, it must be kept until Smith could arrive in Africa to inspect the find. The professor's offer set off a worldwide hunt for another of these creatures from the eons.

Other scientists laughed at Smith. "You're wasting your time and your money. The drawings are fake, or inaccurate. The only coelacanths are fossils." Smith's fellow scientists could be right. Coelacanths date back to 360 million years. The ridicule from these scientists stung Smith, but he kept his faith that he'd find another. He did have the interest of the world to support him.

For years no one found another coelacanth. Because everyone began to doubt Smith's theory, they lost interest, but he never gave up hope. Fourteen years later he received a telegram. With shaking hands he read that a fish had been caught that looked like the one in his poster. Smith flew to South Africa. He felt giddy as he walked, almost with drunken steps, toward the native hut where Marjorie kept the find. Shivering he pulled back the cloth that she had wrapped around the prize. The hair on the back of his neck rose, and he felt a chill rush through his body. He laughed while tears swelled in his eyes. He shouted with delight at the sight. It was December 29, 1952, summer in the in Comoros.

The specimen was exactly like Marjorie Latimer's drawings. It was truly a coelacanth—an ancient fish from the eons. Despite the mocking laughs from his peers, L. J. B. Smith was rewarded for his courage in holding fast to what he believed.

NOTES

1. Richard A. Boning, *Getting the Facts: Book E* (Barnell Loft Books, 1997).

2. *Coelacanth Information*, accessed May 23, 2016, http://www.dinofish.com/.

3. "Coelacanth—The First, Astonishing Find," F.C. Nicholson, *Science Encyclopedia*, accessed May 23, 2016, http://science.jrank.org/pages/1566/Coelacanth-first-astonishing -find.html. (Dominik Mazur.)

4. Mark T. Holder, Mark V. Erdmann, Thomas P. Wilcox, Roy L. Caldwell, and David M. Hillis, "Two living species of coelacanths?" *Proceedings of the National Academy of Sciences of the United States of America*, vol. 96, no. 22, (1999), http://www.ncbi.nlm.nih .gov/pmc/articles/PMC23015/.

LIVING A CHARMED LIFE

At the age of eight, Eddie Rickenbacker and his Horsehead Gang built a roller coaster. It was a cart that he and the others would ride down the one-hundred-foot slope of the local gravel pit. Too late, he learned that most vehicles need brakes, something they had failed to install. Whether it had adequate steering was a matter of debate also. He learned that danger and peril often come while seeking adventure. The roller coaster stuck in the loose gravel and flipped. With arms like a windmill, Eddie and the boys tumbled downhill like rag dolls blown before a strong wind. The contraption rolled over Eddie, leaving a lot of bruises and scratches. A metal wheel cut his leg to the bone. Eddie earned his first scar; this encounter would not, however, be his only brush with death. On his road to fame and fortune, he would meet death face-to-face several times.

It became one of the parts that defined his life. Yet, from childhood, he loved machines. He was always around them, tinkering, repairing, and planning. He was saddened by the sudden death of his father, but he did not have time to grieve much; to help support the family, he began work at a garage. He loved repairing automobiles.

Accidents continued to plague him. In any one of them he could have lost his life: being run over by a horse-drawn carriage, enduring a botched surgery, walking away from several airplane crashes. These milestones in his life did prepare him for the near-death scrapes he would encounter as a race car driver and as a pilot in World War I.

When he drove in speed races, he drove his employer's cars. With cars only in their infancy, achieving any real speed was difficult. Yet Eddie always felt a thrill when pulling on his race clothes, beret cap, and goggles. As he climbed into the driver's seat, the adrenaline coursed through his veins as fast as he raced the car around the track.

When he pressed the accelerator, he heard the engine roar louder than a semi truck. It rumbled in his ears. He was always thrilled by the raw power of the car on the track. As he worked the clutch and geared it down, he felt the powerful machine leap forward like a lion on the hunt. Eddie was propelled down the track. He had quickly learned how to get the most out of his racer. He gripped the steering wheel so hard that his knuckles turned white. His heart beat a tattoo against his chest. He could actually hear it above the engine roar. Every time he climbed into a race car and jockeyed it into the pack, the hair rose on the back of his neck. At full throttle, every time he pressed the accelerator all the way down, he felt the thrill of his life.

Race cars in the 1900s looked like boiler tanks with a cut out section for a driver's seat. The engine hoods were strapped on. Wire spokes radiated from the hub to solid rubber tires. They had no cages, no seat belts, and no roll bars to protect the drivers. He was fully exposed, and crashes were often deadly. Eddie, living the charmed life that he was, always walked away unharmed, even when he crashed into the wall or tangled with other race cars.

He drove a Peugeot 7 and a Firestone Columbia, but preferred his Maxwell. He was a daring race car driver in all of them. He raced all over Iowa and Nebraska and won his first race in 1913. This established his fame as a good driver. He won five more races with his Maxwell. With cars still unable to reach great speeds, as they do today at four hundred miles per hour, when Eddie drove faster than a mile a minute, he was given the nickname "Fast Eddie." Although he set the speed record at 134 miles per hour, and raced three separate years in the famous Indianapolis 500, he never won the Indy 500. He did place tenth in 1914. For six years he was one of the nation's top race car drivers. He left racing only one regret: never winning the Indy 500.

The threat of war was brewing in Europe. Eddie was one of the few who knew that war would come and the United States would probably be in it. When the United States declared war on Germany in 1917, Eddie was already training in France. With the help of Colonel Billy Mitchell, he was able to get into the Ninety-Fourth Aero Squadron. On his first mission he flew a Nieuport 28e biplane, a plane with two wings. He and Captain James Hall were in their planes on the runway with propellers spinning. Eddie scanned the skies. He saw a tiny speck against the clouds. The two pilots agreed that it was an enemy plane. They opened the throttles and moved across the wet field.

Hall led them into the sun, a good position from which to attack. Eddie cut off any retreat while Hall dived at the enemy with the sun at his back. As the enemy flyer spun off to the left to escape, Eddie opened the throttle and was on target. He pressed the machine gun trigger and tracer bullets streaked into the enemy plane. Fire erupted causing the plane to make a lazy curve and head toward the ground. It crashed in a ball of fire at the edge of some woods inside the German line. Eddie had brought down his first enemy plane.

The men of World War I fought in canvas and wood frame biplanes. They were small craft with a single propeller. These planes could barely get up to speeds of one hundred miles per hour. High above the trenches men fought heroic battles with these primitive aircraft. It was in this kind of plane that Eddie scored his second victory. He and a fellow pilot took off before dawn to catch the enemy off guard. Eddie spiraled off by himself to have a look at the enemy airfield. He saw three planes taking off. He flew lower, still unseen by the enemy. He dived at them with machine gun spitting a hail of bullets, stopping the takeoff of all three.

When Eddie pulled out of his dive, the Nieuport cracked and the upper wing covering tore off. He spun down, headed for certain destruction and death. If fear gripped him, he did not have time to think about it. Frantically he worked the throttle and pulled on the stick. No response. He kept trying. Harder. More throttle! Harder on the stick. He had to pull out! The engine sputtered, a half-hearted try. It finally came to life. He landed safely with another victory.

Eddie went up in a new Spad XIII when these improved planes arrived at the front. They were faster, had a hardy construction, and could dive at high speed. He found them to be one of the best dog fighters in the sky. With his new Spad, Eddie ran up his victories to twenty-six and became the top pilot of the war. The guys nicknamed him "Ace of Aces." When the war ended, he returned to the United States to cheering crowds. He became the owner of the Indianapolis Motor Speedway. Soon he was general manager of Eastern Airlines. On a business trip to Atlanta, Georgia, in 1941, his plane crashed and he was nearly killed. His injuries were serious, but when they were barely healed, they did not keep him from helping out when America went to war again that year.

One of Eddie's most famous near-death crashes came while he was flying a secret mission to the Pacific area. He was to review conditions and operations and report to General MacArthur. His B-17 overshot the island by one hundred miles. When the fuel ran out, the pilot put the plane down in the ocean. The men lashed three inflated rafts together. After several days the men in two of the rafts decided to cut themselves free and try to find land. This left Eddie and the others in his raft to fend for themselves.

On the twenty-first morning they had but a little water left from the rains that had drenched them days before. Late that afternoon two planes appeared but passed into the sunset. A half hour later they came back. They flew directly for the raft. The first dived right over the half-starved men. The plane was so low that Eddie could see the pilot's smiling face. He was like an angel from heaven.

Light was draining from the sky. They would have to be rescued soon or darkness would overcome them. They might not survive another night without food and water. One of the planes flew off while the other made a cautious landing on the smooth sea surface. The pilot throttled the plane closer. Eddie and the others paddled to the plane. America's Ace of Aces had cheated death once again. No one could disagree that Eddie Rickenbacker was living a charmed life.

NOTES

1. http://www.af.mil/information/heritage/person.asp?dec=&pid=123006466.
2. "Eddie Rickenbacker—America's "Ace of Aces," Pamela Feltus, *U.S. Centennial of Flight Commission*, accessed May 23, 2016, http://www.centennialofflight.net/essay/Air_Power/rickenbacker/AP9.htm.
3. "Rickenbacker, Edward Vernon," Bibliography Branch, *Air University*, last modified March 10, 2014, http://www.au.af.mil/au/aul/bibs/great/rickenbacker07.htm.
4. "Captain Eddie Rickenbacker: America's Ace of Aces," *Home of Heroes*, accessed May 23, 2016, http://www.homeofheroes.com/wings//part1/4_aceofaces.html. (Doug Sterner.)
5. "Eddie Rickenbacker Papers, RG 101 Edward Vernon "Eddie" Rickenbacker," *Auburn University Special Collections and Archives*, accessed May 23, 2016, http://www.lib.auburn.edu/archive/find-aid/101/eddie.htm. (John Barnes: Auburn Library.)
6. "Eddie Rickenbacker in a Maxwell racecar," *America on the Move*, accessed May 23, 2016, http://amhistory.si.edu/onthemove/collection/object_341.html.
7. "Tuvalu: Lost at Sea—the Rescue of Eddie Rickenbacker," *Jane's Tuvalu Polynesia*, accessed May 23, 2016, http://janeresture.com/rickenbacker/index.htm.
8. Captain Edward V. Rickenbacker, *Seven Came Through, Rickenbacker's Full Story*, (Doubleday, Doran and Company, 1943).

BRING 'EM BACK ALIVE

The big cat crouched and growled fiercely. It struck at the men with its huge paws, its claws flexed out. Three men held stiff, sturdy poles with loops at the end to encircle the big cat's neck. Carefully they maneuvered the animal into the bamboo cage. Another helper dropped the door into place. The tiger continued to growl and bear its fangs, but it was on its way to a new home.

This was a time before tranquilizer darts. Out in the wild, the animals were quite alive and alert. They fought back. With sharp claws and teeth, they lunged at their captors. Boa constrictors could wrap themselves around a man and squeeze the breath out of him. Kangaroos could give a man a kick with their powerful hind legs and crush his ribs or break an arm. Snakes with deadly venom could sink their fangs into an arm and send a man into a coma.

The San Antonio Express News said, "Picture a cross between Clark Gable and that enthusiastic Australian fellow who frolics with alligators on TV and you get something of a picture of Frank Buck." That may be putting it mildly even then. "Fans remember Frank Buck as a devoted conservationist. He fretted often about the survival of rare species." He was a bold adventurer, whose deeds in Borneo, Sumatra, India, and the Philippines amazed everyone.

You name it—Buck caught it. For eighteen years he traveled the world to exotic places to bring back animals and birds of every kind.

Frank Buck was born in Gainesville, Texas. As he grew he developed a love of geography. He studied it at the expense of all his other subjects.

In fact, he utterly failed every other class. During his childhood he collected birds and small animals. He became a cowpuncher, a name given to men who prodded cattle to keep them moving, but being a cowpuncher was not what he really wanted to do. He had a chance to ride a cattle car to Chicago, but he did not take the train back to Texas. In 1911, he won some money and sailed for Brazil, the beginning of a lifetime of world travel. He returned with many exotic birds that he was able to sell at a large profit. Then he was off to Singapore and more dangerous adventures.

In Buck's day, capturing wild animals meant working very close to them and it was a dangerous activity. Because the black leopard is a mean animal, catching one is never easy. A trap would consist of a large chunk of raw meat in a cage. The animal would pass by the opening, but then return and go after the meat. Down falls the gate.

A friendly ruler gave Buck a pig, which he housed in a pen. A thirty-foot python slithered into the pen and swallowed the pig but was unable to escape. Buck won himself a prize catch without endangering himself. Once, he cut a hole in a coconut shell and placed rice inside. When a monkey reached into the shell, it would not let go of the food and could not withdraw its fist: another wild animal for his collections.

A cobra escaped from its cage and spewed deadly venom in Buck's eyes. Attacked by another cobra, he danced around it until he could throw his coat over the snake and pounce on it. He held it beneath him as it wiggled to get free until helpers could pull it out like an eel from its cave. He herded wild elephants into a corral and rode one across a river. With ropes and lassoes he lifted a man-eating tiger from a pit, all the while the animal growled, clawed, and tried to sink its teeth into Buck's body. In a test of nerve and courage, he grabbed a python, which twisted and sprang like a coil, and tried to stuff it into a crate. The snake wrapped itself around him, suffocating and crushing Buck, yet he was able to free one arm to reach for his pistol. He fired three shots into the snake before it released its grip. On another occasion, a six-hundred-pound tapir that he was treating turned on him and nearly killed him.

Frank Buck lived an exciting and courageous life, one filled with danger and peril. He brought the world of exotic and faraway animals home for young and old to admire. Today, animal rights activists say he was wrong. Most others, including doctors, say he was ahead of his time in the humane treatment he gave his animals. He treated them like babies.

Frank Buck brought 'em back alive. His monkeys helped in the defeat of polio. For his courage and foresight, we owe him a vote of thanks.

NOTES

1. Frank Buck, *Bring 'em Back Alive: The Best of Frank Buck* (Texas Tech University Press, 2006). (Joanna Conrad.)
2. "Frank Buck," Charles Fisher Cooper, *CooperToons*, accessed May 23, 2016, http://www.coopertoons.com/caricatures/frankbuck_bio.html.
3. Frank Buck and Edward Anthony, *Bring 'em Back Alive,* directed by Clyde E. Elliot (Van Beuren Studios, 1932), DVD.
4. Frank Buck and Edward Anthony, *Wild Cargo,* directed by Armand Denis (Van Beuren Studios, 1934), DVD.
5. "How Frank Buck Filmed His Tiger-Python Battle (Nov, 1932)," *Modern Mechanix,* accessed May 23, 2016, http://blog.modernmechanix.com/how-frank-buck-filmed-his-tiger-python-battle.

"I FEEL TEN FEET TALL"

By the time he was seven, Cody had gone through five pairs of legs. He actually has pairs of legs for almost any occasion. When he's sitting or climbing, he dons short ones. If he wants to run like a young colt, he puts on longer ones. Since Cody was born without useable legs, doctors amputated them above the knee when he was a baby. He suffered from a rare disease called sacral agenesis, a deformity of the spine. He had no tibia or knee bones. His mother, Tina, said "Hardly anyone takes to prosthetics so well. . . . It was as if Cody had been waiting to have new legs so he could walk."

He was also born six weeks early with kidney problems and other difficulties. During the first two years of his life, he survived operations for gall bladder, intestinal, and stomach problems, as well as surgeries for a dislocated hip, a hernia, and difficulty breathing. Doctors told his parents he might not live.

At seventeen months he was walking like any other toddler. At five he got his first pair of running legs. Can he run? Swim? Play soccer or golf or ice hockey? You bet! He even joined the Boy Scouts and went rock climbing. Artificial legs are expensive and Cody outgrows them faster than a robot counts numbers. Luckily, the Texas Scottish Rite Hospital for Children provides prosthetics for him. The family agrees that they are truly lucky and grateful to have the specialist center that donates his running legs.

Marathons and Olympics draw Cody like a bear to honey. To help repay the costs of providing the artificial limbs for Cody, he and his parents participate in the marathons and races to raise money. Over the years they have raised thousands of dollars. Participating has been a benefit to Cody. In addition to the funds, he has also established great racing times in his age range. "I'm a nonstop runner," he announced. "No one can keep up with me. With my walking legs I take big steps. In my running legs, I can run very fast and jump on one leg." Already, he can run sixty meters in twenty seconds and one hundred meters in thirty seconds. He did this at the Endeavour Games (an international competition people with disabilities) when he was only six years old. What is amazing is that he was just seconds away from the record holder, who is nine years old.

Cody is also on the swim team at his school. He competes against able-bodied classmates in running and swimming and sometimes beats them. His ability in swimming has improved by half a minute. "I'm going to compete in swimming. I will definitely take part one day and win a gold medal." His dreams don't stop there. When Michael Phelps won the Olympics, Cody said, "I'd love to swim in a race against Michael Phelps one day." This year he got to meet his swimming idol—double amputee Rudy Garcia-Tolson, who won gold in the 2004 Paralympics and became a world-class swimmer. Cody hopes to swim in the Paralympics for Team USA.

There are athletic events for amputee participants, but it is classified as those with one artificial leg. Cody and others like him have to compete in this category even though they are double amputees. He hopes that the rules will someday be changed to create a category for double amputees.

He is not shy. He marches right up to grown men and says, "You can do all the things I do." Soldiers are Cody's heroes. When he's not competing in athletic events, he loves nothing better than to visit disabled veterans' hospitals. He motivates the wounded. It's anybody's guess who is the real hero, the disabled veteran or Cody with no legs. He is their hero as much as they are his.

Courage can come in small packages. Cody's courage explodes like a grenade in the face of everyone who meets him. His enthusiasm is disarming and contagious. He is like a welcome ray of sunshine after a storm. He concludes, "With my five pairs of legs, I feel ten feet tall."

NOTES

1. "Cody McCasland," *Challenged Athletes Foundation*, accessed May 23, 2016,http://www.challengedathletes.org/atf/cf/%7B10e89006-a432-401e-bc7-805e68ce5c27%7D/CodyMcCasland.pdf.
2. "With five pairs of legs, I feel 10 feet tall! The boy, 7, who doesn't let a double amputation hold him back," Daily Mail Reporter, *Daily Mail*, published March 12, 2009, http://www.dailymail.co.uk/news/article-1160954/With-pairs-legs-I-feel-10-feet-tall-The-boy-7-doesnt-let-double-amputation-hold-back.html. (Danny Howell.)
3. Personal communication with Tina McCasland (September 2009).

ROUGH RIDERS AT SAN JUAN HILL

At 9:40 p.m., on February 15, 1898, the powder charges stored in the forward part of the USS *Maine* exploded. The entire front third of the ship was blown apart. Directly above the explosives were the crew's sleeping quarters. Since the captain had not allowed shore leave, the crew was asleep in their bunks. 260 sailors vanished as if vaporized.

A board of inquiry was immediately formed. Their investigation of the wreckage at the bottom of Havana Harbor led them to believe the *Maine* had been sunk by a mine. When this news was announced, the American public was outraged. Their feelings were fed by news articles that blamed Spain for the disaster. Relations between the two countries were already at the boiling point. The sinking of the *Maine* lit the fuse to war.

Spain controlled the Cubans, who had tried for ten years to free themselves of Spanish rule. Americans sided with the Cubans, which strained Spanish and American relations. War almost broke out earlier when the Spanish attacked the *Virginia* at sea and murdered the entire crew. The Cubans made a second bid for freedom but Spain sent a general to pacify the people.

He became known as the Butcher. By random selection he killed more than two hundred thousand Cuban citizens. The American press kept up its crusade to liberate Cuba from Spanish tyranny. Riots in Cuba made President McKinley fear for the safety of Americans on the island. To ensure their safety, he sent the *Maine*.

Although President McKinley tried to solve the Cuban problem, he could not get Spain to agree to Cuban freedom. Spain hardened its position against it. McKinley pushed for intervention and ordered a blockade of Cuba (using ships to prevent other forces from entering or leaving the Havana Harbor) that caused Spain to declare war. Congress responded by declaring war two days later. The destruction of the *Maine* was the catalyst that drove the United States into full-scale intervention and finally into the Spanish-American War.

One of the first Americans to jump into the fray was Theodore Roosevelt. He prepared to attack both Cuba and the Philippines. As assistant secretary of the navy, he placed George Dewey on high alert and told him, "Be prepared to keep the Spanish fleet from getting into Cuba." Since the standing army consisted of only twenty-eight thousand men, Roosevelt came up with the idea of volunteer units. These units "will be composed exclusively of frontiersmen who possess skills as horsemen and marksmen," (men who could shoot a rifle with great accuracy). Roosevelt resigned his government job to lead one of the volunteer units. They were called "Rough Riders."

The navy had the island under blockade. The army set up a bombardment of Santiago, Cuba, while marines landed at the southern coast of Cuba. Two days later Roosevelt's Rough Riders fought their first battle. They were assigned as a diversion while General Lawton's infantry captured El Caney. At thirty-nine years old, Teddy, as he was called, was the roughshod, take-charge leader in the glory of his youth and service to his nation. In his defining moment, he decided to lead a charge up San Juan Hill against the heavily fortified forces of the Spanish. It was also the bloodiest battle of the war.

Under a hailstorm of bullets, tropical heat, larger-than-life insects, wet clothing, and empty stomachs, the Rough Riders were, nevertheless, a colorful unit. Screaming, brandishing sabers and rifles, they charged up the hill. At point lead was Teddy Roosevelt. Men fell beside him, cut down by enemy fire. Yet the Riders had one purpose—capture the blockhouse on the hill. As they neared the top, two other officers were shot from their horses. Even Teddy was forced to dismount and climb to the top on foot. The Rough Riders won the day.

Theodore "Teddy" Roosevelt came home to become president of the United States. He would be awarded the Medal of Honor some eighty years later. The legacy of his Rough Riders lives forever.

NOTES

1. "Topics in Chronicling America—The Sinking of the Maine," *Newspaper & Current Periodical Reading Room*, accessed May 23, 2016, http://www.loc.gov/rr/news/topics /maine.html.

2. *Theodore Roosevelt Association*, accessed May 23, 2016, http://www.theodoreroosevelt .org/site/c.elKSIdOWIiJ8H/b.8090799/k.C003/Home.htm.

3. "T.R. the Rough Rider: Hero of the Spanish American War," *National Park Service*, accessed May 23, 2016, https://www.nps.gov/thrb/learn/historyculture/tr-rr -spanamwar.htm.

4. "The Destruction of the USS *Maine*," *Naval History and Heritage Command*, published October 5, 2015, http://www.history.navy.mil/browse-by-topic/disasters-and -phenomena/destruction-of-uss-maine.html.

5. David Wallechinsky and Irving Wallace, *The People's Almanac*, (Doubleday, 1975), 209, 273.

6. "Theodore Roosevelt," in *The Presidents of the United States of America*, Frank Freidel and Hugh Sidey, *The White House*, accessed May 23, 2016, https://www.whitehouse .gov/1600/presidents/theodoreroosevelt.

SACRIFICE FOR HONOR

It was October 1963. Captain Rocky Versace was with a patrol along a Vietnamese canal. The team left their camp at Tân Phú for the village of Le Coeur to drive out an enemy command post there. When they reached the village, they found the enemy gone. The patrol decided to follow but ran into an ambush. The Americans fought for more than six hours until they were overpowered. Captain Versace and two close friends were captured and imprisoned.

When France pulled its military forces out of Vietnam, the United States was left to deal with the Vietnam problem. The government sent two hundred American soldiers as advisors in 1954. The first Americans were killed in 1959. The North was rattling its sabers and threatening invasion and war; it was about to be a replay of the Korean War.

The United States Army Special Forces was formed in 1962 to advise and assist the South Vietnamese in organizing, training, and equipping the Civilian Irregular Defense Group. Military personnel in Vietnam in 1963 totaled 674, most of them Special Forces men from the United States.

This force had armed and well-placed camps located along the borders, each with an airfield. The forces soon became combat fighting units. They had to patrol the borders, but their isolated locations in the middle of known enemy units made the camps easy prey to enemy attack. It was from one of these border camps that Captain Rocky Versace and his friends left on patrol.

When they were overrun by superior enemy forces, Rocky went down with three bullet wounds in his leg. When the Viet Cong (a Vietnamese political organization) captured him and his friends, Lieutenant Rowe and Sergeant Pitzer, they took their boots and led them barefoot deep into the jungles. The place was a dark maze of mangroves, canals, and swamps. Mosquitoes nearly ate them alive. The enemy did not treat Rocky's leg wounds, and his leg became badly infected. Even with his leg wounds, within three weeks he tried to get away, dragging himself on hands and knees. Guards quickly found him crawling in the swamp and returned him to his bamboo cage—six feet long, two feet wide, three feet high. He lay flat on his back with leg irons clamped around his ankles. Kept in cages, the three men suffered sunburn during the day and insect bites that nearly drove them mad at night.

Some years before, Rocky chose the army over the priesthood for a career. When he won an appointment to West Point, he decided that God wanted him to be a soldier. He spoke French and Vietnamese, in addition to his native English. It was evident from the beginning that he would be a problem prisoner for the Viet Cong. Actually, he loved the Vietnamese as a people, but could not accept the Viet Cong's acts of revolution and the communist agenda. Yet, even as a prisoner, he did not regret his career choice.

The enemy set up schools that prisoners had to attend. Rocky went only when the guards poked him with bayonets. He resisted all attempts by the Viet Cong to force him to embarrass his country. For him, duty, honor, country, and liberty—the big four—were his life. He talked loud and long against the Cong. He told his captors that as long as he was true to God and true to himself, what was waiting for him after this life was far better than anything that could happen to him now. He stood toe-to-toe with them. For his defiance, he was beaten, starved, and humiliated, but he held true to his country and himself.

Rocky developed the strength to resist at a young age. He was the oldest of five children in a close but strict Catholic family. He took on the role of father when his own father had to be away with the army. He developed a firm sense of duty and morality. His brothers said, "If Rocky thought he was right, he was a pain in the neck. If he knew he was right, he was absolutely atrocious." Knowing that he was right, he also knew who he was and what he was. He had strong, firm courage.

Rocky's defiance grew even as his condition became worse. This infuriated his captors. They tried anything to break him. They tied a rope around his neck and yanked him from village to village. His head swelled, his hair turned completely white, and his skin turned yellow with jaundice. He wore no shoes; his feet were cut and bleeding. The villagers liked him despite what the Cong wanted them to believe. They liked his funny expressions and his friendly smile. When he spoke, they listened because they couldn't help themselves.

Frustrated and angry, his captors separated him from his buddies. He was placed in isolation and confined by himself for days. He never saw his friends except from time to time, but they noticed that neither his spirit nor his will to live was broken.

One of the codes of military honor requires prisoners to try to escape. Rocky did time after time. For his efforts he was always tortured. The Viet Cong guards twisted his wounded leg, but he refused to cry out from the pain. The Cong fed him only rice and salt. He became as thin as a fence post. When he came to Vietnam he was a tall, dark-haired, and very handsome man. Marine officer Don Price said, "If you're going to ask for a West Point cadet from central casting, Rocky is it." By January 1965, he was barely recognizable.

Rocky was a soldier's soldier. He lived and breathed the code of duty and honor and country. Later, his friend Rowe would say, "The alien force of the Viet Cong, applied with hate, could not break him. They failed to bend him. Though solitary confinement gave him no contact, he drew upon his inner self to create a force so strong that those who tried to destroy him failed."

While the Viet Cong tortured their prisoners, they wanted to get the men to confess to war crimes to use their confessions as propaganda against the United States. Rocky's captors had no idea with whom they were dealing. He gave them only name, rank, and serial number. He repeated the rules of the Geneva Convention, the treaty, chapter, and verse over and over. This only made the Cong angrier. He resisted loudly and strongly. His captors focused all their anger toward him, not bothering to torture his friends Rowe and Pitzer. Rocky was a hard line resister.

Not only did Rocky resist, but he also fought back at the top of his voice. He countered their claims of war crimes so that the local villagers could hear. The rice farmers smiled at what he did and were surprised at his strength and honor in the face of torture. His loyalty to God and his country stood out against the attempts of his captors to break him.

Finally, he was separated from his friends completely. Yet even in isolation, he continued to inspire others. One night, Nick Rowe stirred uncomfortably in his cramped bamboo cage as he heard noises in the darkness. The noises were coming from the distant area where Rocky was caged. Nick was weak, suffering from frequent bouts with dysentery and wasting away to mere skin and bones. Dan Pitzer was in no better condition, but they were better off than Rocky.

Nick could hear Rocky's voice rising above the noise still defying his captors. From the darkness of the U Minh Forest, he could hear Rocky singing. At the top of his lungs, Captain Rocky Versace belted out the words of a song, then it became quiet. The following morning as Nick Rowe walked past the area where Rocky had been, he saw what remained. A twisted piece of metal that had been Rocky's cup and pan, a pile of bloody rags—Rocky's gray POW pajamas. The cage was wrecked. Later, a guard told Nick that they had to take drastic measures against Captain Versace because he would not do what they wanted.

On Sunday, September 26, 1965, *Liberation Radio* announced the execution of Captain Rocky Versace. Very shortly, a flight of helicopters flew into the area and Rowe overpowered his guards, ran to the copters, jumped aboard, and flew off to freedom. Yet he will ever hear the voice of his friend, and he will never forget the courageous warrior's last words sung defiantly into the darkness of that Vietnamese jungle—"God Bless America."

NOTES

1. "Humbert Roque Versace," *Arlington National Cemetery*, last modified January 27, 2007, http://arlingtoncemetery.net/hrversace.htm. (Michael Patterson.)

2. "Rocky the Reactionary," *Home of Heroes*, accessed May 23, 2016, http://www.homeofheroes.com/profiles/profiles_versace_pow.htm. (Doug Sterner.)

3. "Vietnam War Medal of Honor Recipients: Versace, Humbert R.," *U.S. Army Center of Military History*, last modified May 7, 2015, http://www.history.army.mil/moh/vietnam-m-z.html#VERSACE.

4. *P.O.W. Network*, accessed May 23, 2016, http://www.pownetwork.org.bios/v/v017/htm.

5. "Distinguished Member of the Special Forces Regiment," *United States Army Special Operations Command*, accessed May 23, 2016, http://www.soc.mil/swcS/RegimentalHonors/_pdf/sf_versace.pdf.

6. "Special Forces Advisors Republic of Vietnam," *US Army Special Forces Vietnam, Provisional*, accessed May 23, 2016, http://www.groups.sfahq.com/adv_rvn_61_63.htm.

7. "Bush Awards Medal of Honor to Vietnam War Hero," Linda D. Kozaryn, *U.S. Department of Defense*, accessed May 23, 2016, http://archive.defense.gov/news/newsarticle.aspx?id=43679.

CHRISTIAN MARTYR

It was late afternoon of June 27, 1844. The shadow cast by the two-story, brick jailhouse at Carthage, Illinois, shaded the courtyard below. Two hundred armed men, with their faces painted black with wet gunpowder, surrounded the building. They were an unruly mob, shouting and swearing and waving their weapons. As the mob approached the single doorway that led to the narrow flight of stairs to the cells on the second floor, the jailor warned Joseph Smith of their coming. Joseph, his brother Hyrum, and two other members of their church, were in jail based on false charges. Now, even without a trial to deny the charges, they were about to be murdered by a lawless mob that had crossed the Mississippi River from Missouri.

Only fourteen years earlier, Joseph Smith had founded the Church of Jesus Christ of Latter-day Saints. Heavenly beings, in a series of visits, gave Joseph a charge to translate writings from golden plates hidden in a hill in western New York. From the beginning, mobs persecuted Joseph and the members of the church. He moved to Kirtland, Ohio, where he set up the church office. The members began building a temple. As the church was growing, Joseph sent some members to Missouri to establish a settlement. Two years later, the members of the church came under attack.

With faith and courage, the people responded to the persecutions. In the town of Far West, the mobs came nightly. At various times they shot and killed a pet dog or cut the tail off a member's cow and then stuck it in a crack of the front door. A member said, "Our neighbor had a fine horse. We saw that same horse passing one day missing both its ears and tail.

The mob had cut them off!" The mobs tore a roof off a house and smashed the windows with rocks. Night after night the mobs came. When one member of the church stood up to them, they marched him down to some dark woods to whip him to death. They coated others with melted tar and covered them with feathers. They put others in a rat-infested jail. At another time, the mobs rode up on their horses, firing their guns and shouting, "Bring out them Mormon brats so we can kill 'em! Git 'em out here! We're gonna' kill 'em!" At Haun's Mill, the mobs *did* ride in and murder many men, women, and children. Mobs routed them from their homes and businesses and butchered them in the streets. The raiders took over church member's property.

In the winter of 1838, and 1839, the Missouri State Militia received extermination orders from the governor to drive the Mormons from the state or kill all of them. The people sought safety in Illinois. Mobs arrested Joseph again and placed him in Liberty Jail—a contrary name for a jail to say the least. He was helpless to aid the people. That winter the members suffered terrible conditions. They walked the two hundred miles out of Missouri, many with feet wrapped in rags because they had no shoes. The mobs took the few decent wagons and horses they had. At night the people slept in the open in the freezing snow.

April arrived. Prison officials moved Joseph and the other prisoners from Liberty Jail to Gallatin, Missouri. After court appearances, guards moved them to Columbia, Missouri. About two weeks later, while being moved yet another time, sympathetic guards let Joseph and his fellow prisoners escape to join the main body of the church in Quincy, Illinois. Joseph praised the others for the endurance of their suffering.

On the banks of the Mississippi River, in a lowland swamp, the members of the Church built a new city—Nauvoo. It blossomed like a giant flower from the wastes of the Mississippi swamp. Within four years, the city of Nauvoo grew to the size of Chicago.

Up to the event of Joseph Smith's final arrest, he was involved in two hundred lawsuits, but every time he was set free because the charges were always false. In 1844, several of Joseph Smith's former associates left the church to publish a paper attacking him. In response to public outrage caused by their writings, the Nauvoo city Mormon leaders declared the newspaper to be a public nuisance and enacted a law that allowed them to destroy the libelous press. As proof of their action, they used William Blackstone's book on the law. He said that a libelous, or untruthful, press is a nuisance. Under the council's new ordinance, Joseph Smith, as mayor of Nauvoo, ordered the city marshal to destroy the paper and the press.

Many of those who persecuted the church said Joseph Smith had violated freedom of the press. They filed charges against Joseph for inciting a riot. The mob made more violent and vicious threats against Joseph and the church. On the strength of another editor's printed lies, the mob rose to action, and officials issued arrest warrants from outside Nauvoo.

The governor of Illinois called for a trial by a non-Mormon jury in Carthage, promising to protect Joseph. Members persuaded Joseph to turn himself in. Although afraid of what might happen, he agreed. He was not sure that he should give himself up, but he went like a lamb to the slaughter, yet as calm as soft snow in the face of possible death. He knew he had done nothing wrong, but he also knew he would be murdered in cold blood. The truth of his words would be fulfilled sooner than anyone thought. Joseph, his brother Hyrum, and other city council members surrendered on the charge of riot, but no sooner had they given themselves up when they were charged with treason. The council members were released on bond, but the judge ordered Joseph and Hyrum held in jail.

This courage and bravery were part of Joseph Smith's very nature. When he was seven, Joseph and his brothers and sisters were stricken with typhoid fever. In a short time they recovered, but Joseph did not. A painful abscess grew on his leg and would not heal despite doctors' efforts to make him better. They told his parents that they would have to remove the leg. One doctor offered to try a new procedure. They brought rope to tie young Joseph to the bed. There was no anesthetic to ease his pain, and they could not run the chance of having Joseph move. "I will not be bound," the seven-year-old said. "I can bear the pain much better if I have my liberty." He asked that his father sit beside him and hold him in his arms, then he did what they asked. The operation was a success.

As he had endured the possibility of death at age seven, Joseph Smith now faced it again. He and his brother Hyrum and two others were beaten and dragged through the streets. They spent days that ran into weeks that ran into months in filthy jails. Now in Carthage Jail, with no way of escape, they faced the angry mob that came storming up the stairs. The militia that the governor said would protect the prisoners would in the end, join the mob.

The mob tried to push the heavy wooden door open. Joseph and the others held it firm. Shots came through the door. A ball struck Hyrum directly in the face. He cried out, "I am a dead man," and dropped to the floor. Unable to keep the stronger force out, the men inside yielded. More shots. Blue smoke filled the room. The mob fired five more bullets into Hyrum as he lay defenseless on the floor. Bullets hit another man as many times; he fell and rolled under furniture. Joseph ran for the window. As he prepared to jump, the mob shot him twice in the back. A third bullet hit him from the courtyard. He fell into the shaded patio. At just thirty-eight years old, Joseph became a Christian martyr for standing up for what he believed and what should be his right to believe.

NOTES

1. "Martyrdom of Joseph Smith," Joseph I. Bentley, *Light Planet*, accessed May 23, 2016, http://www.lightplanet.com/mormons/people/joseph_smith/martyrdom.html.
2. *Mormonwiki*, s.v. "Martyrdom of Joseph Smith," last modified June 23, 2011, http://www.mormonwiki.com/Martyrdom_of_Joseph_Smith.
3. http://www.ldsces.org/inst_manuals/chft/chft-21.htm.
4. http://www.ldsces.org/inst_manuals/chft/chft-22.htm.
5. "Joseph Smith Martyrdom," *The More Good Foundation*, accessed May 23, 2016.
6. "Joseph Smith: Early Life and Martyrdom," *History of Mormonism*, accessed May 23, 2016, http://historyofmormonism.com/joseph-smith/life/joseph-smith-early-life-martyrdom/.

GRIDIRON LEGEND

Not long after he was born, Vince Lombardi began playing football. When he was old enough to carry a ball, he organized the neighborhood kids into a sandlot gang. Although they volunteered, they had to play by his rules. His demands were as subtle as a sledgehammer. In these breakneck escapades, he was encouraged by his father. On the opposite side of the field was his mother—she feared that he might be injured.

His love of the sport grew as fast as his shoe size. Vince wasn't a halfway player. He had learned from his father the importance of hard work. At a young age, he helped his dad in the family butcher shop and became adept at hefting large sides of meat around the shop. Along with his talent as a football player, he strengthened his body. He sped up this development by pumping iron (lifting heavy iron weights). All this muscle building at the gym became an asset to him later in his pursuit of athletics and eventual football career.

In high school Vince had a chance to try his athletic skills. He was selected as center for the basketball team. Centers were expected to be able to jump and control the ball. Although he was short for this position, he excelled. On the baseball field he played outfielder and catcher. Here he did not play as well, yet he was admired by his coach for his hard work and drive. When he transferred to another high school, he won a place on the football team. At five feet eight inches and 185 pounds, built like a Sherman tank, he was aggressive and powerful on the field. His dream of winning a college scholarship came true. With the help of teachers and coaches, he won a football scholarship to Fordham University where his skillful playing, both offense and defense, made him a New York hero.

Fordham became but a stepping stone for his greater ambition—to coach for the big boys. His chance came in 1948. With meteoric speed, he moved through the football channels toward the position of assistant coach for the Academy at West Point. Like the financial stock market, Vince had his ups and downs. In the five seasons he coached, he had three wins and two losses. Regardless, these years prepared him for the move to professional football. At age forty-one, in 1954, he took on the daunting job of planning offense for the New York Giants. Their previous season was a sad 3-9 record, but Vince turned them into a winning powerhouse. The Giants defeated the Chicago Bears to take league title. Under his coaching, glamorous gridiron star Frank Gifford played halfback. Coach and player shone on the field.

Like an itinerant preacher, Vince didn't stay long with the Giants. Four years later he took a position as head coach and general manager of the Green Bay Packers. He called on his early tutoring: "It's all in how you do it," he remembered. He had a knowledge of football as strong and focused as a P-51 pilot with an enemy in his gun sights. Since the Giants and Packers played in different leagues, Vince had not been able to watch them play, so as always, he devoted the first months just getting to know his players. With the Giants, he had been clever enough to choose Gifford, who often carried the day. Now, he had the same luck choosing a key player for the Packers. Instinct said, *choose Hornung,* a Heisman Trophy winner from Notre Dame. Paul Hornung was thinking about leaving because he did not want to go through another miserable season like his first had been, but this new coach caught his attention. He decided there was something about Vince Lombardi that told him to give it another year.

Lombardi dished out painful training routines with practice on the field as punishing as being stretched on a medieval torture rack. He demanded on 100 percent loyalty. No time for other things. No time for partying. Nothing less than a 120 percent performance was acceptable. Lombardi's know-how came through in a way the players could see and admire. They knew that the difference between being a good football team and being a great football team was their coach Lombardi. What they liked most was the way he cut to basic elements. He threw out the endless gibberish that other coaches forced their players to swallow. He replaced their complicated codes with a one-number system, reducing the playbook to a third of the size of other teams'. His rules were as strict as the orders of an army sergeant. Players learned *his* system of football.

"The only way I know how to coach the game is all the way," Vince said. Although he was a thoughtful man, he had uncommon passion for what he did. He could talk a team into winning. In fact, "Winning is the name of the game," he told them. "Be a hard loser." Certainly, he was a leader, and he taught that skill to his team. "The leader must always walk the tightrope between the consent he must win and the control he must exert." Not only did he drive these ideals home to his players—he lived with urgency, passion, and conviction off the field as well.

"You don't do things right once in a while. You do them right all the time." He drove these ideas into the minds of his players. He convinced them that they could win. "Confidence is contagious," he said. "Yes, mistakes and errors are the necessary steps in the learning process, but once they have served their purpose, they should be forgotten." He taught his team not to make the same mistake twice—good advice for our own lives. There is an irony in many of the words Vince Lombardi spoke during his football career: "We didn't lose the game; we just ran out of time." "Winners never quit and quitters never win." "Leaders are not made. They are born." To those who scoffed at winning as an end, he retorted, "If it doesn't matter who wins or loses, why do we keep a score?" To those who think that they alone are the cause for winning, he said, "You're playing for the group effort, that is what makes a team work, a company work, a civilization work." The one thing to be remembered is that everyone has to work together as a team. Then, "It's not whether you get knocked down, it's whether you get back up."

Getting up is just what Vince did with the Packers. When he took the helm in 1959, the Packers had lost ten of their twelve games the year before. Under Lombardi's coaching, they finished the season with a 7-5 record. In the second year, Lombardi led the Packers to an NFL Championship contest with the Philadelphia Eagles, but he would not win the league. Fullback Jim Taylor darted like a rabbit for the goal but was stopped only feet short of a touchdown. As luck would have it, time ran out. If you ask Vince, that was the only reason they lost the game, but losing a championship game was not an option. Lombardi promised, "It won't happen again."

In 1967 the Green Bay Packers played one of the most notorious games ever played in football. They were hosting the Dallas Cowboys in Green Bay on New Year's Eve. Yes, it was bitterly cold. Game time temperature was minus thirteen degrees. In fact, the event became known as the Ice Bowl.

The time left on the scoreboards read sixteen seconds. Lombardi called for the Packers' last time out. They were behind by three points. In play, it was third and goal for the Packers on the Cowboys' one-yard line. In the previous two plays, halfback Donny Anderson had hit a wall of Cowboys' defense. No gain. Time was slipping away like sand through an hourglass.

In the time out, the plan agreed upon called for Starr, the Packers quarterback, to hand the ball to Chuck Mercein, their fullback. He was an unknown quantity from Yale but had been a driving force in getting the ball to the Cowboys' one-yard line. The play, suggested by Starr, was a clever maneuver from Lombardi. The Cowboys knew the Packers had no more time outs, and the clock was about to run out of time. The situation called for the Packers to pass the ball. The Cowboys could set up a block that would result in an incomplete pass. That would stop the clock. The only move then would be to attempt a field goal. If the Cowboys could stop Mercein short of the goal, they knew Starr could not spike the ball, as that would move the game to a fourth down.

Center Ken Bowman and right guard Jerry Kramer brought down the Cowboys' defensive left tackle, Jethro Pugh. Starr noticed the playing field covered with ice. Trying for a fourth down was all risk since his footing would be unsteady. He tucked the ball firmly under his arm and bolted across the goal line for the winning touchdown. His teammates were visibly surprised. The Cowboys were stunned. Mercein had thrown his hands into the air to receive the handoff. The move also signaled to refs that he was not assisting Starr in his unscheduled play.

Lombardi later explained why he had not gone for the field goal. His answer seemed too simple for the importance of the event. He merely said, "We gambled and we won." He also kept the pledge that he made following the loss to the Eagles: "It won't happen again," and it didn't. Two weeks later, in a show of pure professional football, the Packers defeated the Raiders in Super Bowl II. It was also Vince Lombardi's swan song as coach of the Green Bay Packers. After the season, he announced his retirement.

That lasted about one year. Under his leadership the Packers had dominated professional football, achieving six division titles, five NFL championships, and two Super Bowls. Not a bad record. Now Vince would try his skills again with the Washington Redskins. In doing this, he never let go of the traditions that had guided him to past victories. Under Lombardi's guidance, the Redskins ploughed to their first winning record in fourteen years. At age fifty-seven, he became football's coach of coaches. No man had achieved what he had in a career in football. His overall record stood at an astonishing 105-35 with no losing season.

As Vince once said, "Some of us will do our jobs well and some will not, but we will be judged by only one thing: the result." If result is how you judge a person, Vince Lombardi did his job well—and his mother need not have worried about her son's football career.

NOTES

1. "Vincent Thomas Lombardi," *GreenBayAntiques*, accessed May 23, 2016, http://greenbayantiques.com/lombardi.php.

2. Patrick Hughes, *American Weather Stories* (Fredonia Books, 2006).

3. "The Ice Bowl," Mary Kornely, *Wisconsin Weather Stories*, accessed May 23, 2016, http://weatherstories.ssec.wisc.edu/stories/icebowl. (Margaret Mooney.)

4. "Vince Lombardi—The Early Years," *Famous Sports Stars*, accessed May 23, 2016, http://sports.jrank.org/pages/2890/Lombardi-Vince-Early-Years.html. (Dominik Mazur.)

5. Steve B. Davis, "Vince Lombardi: Super Bowl Coach Personified," *Writings & Ramblings*, https://stamperdad.wordpress.com/2008/01/28/vince-lombardi-super-bowl-coach-personified/.

SHE DESIGNED GLAMOUR

Seven-year-old Rose Marie picked up the potato fork and followed her dad to the field. The potatoes lay like irregular brown stones in disarray, belched from the loose dirt of the newly plowed earth. It was harvest time, and Rose Marie was expected to help fork the potatoes into the rough burlap sacks. Of course, in Idaho, these woven bags were called gunnysacks. In early America, kids worked on the family farms right along with their parents. The one thing they learned was how to work, and they were not afraid of it. They grew up with work as part of their daily lives. They also learned independence—how to care and think for themselves.

Rose Marie's family was no exception. They owned a small grocery store where Rose Marie worked at age fourteen, learning how to run a business. She also learned sewing from her mother at a level equal to professionals. Some years later she married Jack Reid and moved to Canada.

In the early 1900s men's bathing suits were made of wool. You've probably never worn a wool bathing suit, but if you ever do, you'll find they are extremely irritating. They scratch and itch, become waterlogged, baggy, and heavy when gorged with water. They are unsightly, and stink like a mangy dog when wet. Rose Marie's husband had such a pair of trunks. He complained about them every time he wore them.

Rose Marie pulled out an old duck fabric coat, long since pushed to the back of a closet. As precise as a surgeon, she deftly cut the material and laced the sides for a close fit. Jack was more than pleased. He showed them to a local department store owner who arranged to carry the item in the

94

store's athletic wear department. Her husband also told the store owner Rose Marie had the same kind of swimwear for women. This, of course, was not true. Anyway, the nonexistent product was soon created and Reid Holiday Togs, Inc. was born.

The Rose Marie Reid swimsuit empire had modest beginnings. In her first year, she produced six styles in the face of daunting obstacles. Here was a woman, and a Mormon at that, competing in the business world, a world controlled and run by men. With the virtues of hard work learned as a child, determination, and self-reliance, she pushed sales from a paltry $32,000 dollars in 1938 to a handsome $800,000 in 1946. She remained steadfast in her goal to succeed. She began a more aggressive competition with the big swimsuit companies.

By 1959 she was selling swimsuits in forty-six countries. She was the first swimwear manufacturer to come out with more than one line a year. One of her designs was the "glistening white" with a lobster sewn on it. She also designed a gold metallic piece that sold for ninety dollars. The going price for a woman's swimsuit at the time was about seven dollars. Rose Marie Reid became the largest producer of women's swimwear in the world. She was featured in leading fashion magazines. One of the smartest design ideas she came up with was the "hourglass" suit. This design shot her into the international market and worldwide fame. She was a phenomenon—a Mormon woman at the top of the business world.

Glamorous movie star, Marilyn Monroe, gave Rose Marie a warm thank you. "You've done as much for my career as Mother Nature." When Rita Hayworth bought one of her suits, Rose Marie's success skyrocketed even higher. Other star celebrities paid the price for Rose Marie Reid glamour—Yvonne de Carlo, Rhonda Fleming, Joan Crawford, and Jane Russell. By now her hourglass swimsuits were selling at one hundred dollars apiece. Her swimsuit sales reached $18 million in 1960.

During this time, she fought biases, detractors, and stubborn, hard-nosed businessmen who refused to acknowledge that a woman could succeed in a man's world. She also faced religious bias. Everyone asked, "Why is a Mormon woman running such a business?"

Demands on her time kept Rose Marie away from her husband and family for long periods. This caused a strain on their marriage, coupled with her husband's mental abuse and demands that she work. She obtained an annulment while living in California, but her husband Jack was able to drain all the money from their Canadian company. He also kept their children as ransom, demanding more money from Rose Marie before he would let the children join her. The court battle lasted years. She continued to suffer monetary loss from the custody fight as well as the other lawsuits and court battles that made her life a nightmare.

From the beginning Rose Marie was a very trusting person. While enduring the family crises she was now facing, the truth about her financial advisor Michael Silver came to light. He had obtained power of attorney early on and was now refusing an accounting of the large sums of money she had entrusted to him. Rose Marie was forced to sue him. Her attorney learned that Silver had embezzled one and a half million dollars from her accounts. In 1990 money values, that was equal to six and a half million dollars. He was also involved in illegal deals that netted him even more money that benefitted his friends. He had even written checks on other people's bank accounts. After all the legal actions, Rose Marie gained nothing.

Some of Rose Marie's so-called friends, who were also business associates, saw in Rose Marie her trusting nature. An original agreement called for them to provide $25,000. Rose Marie was to contribute her skill and expertise to create and market swimsuits. The friends, Jack and Nina Kessler, manipulated the stock to their control, quietly and without Rose Marie's knowledge. They lied about the original agreement to win large sums of money from her. They said that Rose Marie had agreed to put up the same amount of money as themselves. She would also provide "her expertise, designs, and patents without pay or credit for value." The judge thought that was unjustly one-sided. He ruled against the Kesslers; however, they were able to keep most of the stock.

There was a bright side to Rose Marie's life. While so-called friends and advisors bilked her of millions, she continued to rise in the swimsuit business. Other companies copied her styles. Cole Industries offered a suit they named *Rose Marie.* Their daring action was partly to cover the fact that they had stolen the design. Even so, with the theft of designs and bank accounts, Rose Marie Reid ruled the swimsuit empire.

Her life was a whirlwind. At times neither she nor workers could finish tasks before her swimsuits had to be modeled. In one fashion show, she had no time to price the suits. She solved the problem rather easily. To the models she said, "What would you pay for the suit you are wearing?" After deciding on a price, the models relayed it to buyers.

Rose Marie always put modesty first. Her designs were glamorous but always one piece. Along came the 1960s and the bikini. The Rose Marie Reid swimsuit train was put on the sidelines while the bikini express roared into existence. Her company, under the control of outsiders, brought in foreign designers. Products bearing her name were no longer hers.

Munsingwear bought what was left of Reid Holiday Togs. The new owners stopped operation of Rose Marie swimwear in 1965. Although still licensed today, Rose Marie's company has changed ownership several times, most recently in 1994.

What made Rose Marie swimsuits so popular? The simple answer is swimsuits went from being just a sport style to beauty and glamour. Rose Marie sparked that change.

She once said, "Nothing is so brutally frank as the bare essentials of a bathing suit." Bikinis do not deal with style. They do bare a lot more than the essentials. In contrast, Rose Marie's genius was all about glamour. With impeccable character and courage, Rose Marie Reid designed glamour.

NOTES

1. *Movie Star Makeover*, accessed May 23, 2016, http://moviestarmakeover.com/tag/rose-marie-reid/.

2. April Ainsworth, "Rose Marie Reid: Vintage Designer Bios," *Vintagevixen.com*, http://blog.vintagevixen.com/2011/08/rose-marie-reid-vintage-designer-bios.html.

MAN OF THE FRONTIER

A frontier may be part of a country that faces or borders another country. It may also be a part of a settled, civilized country that lies next to an unexplored or undeveloped region. From the point of view of American colonists, the frontier was anything west of them. In 1750, it was the Appalachian Mountains.

West of this barrier—in what is today, Ohio, West Virginia, and western Pennsylvania—lay endless rolling hills covered with dense forest. At one time the Shawnee inhabited this land. Around the 1660s, they were driven out by the warring Iroquois tribes. They were scattered in many directions through Illinois, South Carolina, eastern Pennsylvania, and the Tennessee Cumberland Basin. Once settled in this new land, they considered the area known as Kentucky to be their hunting grounds. Into this area came a man named Daniel Boone.

At one time he lived with his wife and children on a farm in North Carolina, but he wanted to see what was on the other side of the mountains. He had heard tales about rivers you could drink from, forests full of wild game, and plains that stretched as far as the eye could see. He put on a fringed shirt, trousers made of deerskin, Native American moccasins, and, in 1769, joined five other men for a trek into Kentucky. They took knives, Native American hatchets, rifles, and sacks full of lead bullets. Carrying little, they would live by hunting game in the forests.

With difficulty, they followed an old trail used by local tribes. Five weeks later they reached the top of the mountains and looked out over a vast, beautiful valley. Green hills rolled away like waves in a stormy sea.

They selected a site near a river and built a small cabin for shelter. Day after day they hunted and explored, sometimes going farther and farther west.

One day, on one of their searches, they came upon a large herd of buffalo. The animals raced toward them like a hundred locomotives, their hooves sounding like thunder in the earth. Their eyes were wild with rage. Boone and his companions saw no way to escape. One of the men who knew what the buffalo would do, raised his rifle and shot the lead animal. It plowed head long into the earth just feet from the men. "Get behind the dead buffalo," he yelled above the roar of hooves. The charging herd divided and dashed around either side, as the man knew they would. The animals leaped past them like giant furry shadows.

While on a hunting trip, Boone and one of his friends were captured by the Shawnee. He used quiet courage and patience—unmovable as a stone. The Shawnee were impressed by his bravery and thought he wished to be taken into the tribe. The braves did not keep a sharp watch on the men, so in the stillness of night, they escaped. On their return they found their cabin in shambles. Daniel could only conclude that the Shawnee had raided the place and taken the other men.

Despite the loss of their companions, Daniel and his friend stayed in the wilderness and continued to hunt wild game and trap for beavers. Beaver furs were in great demand at this time. Soon, Daniel's brother joined him. Not long after, the last of the other five men, who had come with them to the wilderness, vanished. In May, Daniel's brother loaded their horses with many animal furs and left for home. The people, learning of the plentiful supply of beaver and other animals, were eager to establish a colony in Kentucky, but the British did not allow settlement of the area. Daniel Boone didn't much care about the rule, and in 1773, he packed up his family and moved with about fifty other families into Kentucky.

At this time, Boone was still an unknown hunter and trapper. The most prominent member of the group was William Russell, a well-known Virginian and future brother-in-law of Patrick Henry. Boone's son James, William Russell's son Henry, and a few other men and boys left the main party for supplies but were captured by a band of Native Americans. The entire group of men and boys was tortured and butchered.

The tribes who killed the boys wanted to send a message to others who might want to settle in Kentucky, so Boone and the other families gave up their plan to settle in the region and turned back. News of the killings sent shock waves all along the frontier. In the summer of 1774,

Boone and a friend agreed to notify surveyors of the outbreak of war in the area. Most people returned to the safety of the settlements east of the mountains. After a brief war and victory by Virginians at the Battle of Point Pleasant in October of that year, the Shawnee gave up their claim to Kentucky. Upon his return to Virginia, Boone helped defend settlements along the frontier. As a member of the militia, his fame grew when he was promoted to the rank of captain.

Boone hadn't given up on his idea for a Kentucky colony. He and twenty-eight other men blazed a trail through the Cumberland Gap. Despite many attacks by bands of Shawnee and Cherokee, the men were able to cut and build the Wilderness Road. He was asked to lead a pioneering party back into Kentucky. Soon hundreds of frontier people moved along the road. Boone's family and relatives were some of the very first to settle there. Everyone pushed to make Kentucky the fourteenth colony.

On one of his many trips into the wilderness hunting and surveying, Daniel was surrounded by tribal raiding parties. The only route of escape led to a high riverbank. He leaped over the bank and landed in the top of a tall tree. Like a squirrel, he scampered down the limbs, boulder hopped along the river, leaped in, then swam like an otter across the wild current, and escaped.

When Daniel and his companions were captured by the Shawnee yet a third time, they were stripped of their clothing and forced to run the gauntlet. Two lines of Shawnee formed between the men and freedom from the gauntlet about fifty feet away. Fear gripped them. The hair on the backs of their necks stood on end. Blood coursed through their veins like wild rivers wanting to burst from their bodies. Daniel clenched his hands into hard fists. He bolted into the lane between the Shawnee, running like a deer, swift and sure. As fast as he was, he could not outrun the clubs that crashed across his back. He dodged most of the heavy blows aimed at him by the Shawnee. As he neared the end of the line, he saw a Shawnee with an arm upraised step into his path. He saw the club being aimed at him. Lowering his head, he charged into the man like a battering ram and knocked his tormentor to the ground. He leaped over the fallen man, dived into a ball like an armadillo, and rolled to safety. The Shawnee were again impressed with Boone's quick thinking and bravery and allowed he and his companions to live. Later, he managed to escape again.

During the Revolutionary War, Daniel Boone and others built a fort at Boonesborough, and he rose in rank in the militia. Captured again by the Shawnee, he was adopted into the tribe. He lived five months as a brother with his captors but learned that the British planned an attack on the fort. Like the escape artist he was, Daniel eluded his captors to warn the settlers and the militia at Boonesborough. They held the fort for ten days.

Daniel Boone was a true American, a frontiersman, pioneer, settler, and explorer who played a very large role in the settlement of Kentucky. Credit must be given to him for defending the western borders of the fledgling colonies. Daniel Boone was a noble leader and brave man. Without him, the route to the West would very well have been delayed many years. He was and is every bit a legend. He was an American with great vision—another of the courageous.

NOTES

1. John Stevens Cabot Abbott, *Daniel Boone*, performed by Allyson Hester, 2010, audiobook, https://librivox.org/daniel-boone-by-john-s-c-abbott/.
2. "George Washington Custis Lee," *About Famous People*, accessed May 23, 2016, http://www.aboutfamouspeople.com/article1173.html. (John T. Marck.)
3. Richard A. Boning, *Getting the Facts: Book C* (Barnell Loft Books, 1997).
4. "Daniel Boone," *Project Gutenberg*, accessed May 23, 2016, http://www.gutenberg.org/ebooks/39927?msg=welcome_stranger. (Reuben Thwaites.)

MASTERS OF THE IMPOSSIBLE

They take us beyond the common. They capture our hearts with magic. They make the world more amazing. Who are they? They are the magicians, illusionists, conjurors, and escape artists. They are people who can do almost anything. They can walk through a brick wall. They can get out of a trunk with chains tied around it underwater. They can make great animals vanish from the stage. They can cut bodies in half and make them come together again. They can defy injury and seem to defy death itself.

Any magician can make a rabbit disappear. They can stuff separate ribbons into a can then pull them out knotted into one colorful string. Yet those simple tricks are not good enough for the best of the magicians.

Harry Houdini placed a large elephant in a box on stage. Seconds later when he opened the box, the elephant was gone! How did he do that? Even today people are asking that question. One of Houdini's magic tricks was billed as the Great Trunk Trick. First, stage helpers tied his hands behind his back. They stuffed him into a large sack like a piece of beef being readied for shipment and then lifted him into a trunk. They hurried about like flitting butterflies as they locked the trunk then wrapped thick ropes around it. Within seconds Houdini popped out like a cork from a wine bottle. He made a deep bow and swung his arm across his body like a pendulum. The audience clapped loudly, ready for his next act.

Harry Houdini became known as an escape artist. In fact, he was more of an escape artist than he was an illusionist or magician. He could escape from any handcuffs offered. No jail cell could hold him either; he escaped from them like smoke through a wire screen. He escaped from handcuffed bridge jumps, from padlocked crates thrown in rivers, from a giant paper bag suspended upside down from a height. He even escaped from being buried alive.

Around this same time, a father and son named Blackstone also performed a magic routine. Harry Blackstone Sr. placed a woman in an open, bird-like cage and covered it with a flower-designed drape. When he removed the cover, the woman had been replaced with a small child sitting in a colorful swing.

Young Blackstone produced what looked like an ordinary light bulb. Through some trick of magic, he suspended the bulb from the ends of his fingers and actually made it light up! Then the lighted bulb began to float free of his hand. The effect caused an eerie spell to fall over the audience. He flipped a large ring around it to prove that it was not attached to anything. Part of the act included an audience member who held the bulb. As Blackstone stood on the stage, he could make the bulb float out over the audience.

Another of young Blackstone's tricks involved cats. A small cream-colored cat, lapping at a saucer of milk, was sitting on a pedestal. In a flash of sparks and light, the cat vanished and a larger, Angora long-haired beauty appeared. It too continued to lap at the saucer of milk.

At age eight, Dai Vernon fell in love with the idea of magic when his father took him to his first magic show. By the time he was thirteen, he had memorized the contents of a book about card magic. Not much later, he met another up-and-coming young magician who asked, "What kind of magic do you do?" Vernon said, "Name a card." He pulled a pack of cards from his coat pocket, turned over the top card of the deck to reveal the named card, and said to the speechless doubter, "That's the kind of magic I do."

As a master of slight-of-hand tricks, Vernon is probably the best there has been. He improved standard tricks and invented new close-up tricks with cards, coins, and small items. He made his Symphony of the Rings his most famous and lasting routine. It has eighteen steps: counting, twisting, linking two rings, spinning the rings, unlinking, sounding, crash linking, pulling them through, making a chain of three rings, linking two single rings and the key ring, unlinking, continuous linking, letting a ring fall, interlocking, creating figures, making a long chain of six rings, unlinking a solid ring, and finally, the last unlinking. The entire routine is performed so smoothly that the rings appear to *melt* into each other. This routine in a magic show continues to be one of the most popular acts.

For centuries magicians have charmed, baffled, and amused audiences with the mysterious linking and unlinking of what appear to be solid rings. Vernon was a master of this artful act. He also became known as the Professor of Magic. He was the only man who fooled Houdini. He lived until 1992, the last thirty years of his life as a resident magician at the Magic Castle in Hollywood.

Doug Henning is credited with reviving the magic show as a form of entertainment in North America, beginning in the 1970s. Until then, it had pretty much died out. Henning changed the image of the stage magician when he rejected the typical magician's costume: penguin tuxedo, top hat, trimmed moustache, goatee, and short hair. Instead he chose long hair, sporting a crown of wavy, wild, shoulder-length hair.

In one act he allowed helpers to lower an amber colored, open-ended box over him. It appeared to be lit from within. The helpers lowered the frame then raised it to reveal Doug standing on his left leg. They repeated this action, this time only his right leg was visible below the frame. On a third lowering and raising—no feet! One assistant flailed his arms under the frame to prove that nothing was there. When the frame was removed, Doug walked out.

One of today's best-known masters of magic is Criss Angel. His acts of illusion, escape, and magic stunts set him apart from the ordinary. He performs in open areas to large audiences so there is no doubt in their minds as to what is happening. In Las Vegas, he walked on water. He floated between buildings as a ghost floats in a haunted mansion, and performed other levitating acts. In one episode he levitated five hundred feet in front of the Luxor Hotel. This he did right in front of the hotel's 42.5 billion candlepower spotlight. The heat from the spotlight would have been as hot as molten sun—enough to fry anything.

David Blaine performs what is called street magic. It is also close-up rather than large-scale productions with lights, sounds, and machines. In one act he has a spectator sign a card. The card is returned to the pack and then appears from between two aces. He is able to take a handful of specially cut paper and magically transform it into money.

His voodoo ash trick requires a spectator to write a name on a page in a notebook. The writer then tears out the page, crumples it up, and places it in an ashtray. The paper is set afire; afterward Blaine rubs the ashes on his arm. The name written by the spectator magically appears! In another trick, he casually lifts a teaspoon from a cup of tea. He is amused by its wiggly and malleable form. He calmly proceeds to bend the bowl of the spoon, backwards and forwards. He continues to be a bit amused by this unusual spoon. With an incredible feat of strength, he twists the bowl free of the spoon handle. He shakes his head in disbelief at the poor quality of the spoon. The handle and bowl are joined, and with a couple twists, the spoon is whole again.

Many other magicians present shows around the world. One named Teller brings a red ball to life. Luis de Matos gets water to turn black and then clean again. Wally Eastwood plays a classical piece of music by dropping juggling balls onto musical keys. Norm Nielson gets a violin to play as it floats free of any visible connections. The list goes on and on.

David Copperfield used to perform two shows daily at the MGM Grand in Las Vegas. His magic is worked on stage accompanied by a half dozen circling lights, lots of white vapor, rousing music, and several assistants. Everything that he uses as props is impressive, state-of-the-art equipment, created just for the particular trick that he is performing. Opening one show, he began by placing a motorcycle under a large white sheet. With the usual levitating or lifting motion of his hands, the sheet rises. He pulls it away. Shazam! Two women in stylish tight-fitting costumes have replaced the motorcycle.

This is followed with a steel-framed, see-through cage being moved about ten feet above the stage floor. Lights glow through it. The door closes for a moment and opens again to reveal Copperfield inside. Next, he lies on a platform. An opaque shield momentarily hides him. From above, a huge rack of silver spikes, each about a foot long, comes crashing down. The shield is quickly pulled away. The spikes have gone *through* Copperfield and the platform beneath him—or it would seem. Of course, he sits up and waves to the audience.

A good magician includes a little humor in his show. Copperfield has Webster, a duck, appear at one place on stage then suddenly reappear in another. The audience is pleasantly amused.

In one stunt filmed over Niagara Falls, Copperfield is encased in a coffin, which is perched on a metal frame over fire. All this floats quickly to the edge and plunges into the foam and rocks below. A helicopter hovers near the bottom. Pilots lower a cable into the water. Up comes Copperfield who is lifted above the falls.

The world of magic is dazzling! Each of these amazing magicians started out as an amateur, but like them, you can study these tricks and become a master of magic.

NOTES

1. "Magicians: Who's Who in the World of Magic!" *AllAboutMagicians.com*, accessed May 23, 2016, http://www.all-about-magicians.com/. (Julio Sevilla.)

2. www.blackstonejr.com.

3. "Houdini's Magic Tricks," *America's Story from America's Library*, accessed May 23, 2016, http://www.americaslibrary.gov/aa/houdini/aa_houdini_magic_3.html.

4. *CompuMagic*, accessed May 23, 2016, http://www.compumagic.com/magic/dh /collage.html. (Kevin Gough.)

5. *Wikipedia*, s.v. "Criss Angel," last modified May 11, 2016, https://en.wikipedia.org /wiki/Criss_Angel.

6. *Wikipedia*, s.v. "Dai Vernon," last modified February 13, 2016, https://en.wikipedia .org/wiki/Dai_Vernon.

7. *Wikipedia*, s.v. "David Blaine," last modified May 9, 2016, https://en.wikipedia.org /wiki/David_Blaine.

8. *Wikipedia*, s.v. "David Copperfield," last modified May 19, 2016, https://en.wikipedia .org/wiki/David_Copperfield.

9. "Harry Houdini," *Appleton Public Library*, accessed May 23, 2016, http://www.apl .org/book/export/html/1003.

10. "David Copperfield," Ram Samudrala, *ram.org*, published December 28, 2002, http://www.ram.org/ramblings/plays/david_copperfield.html.

THE ODDS DIDN'T MATTER

The story of Michael Murphy is but one of the thousands related to Afghanistan, but Michael's story is different—Michael was awarded the Medal of Honor. In fact, he was the first to receive the award since Vietnam. His father described him as a protector. He just jumped in where he saw a need. In middle school, he took on three bullies who were trying to push a disabled student into a locker. The odds didn't matter.

Michael's story is about courage and bravery beyond the call of duty. In early 2005, Michael was assigned to SEAL Delivery Vehicle Team One. He was the officer in charge of Alpha Platoon. The platoon was sent to Afghanistan to support Operation Enduring Freedom. By June he was in the thick of the fighting in Afghanistan and Iraq. His Navy SEAL training would soon be put to the test, and again, he would jump in to save others.

He and three buddies—Marcus Luttrell, David "Danny" Dietz, and Matthew "Axe" Axelson—were dropped from a helicopter in the remote and treacherous mountains east of the city of Asadabad in Kunar Province on the Pakistan border, near the famous Khyber Pass. The pass looks as if it were cut by a giant sword through the mountains. Its history dates from the invasion of Darius I and the subsequent invasion of Alexander the Great to the British entry into Afghanistan. Said a member of the British forces in 1979, "Every boulder in the Khyber Pass has been soaked in blood." The truth of the matter is nothing has changed. In 2005 and ever since, the boulders of Afghanistan are still being soaked with blood. This time it's with American soldiers' blood.

Michael and his squad met three men. The wild and suspicious look in their eyes should have warned the team. Instead, they let the three "goat herders" continue on. As soon as the three were out of sight, they ran to tell the Taliban of their meeting with the Americans. (The Taliban is the terrorist force fighting guerilla war against the government of Afghanistan.) NATO forces, mostly American, were sent into the area to stop them. One of the critical problems in finding Taliban terrorists is that they wear no uniforms. American forces could not determine who were civilians and who were enemy fighters. Michael's team was on a mission to find and capture a Taliban leader. Within minutes, the SEAL team was surrounded by one hundred wild-eyed, scraggly enemy fighters.

The team was pushed down the mountain by heavy enemy rifle fire. Danny was hit and died almost instantly. Michael, called Murph by his buddies, was hit a couple of times. Matt and Marcus also received bullet wounds. Murph tried to make cell phone contact to call for support, but the huge boulders, strewn about the mountainside like giant marbles, and a wall of trees blocked the radio waves. Murph crawled out onto a boulder to contact the base, placing himself in line of direct enemy fire. Immediately, he was struck with bullets front and back.

He fell back but continued trying to make contact. The team was running out of ammo. During the firefight, Matt was hit by several bullets. He too died on the mountain slope. Finally Murph was able to contact base. A helicopter with sixteen men aboard was sent to rescue the team, but it came under heavy rifle fire and crashed, killing all sixteen men inside. At the same time, Murph received a fatal hit. His body would not be found until almost a year later, but the odds didn't matter.

As fate would have it, Marcus was rescued and came home to a hero's welcome. He said, "Murph was the consummate professional, a real go-to guy, always with a smile. He was a great leader and friend. Everyone tried to emulate him." Sometime later, Michael "Murph" Murphy was awarded the Medal of Honor in ceremonies at the White House. His citation reads, "For conspicuous gallantry and intrepidity at risk to his own life and beyond the call of duty."

To his buddies he was Murph. To his high school friends he was Mike. To his parents he was the Protector, always looking out for the other guy, and the odds didn't matter.

NOTES

1. Mike, "Memorial Day Murph," *CrossFit Assault*, https://crossfitassault.wordpress.com/2011/05/23/memorial-day-murph/.

2. *Wikipedia*, s.v. "Michael P. Murphy," last modified April 25, 2016, https://en.wikipedia.org/wiki/Michael_P._Murphy.

3. "Afghanistan War Medal of Honor Recipients: Lieutenant Michael P. Murphy.," *U.S. Army Center of Military History*, last modified March 16, 2016, http://www.history.army.mil/moh/afghanistan.html#murphy.

4. "Navy SEAL to be awarded Medal of Honor," Michelle L. Kapica, *America's Navy*, published October 11, 2007, http://www.navy.mil/submit/display.asp?story_id=32528.

5. "Lt Michael P. Murphy Awarded the Congressional Medal of Honor Posthumously," *sealtwo.org*, published October 12, 2007, http://www.sealtwo.org/michaelpmurphy.htm.

THE SUB THAT SANK A TRAIN

Commander Eugene Fluckey, who had just been awarded the Medal of Honor, worried that some of his men might not make it back from their daring plan to blow up the Japanese train. He had his submarine, the *Barb*, drifting in about thirty feet of water off the coast of Karafuto, Japan, at 4 a.m. on July 18, 1945. He and the crew were part of the *Barb*'s twelfth mission. They had hit on a crazy idea to blow up the track and an ammunition train that ran along the shore close to the ocean. The plan required a man to stay on the beach to set the charge as the train passed. The commander was not about to lose a man this late in the war just to blow up a train. He hadn't lost a man so far. It was Billy Hatfield to the rescue.

"Why not let the train blow itself up?" he asked. "I used to crack walnuts on the railroad tracks when I was a kid. I'd place the nuts between two ties so the sagging of the rail under the weight of the rain would break them open." He grinned like the Cheshire cat. "Just like cracking walnuts. To complete the circuit to detonate the bomb, we hook it to a micro switch between two ties. We don't set it off, the train does!" He added, "It's my idea, so I get to go."

Everyone volunteered. As eager as they were, the moon was too bright. They needed cloud cover. Fluckey also set a condition: no married men. All departments were represented, some from regular navy and some from reserves. "Half of you must have been Boy Scouts," he concluded. "You'll need experience in handling yourselves in a medical emergency. I'll lead the mission."

In the end, Commander Fluckey's officers outvoted him. "As commander, you belong with the *Barb*." One man even threatened to send a wire if he tried to join the saboteurs. The eight were chosen: Billy Hatfield, Ed Klinglesmith, John Markuson, Larry Newland, James Richard, Frank Sever, Paul Saunders, and Bill Walker. Fluckey brought the Barb to about nine hundred yards from shore. They lowered small boats and paddled inland. The hair on the backs of their necks stood up. Goose bumps rose on their arms, and their faces flushed with excitement. They landed the boats and jumped onto the Japanese homeland. They stumbled through tall grass, crossed a road, and followed a drainage ditch to the railroad tracks.

Markuson climbed a watchtower. He froze in his climb when he discovered a Japanese sentry sound asleep in the box. He alerted the others who dug more quietly along the railroad. With the job done, all that was left was for Billy Hatfield to connect his homemade switch. They watched anxiously. It was like watching the bomb squad defuse a live bomb. A little mistake and they'd all be hamburger.

Commander Fluckey had guided the Barb within six hundred yards of the shoreline, where only six feet of water separated the submarine from the bottom of the ocean. Suddenly, a sailor yelled, "Captain! Another train is coming up the tracks!" Fluckey grabbed a megaphone and screamed to the men rowing toward the sub. "Paddle like the devil!" He knew they would not reach to Barb before the train hit the micro switch.

And hit the switch it did. The darkness on the Japanese homeland lit up like a Fourth of July fireworks display. Loud explosions raced across the water. The train's boiler blew up and rained shrapnel hundreds of feet. Trailing boxcars, filled with wartime munitions, plowed into each other and burst into flame. It looked like the burning of Rome.

A few minutes later, the Barb's octet of saboteurs climbed safely aboard and Commander Fluckey eased his submarine carefully into deep water. These eight men were the only wartime American soldiers to walk on Japanese soil. A couple of atomic bombs dropped a few weeks later saving the lives of a million men who would have died invading Japan to end the war.

Commander Fluckey, of course, had already earned his Medal of Honor and four Navy Crosses by daringly taking his sub into a Japanese harbor to sink a half dozen ships. Add to that one train.

NOTES

1. "The U.S.S. BARB SS220," *HAL-5 Bluehawks*, accessed May 23, 2016, http://www .bluehawksofhal-5.org/news_files/USS%20BarbSS220.htm.

2. "USS Barb SS-220 and Rear Admiral Eugene "Lucky" Fluckey The Sub That Sank a Train," *Gene Slovers US Navy Pages*, accessed May 23, 2016, http://www .eugeneleeslover .com/USNAVY/USS_Barb.html.

3. "U.S.S. Barb: The Sub That Sank A Train," *Home of Heroes,* accessed May 23, 2016, http://www.homeofheroes.com/profiles/profiles_fluckey.html. (Doug Sterner.)

LEMONS TO LEMONADE

When life hands you lemons, make lemonade," said Alexandra Flynn Scott, age four.

One day before her very first birthday she was diagnosed with neuroblastoma, a form of cancer that should not be in her body. It is a disease that only children get that starts with very simple nerve cells found in areas where nerves join together, and it can grow anywhere in the body. Doctors do not know why children get this disease. Worse, at the time, they did not have a cure. Because of this cancer, Alex had pains that would not go away. She told her parents, "I want to hold a lemonade stand. I want to raise money to help my doctors find a cure for all kids with cancer." These were big ideas for such a little human being, but her parents were more than willing to help her. Help included giving her money to buy the lemons and the sugar. Alex carefully taste tested each batch so that it was just right. She needed a stand, which her dad quickly built for her. He set it up in the their front yard. Young Alex was in business. She was on her way to raising money for kids with cancer.

That first summer, Alex raised $2,000. Not a miserly amount for a four-year-old. Over the next few years, Alex held her lemonade stand in spite of her failing health. As her story spread across the country, Alex and her family were asked to appear on the *Oprah Winfrey Show.* They came on *The Today Show.* As Alex told her story, many people cried. Over the next four years, with the help of friends and strangers, they raised $200,000.

When 2004 arrived, Alex set a goal that shocked her parents. "I want to raise a million dollars," she announced as casually as one might announce that dinner was ready.

Her parents asked, "How are you going to do it?"

Alex had a very logical answer. "If people all around the country hold lemonade stands and send in the money, I think I can do it." She couldn't have been more right. Thousands of people volunteered, young and old and in between, from all over the country, holding their own lemonade stands. With everyone working together, they reached the one-million-dollar goal.

Sadly, just after Alex saw her dream of raising the one million dollars come true, she died on August 1, 2004. Even more sadly, she died only weeks before doctors discovered a breakthrough for a cure. Since then, thousands of volunteers have held lemonade stands, not only in all fifty states, but all around the world. Volvo of North America got involved and sponsored a fundraising event that added to Alex's success. Many millions have been raised to support finding cures for childhood cancer, earning— at last report—more than $50 million.

Even while her life was ebbing from her, Alex lived her dream to raise funds to help doctors make life better for other children. Her parents now carry on the dream that their little daughter had. They created a foundation to raise money and awareness of childhood cancer causes.

Doctors have discovered cures to save lives. What began as the vision of one little girl with an untreatable cancer became a world of volunteers. Doctors can now use surgery, radiation, and chemotherapy to save the lives of children with this disease. We can thank Alex for this.

NOTES

1. "Meet Our Founder: Alexandra Scott," *Alex's Lemonade Stand Foundation*, accessed May 23, 2016, http://www.alexslemonade.org/about/meet-alex. (Gillian Kocher.)

2. "A&P," *Alex's Lemonade Stand Foundation*, accessed may 23, 2016, http://www.alexslemonade.org/campaign/corporate-partners/ap. (Craig Rechetti.)

3. "Neuroblastoma," *MedlinePlus*, last modified April 20, 2016, https://www.nlm.nih.gov/medlineplus/neuroblastoma.html.

DAREDEVIL ON A TIGHTROPE

Niagara Falls is not the highest set of falls in the world, but they are spectacular. At the border of Ontario, Canada, and New York, they attract millions of visitors every year. In 1859, they attracted a young French acrobat who called himself the Great Blondin because of his blond hair. He announced that he intended to cross Niagara Falls on a tightrope. No doubt people wondered, "Why would anyone want to walk on a tightrope across Niagara Falls? The man must be missing a few marbles."

But Blondin had been walking on tightropes since he was five. He lost his parents when he was nine and turned to daring ropewalks and acrobatic feats to earn a living.

On this particular day, thousands packed the bluffs and banks of the river. They watched as men strung a rope above the angry waters that crashed over the cliffs. People thought the rope did not look strong enough. Because it was three inches thick, its sheer weight made it sag some fifty feet in the middle. For days people had chattered like clucking hens, doubting the possibility of success. Now that they were about to witness the feat, they were stunned by Blondin's daring. Still, they silently and mentally measured the distance from the rope to the jagged rocks at the base of the falls. As Blondin stepped onto the rope, the crowd held its breath.

"Would anyone like to make the crossing with me?' he asked. 'If so, I will carry him on my back." No one accepted his offer, though several laughed nervously. "All right, I will go alone," He took his first step on the rope that was one-fifth of a mile long. Halfway he stopped to lower a bottle into the water far below. The crowd was as still as stone. When water partly filled the bottle, he hauled it up and drank the water and completed the walk, now an upward climb into Canada.

Minutes later he arrived there bathed in sweat. The sound of applause rose above the roar of the falls. Well-wishers offered him a glass of champagne. He returned to the other side in eight minutes.

Blondin was the very first to perform this feat. For the next two years he crossed many times, always performing before large crowds. Once he crossed riding a bicycle. The next time he crossed walking on stilts. He even went at night. Like a monkey, he swung by one arm. At other times he turned somersaults, always landing squarely on the rope. More than once he stood on his head on a chair. He placed a cooking stove in a wheelbarrow and pushed it across. Once he stopped to cook an omelet. To make the crossing even more dangerous and thrilling, Blondin crossed blindfolded. Once he was tied in a heavy sack made of blankets. As if his feet were not good enough, he stepped into large wooden buckets and crossed in a few minutes.

He always asked if onlookers wished to cross with him. He always offered to carry the person on his back. Always, he got no takers. Onlookers only shook their heads, often with embarrassed and sheepish grins.

His greatest feat climaxed his two years of crossing. Since he had never persuaded anyone to cross with him, he cajoled his manager into the privilege. Harry Colcord could not very well refuse, so scared and trembling, Harry climbed onto Blondin's back. His shaking was visible to many, but once they were on the Canadian side, safe and still alive, Colcord said, "Blondin is a piece marble, incredible muscle, tense and rigid." Blondin was as steady as steel beams. He possessed courage beyond recklessness. He had dared the fates and faced death every time, yet he came out the winner.

Tightrope walking is like playing with tigers in a cage. You must never be afraid. You can never show any fear. To everyone whoever saw him perform, Blondin never seemed to be afraid. He walked across the rope with strength and courage. Others came after him, and many did not make it, but Blondin would always have the honor of being the first.

NOTES

1. "The Daredevil of Niagara Falls," Karen Abbott, *Smithsonian*, published October 18, 2011, http://www.smithsonianmag.com/history/the-daredevil-of-niagara -falls-110492884/?no-ist=. (Tad Bennicoff.)

2. Lloyd Graham, "Blondin The Hero of Niagara," *American Heritage Society*, vol. 9, no. 5, (1958), http://www.americanheritage.com/content/blondin-hero-niagara.

3. *The American History Company*, http://www.americanhistory.com/content/blondin -hero-niagara.

4. Richard A. Boning, *Getting the Facts: Book D* (Barnell Loft Books, 1997).

5. "The Great Blondin," *Niagara Falls Information*, accessed May 23, 2016, http://www .niagarafallsinformation.com/daredevils/blondin.html.

THE UNTOUCHABLES

With a sawed-off shotgun cradled in his arms, Eliot Ness and his eight men crashed through the front door of the Cozy Corners Saloon in Chicago Heights yelling, "Everybody keep his place. This is a federal raid!" He waved his badge of authority above his head in one hand and pointed his shotgun menacingly with the other. Suspects dived for cover under tables and behind counters. Others stood as if frozen by a sudden gust of arctic air. The nine men fanned out across the room with their guns pointed menacingly at their targets.

Ness had selected the saloon because it was the brain center of illegal prohibition operations in Chicago. It also supplied illegal alcohol for cities in the Midwest. The raid coincided with similar raids at seventeen other locations. In one night, Eliot Ness and his team shut down eighteen stills (places where whiskey was made) and arrested around fifty suspects. In all, the operation was a rip-roaring success. Headlines praised the team.

Congress had enacted the Eighteenth Amendment. At the same time, the passage of the Volstead Act forbade the making and distribution of alcohol. Paying no attention to the law, some men continued to make alcohol and sell it. Of course, there was still a market. People still wanted alcohol. Gangsters filled that want.

An era was born like no other in American history. Writers and journalists have written many thousands of articles and books about the era of Prohibition. People have made dozens of movies glorifying either the gangster (criminals who broke the law) or the law-abiding citizen. Hero Eliot Ness is one such citizen.

By 1927, a man named Al Capone had risen from a Brooklyn street thug to powerful Chicago crime boss. Police seemed unable to stop his illegal actions. In fact, many officials were in the pay of the gangster, so he distilled alcohol and sold it by the barrel. Speakeasies (places where people danced and drank alcohol) blossomed all over the big cities.

The United States Department of Justice formed a special unit to fight those who violated the prohibition law. They hired twenty-six-year-old Eliot Ness as a special agent of the Prohibition Bureau. He and his eight-man team were assigned the job of breaking up Al Capone's bootlegging network.

The first team member was Marty Lahart, of Irish descent, who was a fitness fanatic and loved sports. Sam Seager had once been a Sing Sing death row prison guard—tough, but kept in the background. Barney Cloonan, another Irishman, was a giant of a man with muscles hard as oak. Lyle Chapman was a brilliant problem solver; he also had the body and strength of a college football player. Fifth choice was Tom Friel, who had been a state trooper and who was streetwise when it came to police work. Joe Leeson was a legend, a genius for tailing suspects in automobiles, but seemed to fade into the scenery. For a short guy with ordinary looks, Paul Robsky had reckless courage and could tap a telephone line before you could dial a number. When it came to absorbing facts and analyzing them, Mike King was a computer ahead of his time. He could also melt into the woodwork like a thin coat of varnish. Finally came Bill Gardner, a huge, solid wall who had played college football. Together they were a menacing, fiercely dedicated team.

Capone's lieutenants tried to bribe the team. In a time when many police departments were corrupt and took bribes, Ness and his agents refused money and turned their backs on Capone. When a journalist learned of their honesty, he wrote a newspaper article. He called them the Untouchables. From that time on the team took pride in the fact that they could not be bought. Ness made sure of that. He had gone through all the records of all the treasury agents to pull together his untouchable team.

The mobster, Capone, was the most powerful man in Chicago. He threatened to kill Ness and his men. He had already killed, or ordered killed, hundreds of men, often rival gang members. Too often, many of these victims were honest, courageous men of the law who dared to go up against him.

As brave as he was, Ness was disturbed by the threat. Doubts darted through his mind like rabbits scattered by a coyote. He wondered how he might enforce a law that the majority of the people did not want. He felt a chill of foreboding for his men. He knew there would be violent actions from Capone. The mobster had his operations everywhere, like the tentacles of an octopus. Ness thought, *We have undertaken what might be a suicide mission.*

For years, Capone operated without interference from the police. They had not caused any serious damage to his breweries. Ness knew that his little band of crime fighters was going to have to adopt a change of game plan—maybe one with more brains than brawn.

Several of his raids turned up to be dead end runs. The newspapers ran stories that made fun of him. Determined to be more careful, he and his Untouchables chose another of the gangster's stills. Again, armed with his trusty sawed-off shotgun, he and his team arrived with axes and crowbars to smash the locked door. Their hearts pounded while sweat formed on their faces. To their surprise, behind the shattered wooden door was another made of steel. They fired their shotguns at the lock to break it open. They rushed into a large room to find large vats of beer and trucks half loaded with barrels of booze. The suspects, warned by the noise, had escaped. Even so, the valiant eight smashed another Capone operation.

Ness decided he needed a new weapon. He got his hands on a steel-framed, ten-ton truck and attached a wide snow plow to the front. Now he could smash through doors quickly.

At 5:00 a.m. one morning, he gave the signal, and one of the men gunned the armored truck straight for the doors. They splintered into matchwood and the truck came to a stop inside another illegal Capone operation. Ness had stationed men on the roof and at the back door. This time no one escaped. The team captured key men in the gangster's network.

Over the following months, Ness and his close-knit team raided brewery after brewery. Each time they took prisoners and equipment. They confiscated thousands of barrels and vats of beer and took trucks that caused a loss to Capone in excess of $1 million. Ness was like a hornet, buzzing at his prey, stinging Capone until it hurt.

Capone fought back. One evening Ness dropped his girlfriend at her house and drove away. He noticed a car parked the wrong way on the street. As he approached, he saw a bright flash from the front window. He ducked as a bullet shattered his windshield. The car leaped forward when he tromped on the gas pedal. As he passed, he saw another bright flash from a gun, the bullet smashing his left window. The tires squealed as he hurtled around the next corner. Driving madly, he circled the block. Taking his pistol from his shoulder holster, he turned back onto the street where he had sighted the car, but the would-be assassin had faded into the night.

Since enforcement of the prohibition law was mostly the job of the Treasury Department, it went quietly about finding evidence against Capone. The IRS looked for evidence that the gangster was not paying taxes. Capone defended himself saying that reporting income from illegal activities was self-incriminating. It didn't take the court long to strike down that tax dodge. Criminals who did not have bank accounts, yet who lived lavish life styles with no means of income could not hide anymore.

Ness was fighting the battle on two fronts: Capone's battalion of henchmen and the corrupt police and agents who were paid to look the other way, so much so that corruption became nearly synonymous with prohibition agents. Armed with the piles of information the department gathered about the stills and breweries, the government put Capone in prison for eleven years on evidence of tax evasion. Eliot Ness's band of untouchables had done its job.

NOTES

1. "A Byte Out of History," *The Federal Bureau of Investigation*, published January 3, 2007, https://www.fbi.gov/news/stories/2007/january/ness010307.
2. "Law Hero Eliot Ness," *USA Hero*, last modified November 9, 2013, http://www.usa -hero.com/ness_eliot.html.
3. Jack S. Blocker Jr., "Did Prohibition Really Work? Alcohol Prohibition as a Public Health Innovation," *American Journal of Public Health*, vol. 96, no. 2, (2006), http:// www.ncbi.nlm.nih.gov/pmc/articles/PMC1470475/.

STAR OF THE FORTIES

orn in the small, obscure town of Roosevelt, Utah, Laraine Day rose to motion picture prominence in the 1940s. She had leading roles opposite several powerful and very popular male movie stars, including Robert Young, Cary Grant, Gary Cooper, Kirk Douglas, and Ronald Reagan, who was twice elected president of the United States.

Her family moved to California, where she joined the Long Beach Players. A man showed up and wrangled a part in a play she had written. They had serious differences about artistic values. Her Mormon background precluded her writing plays or performing roles that violated her moral ethics. He couldn't sway the straight-laced actress so he rewrote the play, staying to write a few of his own as well. In a way, Laraine indirectly had a role in the early success of this man, Ray Bradbury, who became a well-known science-fiction writer.

Laraine appeared in her first film in 1937 at age seventeen in a small part in *Stella Dallas*, a story of motherly love. Laraine would continue to play roles that showed off her attractive talents. She always conveyed an intelligent and forthright image. Whether it was in *Oater,* a western with George O'Brien, or in film noir, Laraine played leading ladies with likable presence.

She broke into feature films in 1939 when she signed with MGM Studios. From then on her film career soared. Early on, MGM cast her in the popular *Dr. Kildare* series as Lew Ayers' love interest. When she was permitted to work with strong directors, she gave strong performances in such films as *Foreign Correspondent, Mr. Lucky,* and *The Story of Dr.*

Wassell. She took time out to once again appear with Lew Ayers in the underrated *Fingers at the Window.*

She was like a playful kitten when she costarred in a movie with John Wayne. She got a whole bunch of keys and had little tags made that read, "If lost, please return to John Wayne, RKO Studios. Reward." She dropped them all over Hollywood. The result was that Wayne got a lot of telephone calls and people showing up at the studio. He never found out who did it.

Toward the end of her film career in 1954, she was among the star-studded passengers in *The High and the Mighty,* again with John Wayne. The story was about an ill-fated plane headed for certain disaster. The public loved it, and it spawned dozens of other disaster films.

When she met baseball manager Leo Durocher in 1947, she didn't know who he was, but it wasn't long before she married him. He entertained her with exciting stories and incredible tales about players, powerful batting, miraculous saves, talented pitchers, and breathtaking one-point wins. She was converted. Long before it was popular, she became one of TV's first female sports reporters, hosting *Day with the Giants* (the title a play on her last name).

The show's format featured Laraine chatting with team players. She boosted her husband's baseball career with the show and at the same time attracting hundreds of female fans. At one time she said, "Baseball is not a lot of statistics, it's blood and tears."

Since superstardom had eluded her, she said, "Let someone else be the world's greatest actress, I'll be the world's greatest baseball fan." That comes somewhat as a contradiction since as a young girl, Laraine hated baseball. She had never attended a game, but just the same she became a real fan. Even while traveling with Leo and the Giants, she still continued to appear in movies.

Her beauty, warm personality, and late acquaintance with baseball made her the First Lady of Baseball, but she will always be remembered as a Star of the Forties.

NOTES

1. "Actresses Photos and Brief Biographical Info," *LDSFilm.com,* last modified August 19, 2004, http://ldsfilm.com/bioActress.html. (Steve Sidel.)

2. "Laraine Day," Tom Vallance, *Independent,* published November 12, 2007, http://www.independent.co.uk/news/obituaries/laraine-day-400125.html. (Joanna Chaundy.)

SO OTHERS MAY LIVE

Of the 2,753 innocent people murdered by Islamic terrorists on September 11, 2001, in the World Trade Center towers, 343 were firefighters and paramedics. True to one of their mottos, they were first in and last out. One group in particular was the Ten House six: Gregg Atlas, Jim Corrigan, Steve Harrell, Jeff Olsen, Paul Pansini, and Sean Tallon. Their station was across the street from the Towers within Ground Zero, so they were first to respond. They dashed through burning paper and computer parts, falling bodies, and chunks of concrete cascading from above. Weeks later, searchers found their bodies and the wreckage of Ladder Company Ten under forty feet of rubble.

On August 30, 2011, following Hurricane Irene, the Passaic River in New Jersey crested at more than fourteen feet. In the prior three weeks, dark clouds dropped up to sixteen inches of rain, which created conditions for record flooding. More than four hundred people escaped before floodwaters rose several feet above their houses' foundations. In a futile hope to save their homes, others filled sandbags and laid them around their properties to stop the river at the edge of the floodwater.

Not all residents got away. Local firefighters received frantic calls to report a man clinging to the side of a bridge. Led by Captain Frank Liscio they arrived in time to see the mad waters rise up and wash over the bridge. The man vanished. The crew dashed along the river to find him in swift current now clinging to a tree. They could see the terror in his eyes.

They tried several times to reach him with a rigging system, but they couldn't because live power lines prevented helicopter rescue. The firefighters built a "lowering" and "hauling" device while Frank jumped onto a tree and hung by a limb to guide the boat to lift the victim to it and signal the rescue team to pull the boat back to a safe area. Once they had the waterlogged man safely ashore, they formed a human chain for Frank and pulled him in like a fish on a line.

On September 21, 1882, the owner of the Locust Hill Oil Works arrived to find a six-hundred-barrel oil tank afire. He saw that the only way to save some oil was to draw off the oil. By five in the morning he and several firemen had drawn off about half. Working near the tank was firefighter Charles Keegan of Ladder Company 12. He was dressed in his high-fronted hat that tapered in back and a uniform that looked much like the uniforms worn by Civil War southern generals. A mass of curly hair grew down over his ears and a profuse mustache adorned his upper lip.

He worked at the fire even after the heat drove others away. Suddenly, the burning oil boiled over and spilled onto the ground, spreading quickly to light a nearby boatman's clothing afire. A man from Ladder Company 12 ran to pull him from the mud where he stood.

One of the workers said, "It's getting warm—we have to turn off the water from the boat." The foreman then shut off the valves to the tank. One man ran toward the creek. Charles, standing only twenty feet from the flaming oil, ran into a passage between the radiators and the pumping house. Another worker saw the burning oil follow Charles into the passageway, so to escape the flames, Charles ran along the string piece of the dock. No one saw Charles again.

Later, at an inquest, the coroner had something to say about expecting firemen to risk their lives to save a few barrels of oil. "The fatal result of the fire showed great lack of judgment on the part of somebody. In my judgment, it is improper to risk a man's life to save a little oil. We have lost a good citizen and fireman. No one has a right to expect such a thing." His feelings are probably correct; firemen exist "so others may live."

The fire began in a connecting loading dock of the Sofa Super Store in Charleston. The structure had no fire sprinkler system but was open, with employees unaware of the fire.

Firefighters arrived three minutes after they received an alarm. They attacked the fire in the loading dock area and began a search for people. In the showroom, they found only light smoke, but someone opened an exterior door near the fire allowing it to burst in and spread across the room like searching fingers.

A 911 call came from an employee trapped in the warehouse. Several firefighters ran to rescue the employee but could not get to him at first. A couple of quick-thinking men used their axes to smash a hole through a wall to bring the frightened man to safety. Firemen working in the blazing showroom were not so lucky. A flashover that spread across the ceiling weakened the structure and minutes later caused the roof to collapse. Of the sixteen firefighters caught in the sudden change of conditions, Louis Mulkey, Mike Benke, Mel Champaign, Billy Hutchinson, Brad Baity, Jim Drayton, Mark Kelsey, Mike French, and Brandon Thompson did not make it out. They made several calls for help. Their fellow firefighters attempted to rescue them but were not successful. By the time the fire was contained, nine Charleston firemen had sacrificed their lives. Their deaths were due in part to careless motorists, who drove over water hoses that snaked across streets from hydrants blocks away, causing a severe water supply problem. When the fire was only smoldering rubble, onlookers left, and motorists continued on their way, completely unaware of the nine courageous firemen who lay dead in the burned-out building.

Some elevators are posted with signs that read "Do Not Use In Case of Fire." On May 24, 1997, a seventeen-year-old worker stepped into the elevator at the Bargains Galore business, unaware that a fire was raging in a dumpster outside. It quickly raced through the elevator controls area and disabled the elevator. He was trapped on the second floor with flames inching toward him.

Portland Fire Bureau employee Gary Boyles groped his way through the second floor smoke to the trapped youth but could not open the doors. When firefighters arrived, he pointed them to the first floor where they were able to force the doors open. They sprayed water up the elevator shaft to cool the bottom of the cage. Gary worried that heat from the flames might weaken cables and send the car crashing down on the firefighters working below in the elevator shaft.

Firefighter Don Beahm stumbled through the dark basement to an access to hack at the lines until they broke to lower the elevator car to the open doors on the first floor. The terrified worker jumped to safety. In a combined effort—firefighters who risked their lives to spray water in an elevator shaft under a car with broken cables, Gary who stayed in the smoke-filled second floor until the car was released, and Don who dared the flames to force the car down—these courageous firemen risked their lives so that another might live.

On June 16, 1928, Hook and Ladder Company 104 of South Second Street in Brooklyn arrived first at the four-story tenement to see flames shooting from the two upper floors. When wind blew away the smoke that hid the front of the building, firemen saw a man perched on an electric sign.

Firefighter Patrick Barnett climbed up the front of the building to reach the trapped tenant. He helped the man get to a ledge to pass him to another fire on a raised ladder, but was overcome by smoke. As he was about to topple to the ground, he was saved by a fellow firefighter.

NOTES

1. *Wikipedia*, s.v. "Charleston Sofa Super Store fire," last modified March 25, 2016, https://en.wikipedia.org/wiki/Charleston_Sofa_Super_Store_fire.

2. *Firehouse*, April 2012, http://www.firehouse.com/magazine/fh/issue/2012/apr.

3. *Firehouse*, accessed May 23, 2016, http://www.firehouse.com/podcast.

4. "Fires in Brooklyn," transcribed by Nacy E. Lutz, Mimi Stevens, Gladys Jensen, Nina Craven, Joy Bold, and Cherie Sampson, *Brooklyn Genealogy Information Page*, accessed May 23, 2016, http://bklyn-genealogy-info.stevemorse.org/Fire/FireNews .html. (Nancy Lutz.)

5. "Firefighter Rescues Teen in a Devastating Fire," accessed May 23, 2016, https://characterqualitystories.com.

6. "Power Lines Ignite Debris, Destroy Eastside Warehouse," David R. Anderson and Laura Trujillo, *The Oregonian*, accessed May 23, 2016, http://www.oregonlive.com /search/oregonian/.

7. Personal account from Harold Rust.

"I WILL NOT GIVE UP MY SEAT"

Y'all better make it light on yourselves and let me have those seats," said bus driver Blake. He had come to the black section of the Montgomery City bus transit where four black people sat just behind the white section, which consisted of the first ten rows. The white section was full, and a white man was left standing. Now the driver wanted the first row of seats in the black section.

Three of the people complied and moved back. Rosa Parks did not. "Let me have those seats," the driver repeated. "Why don't you stand up?" Rosa Parks responded, "I don't think I should have to move. I'm not in a seat reserved for whites." When Rosa remained seated, the driver said, "Well, if you don't stand up, I'm going have to call the police and have you arrested." The petite—but resolute—woman replied, "You may do that."

This December 1, 1955, incident in downtown Montgomery, Alabama, set off the beginning of the modern-day civil rights movement. At the time, drivers had the authority to assign seats solely for the purpose of segregation. Even though the back of the bus was designated for blacks, drivers could require them to give up their seats if the white section was full and whites were standing.

Ninety years had passed since the Fourteenth Amendment became law, guaranteeing equal treatment, but in Montgomery nobody paid much attention to it.

Rosa Parks was arrested. "Why do you push us around?" she asked the arresting officer. "I don't know," he replied, "but the law's the law, and you're under arrest." Rosa endured the humiliation of police booking, photographing, and finger printing. At her trial she was found guilty of disorderly conduct for refusing to obey orders of a bus driver. She paid a ten-dollar fine. For openly challenging the racial laws of the city, she put herself at great physical risk.

Rosa Parks was not the first person to be arrested for violating the segregation rules on city buses. She was, however, a woman of character and honesty. She was held in high esteem by all who knew and worked with her. She was also secretary of the local NAACP. Someone said, "They've messed with the wrong person this time."

There were many forces in Rosa's early life that forged her character. Her childhood revolved around the small church she attended, where she developed a strong faith and sense of who she was. Listening to the pastor, she learned to believe in equality. Her grandfather kept a loaded double-barrel rifle just in case they had to face Ku Klux Klan violence. At the all-black school she attended, with all white teachers, she learned that not all whites were racists.

During World War II she worked at the Maxwell Field Air Force Base in Montgomery where she rode in desegregated cars and trucks. It was partly this experience that sparked her scorn for the city's segregated bus system.

The day after her arrest, she joined the bus boycott that had been organized and launched by leading black civil rights leaders. For 381 days, blacks—who made up 75 percent of ridership—refused to ride the buses. Cutting into city revenues, the boycott ended successfully in 1956, bringing an end to bus segregation in the city. Rosa moved north to Detroit, Michigan, where she became an aide to Congressman John Conyers. He often joked, "More people visit my office to meet my staff assistant than to meet me."

She didn't set out to make history on that fateful day in Montgomery, but when she would not give up her seat, her words became as immortal as "Remember the Alamo." When she died, she lay in state at the Capitol rotunda. Congress passed a resolution calling her the Mother of Modern-day Civil Rights Movement.

Rosa was modest about her role in civil rights. She gave credit to a higher power: "I was fortunate God provided me with the strength I needed at the precise time conditions were ripe for change. I am thankful to him every day that he gave me the strength not to give up my seat."

NOTES

1. "Rosa Parks Was Arrested for Civil Disobedience December 1, 1955," *America's Story from America's Library*, accessed May 23, 2016, http://www.americaslibrary.gov/jb /modern/jb_modern_parks_1.html.

2. "Teaching With Documents: An Act of Courage, The Arrest Record of Rosa Parks," *National Archives*, accessed May 23, 2016, http://www.archives.gov/education/lessons /rosa-parks/.

3. "Rosa Parks, 1913–2005: Mother of the American Civil Rights Movement," *Manythings.org*, accessed May 23, 2016, http://www.manythings.org/voa/people/Rosa _Parks.html.

4. Lydia D. Bjornlund, *Rosa Parks and the Montgomery Bus Boycott*, (Lucent Books, 2007).

5. Douglas Brinkley, *Rosa Parks: A Life*, (Penguin Books, 2005).

6. "Rosa Parks," Gaius Chamberlain, *Great Black Heroes*, published February 7, 2013, http://www.greatblackheroes.com/civil-rights/rosa-parks/.

7. "Rosa Park: Mother of the Civil Rights Movement," Kenneth M. Hare, *IIP Digital*, published December 29, 2008, http://iipdigital.usembassy.gov/st/english/publication/20 09/01/20090106142830jmnamdeirf0.6788446.html#axzz49XhgZsIX.

8. *U.S. Embassy & Consulates in the United Kingdom*, http://london.usembassy.gov /society163.html.

FREE THE CHILDREN

Who are you to be telling adults what to do?" the woman challenged twelve-year-old Craig Kielburger. Young Craig was speaking about the horrors of child labor and enslavement around the world. Back in 1995, he was searching the papers for the comics section when he came across an article about Iqbal Masih. The Pakistani boy, age four, had been sold into slavery to work in a carpet factory. After he escaped, he was free to speak about the rights of children. Many came to hear him, but Iqbal was killed by those who did not want him to reveal the truth about child slavery. On reading this, young Craig's life changed forever.

Before reading about Iqbal, Craig had never heard about child labor. He didn't really know where Pakistan was. He did recognize the sea of differences between his life and that of the young boy in Pakistan. At that moment, he knew he had to do something to help, so twelve-year-old Craig rounded up eleven of his friends at school. With his friends in support, he founded Free the Children, which began the fight against forced child enslavement.

Craig and his schoolmates signed petitions and faxed world leaders about child labor conditions. They funded their organization through garage sales, car washes, and bake sales run by the children. No one on the board of directors was older than eighteen. Unitedly, they brought to the attention of the world a horror that had been kept secret, that children were being enslaved at early ages to work in factories and sweatshops, working twelve to fourteen hours a day with no chance to attend school. These enslaved children were beaten and mistreated, living behind barbed wire and concrete block walls. They had no future and little chance of happiness. Hundreds of children were kept captive as prostitutes.

Adults were shocked and resentful, but they didn't agree with Craig and what he did about it. For what he was exposing to the world, he suffered attacks by people in positions of power. When he brought child prostitution to light, adults said, "He has overstepped an unspoken boundary—children should not speak of these things." The obvious response was, "If we do not speak of them, who will?" If the horror was to be dealt with, someone had to speak about it, and Craig decided that he would.

At age fourteen, Craig went to the slums, sweatshops, and the back alleys of South Asia to find those enslaved children. He accompanied police on a raid to free children held in a factory. He went with the police when those children were returned to their parents. He talked with families about their hardships and the joy of having their children returned to them. Free the Children talked with government officials, who agreed to investigate the process of labeling imported rugs to identify those not made by enslaved children. The law was changed so that police could charge importers and slave traders with criminal violations.

Spokesmen from these countries made little of what Craig was doing. They tried to hide the horrors. "The solutions to these problems are complex. They require more than a fourteen-year-old boy to solve them. Anyway, why is it that North America always thinks they can save the world?" As Craig had noticed, "No one else will try."

Slave traders make it impossible for children sold into slavery to ever get out. The only way that children can break this bondage is to escape or die, so Craig's group raised money to fund a rehabilitation center for children who have escaped from their slavery. The center provides shelter and schooling. Several countries agreed to ban products made by enslaved children. Craig now dedicates himself to children's rights. Free the Children initiated projects all over the world and opened 109 schools for enslaved and exploited children. Craig and his brother, Marc, founded Leaders Today to teach leadership skills to children around the world.

NOTES

1. "Craig Kielburger (Interview)," interview by Cate Malek, *Beyond Intractability*, July 2005, http://www.beyondintractability.org/profile/craig-kielburger-profile.

2. "Guy Burgess and Heidi Burgess," *Conflict Information Consortium*, accessed May 24, 2016, http://conflict.colorado.edu/burgess.html.

3. "Biography," *peaceheroes.com*, http://www.peaceheroes.com/CraigKielburger/craigkiel burgerbio.htm.

4. http://peacemakers.com/CraigKielburger.bio.htm.

5. Tracy Rysavy, "Free the Children: The Story of Craig Kielburger," *Yes! Magazine* (September 30, 1999), http://www.yesmagazine.org/issues/power-of-one/free-the-children -the-story-of-craig-kielburger.

RYAN'S WELL

R yan Hreljac speaks strongly and with conviction for the people of the world who don't have clean water. From a very young age, he has spoken out as a vibrant voice with a clear message: every person on the planet deserves clean water, and one voice can make a difference.

He was born in Kemptville, Ontario, Canada, a town of about three thousand people. In 1998, when Ryan was in first grade, he learned from his teacher, Mrs. Prest, that nine hundred million people don't have access to safe water and that people were dying because they didn't have clean water to drink. At age six, he decided that raising money for people who didn't have clean water would be a good thing. He worked for four months doing household chores in order to earn his first seventy dollars.

At the time, he thought that seventy dollars would be enough to dig a well, but all it would buy was a hand pump. When he learned that it would cost $2000 to dig a well, he stoically said, "I'll just do more chores." His tenacity touched the hearts of many adults and gave hope to thousands of others.

Ryan's first well was dug in 1999 at a school in a Ugandan village; Ryan was seven. The well serves thousands of people. From that first seventy dollars, Ryan's efforts have resulted in a foundation that has contributed 461 wells in sixteen countries, bringing clean water to nearly six hundred thousand people. The foundation, called Ryan's Well, has raised millions of dollars.

Ryan continued to spread his message of clean water for everyone as he met new people and visited countries—Argentina, Brazil, South

Africa—eventually two hundred in all. He remains dedicated to the foundation and its work. He continues to speak about the need for clean water around the world. He has made presentations at hundreds of schools, churches, and civic clubs. He's attended more than two dozen international conferences and global events. He's even been recognized by UNICEF as a global young leader.

Ryan received many awards for his work, including the World of Children Founders Award, the Ontario Medal for Young Volunteers, the Canadian Meritorious Service Medal, and the Top 20 under 20 Award. He is also the youngest person ever to have received the Order of Ontario. His message has been featured on the *Oprah Winfrey Show* twice, CNN, and NBC. He has been featured in countless magazines. On the radio he has conferred with some of the most prominent people in the world. Of these encounters he says, "The most impressive people I've met are the kids who want to help."

When asked about his achievements he says, "I'm just your regular, average kid," As evidence of this, he plays basketball, ice hockey, and video games. When Ryan first proposed the idea to his family, they helped a little but got bored and stopped. Now they are shakers and movers in the foundation. His older brother, Jordan, works on the foundation's Global Youth Initiative where he makes presentations on behalf of the foundation. Younger brother, Keegan, is the foundation's photographer and gives talks to youth groups everywhere.

Today Ryan has pen pals in Uganda. One of these boys, Jimmy Akana, whom Ryan met while in Africa, became an official member of the Hreljac family. The first time Ryan visited Uganda, he found five thousand children lining the route to the school, all yelling "Ryan! Ryan! Ryan!" He cried, "They know my name!" His escort said, "Everybody for a hundred kilometers knows your name."

And it all began with a little boy's plan to raise seventy dollars to dig Ryan's Well.

NOTES

1. http://www.wordpress.youth-leader.org/2010/08.

2. "Ryan Hrelijac," *Kids are Heroes*, accessed May 23, 2016, http://www.kidsareheroes .org/heroes.htm.

3. "Ryan's well," Judi McLeod, *Canada Free Press*, published December 1, 2003, http:// canadafreepress.com/2003/edesk120803.htm.

ONE STEP AT A TIME

Hurricane Charley moved across western Cuba at sixty miles per hour, picked up speed, turned north, became a category four hurricane, but veered northwest. It made landfall at midnight and swept across the Florida peninsula for seven days at 150 miles per hour, near where six-year-old Zach Bonner lived. Luckily, for the victims of Hurricane Charley, Zach was gifted with a sense of charity, not a common asset of one so young, but he liked doing charity work.

One of the worst problems that hurricanes cause is contaminated water supply. Zach heard that the hurricane had left people with no water or other supplies that they needed. While thinking about people's needs, an idea popped into his head. He had recently received a little red wagon. Without any thought as to the amount of work it was going to demand, he got his wagon from the garage and started down the sidewalk, going from house to house.

At each house he asked the owners to donate water for the victims of Hurricane Charley. Since most people purchased bottled water and stored it, nearly everyone he approached put a bottle or two into his little wagon. Each time the wagon was full, he returned home to empty it. Each time he emptied it, he was back on the beat, going door to door through his entire neighborhood. Days turned into weeks, and weeks turned into months. At the end of four months, Zach had collected not only water, but other needed supplies—twenty-seven truck loads of supplies.

Hurricanes keep Zach busy. His main focus is kids, kids without water, food, or homes. After Hurricane Katrina, people lived in FEMA trailers.

Zach gave backpacks that he named "Zachpacks" filled with supplies, snacks, and toys for the kids who had lost their homes and now lived in the trailers. As of 2008, he had given more than three thousand Zachpacks to homeless kids across the country. He donated eight-thousand-dollars worth of school supplies, toys, sporting equipment, and books.

To get other kids interested in volunteering, he staged something he called 24 Hours. Young people who live in nice houses really have no idea what it is like to live on the streets. Zach gets kids to live in a box on the streets for 24 hours. The event raises funds, donations, and awareness of the plight of homeless kids.

With his interest turned to the homeless, he learned that there are more than a million homeless kids in America. Inspired by the Peace Pilgrim, a woman who walked twenty-five thousand miles for peace, Zach hit upon the idea of walking to raise money for the homeless.

In 2007, at age nine, he began his My House to the White House trek. From his home in Tampa, he walked the 280 miles to Tallahassee. In fall 2008, Zach walked from Tallahassee, Florida, to Atlanta, Georgia. On this walk, he raised money for a homeless Memphis family's Habitat for Humanity home. The grand purpose of his 2009 walk from Memphis to Washington, DC was to build an apartment complex for homeless youth.

Once he had arrived in Washington, he also met and talked with several congressmen.

His mother, sister, and brother gave him moral support along the way; they slept in an RV at night. Cracker Barrel company donated meals. While the trip cost a few thousand dollars, it did end with a $25,000 donation from Elton John. Of course, by this time the family had organized the Little Red Wagon Foundation. It was needed to handle all the money that Zach was generating.

On Christmas Day of 2009, Zach began his 2,478-mile hike across America. He walked about five hours a day and covered about fifteen miles. That's a pace of three miles an hour. His twenty-year-old brother often walked with him. If his brother wasn't walking with him, his sister or mother walked. The sister often drove alongside him, making phone calls, and setting up campgrounds where they would stay. He did homeschooling at night in the RV.

Once he left the humid South and entered the deserts of Oklahoma, Texas, New Mexico, and Arizona, he entered the devil's own playground. Hikers who have crossed Death Valley in the summer wear out two or three pairs of shoes on their short hikes. The heat melted them. Zach wore out eight pairs of Reeboks on his cross-country trek.

On July 28, 2010, near San Carlos, Arizona, a reporter from the *New York Times* took a photograph of Zach walking near a road sign telling drivers to watch out for cattle crossing the highway. Zach was wearing his usual T-shirt and shorts but had added a pair of designer shades. Because temperatures pushed above one hundred degrees, he kept a water bottle handy. He listened to Elton John endlessly. The music and songs helped chase away the boredom. Elton had also pledged $50,000 to Zach's Little Red Wagon Foundation if Zach finished his walk to Santa Monica Pier. When he arrived, Elton invited him to his concert in Tucson that week.

Zach planned to arrive in Santa Monica in September. On his arrival at any place, hundreds greeted him. Those who could, shook his hand. All just wanted a glimpse of the twelve-year-old boy who inspired them and was changing the world one step at a time.

NOTES

1. "Irish American Zach Bonner walking 2,500 miles to help homeless children," April Drew, *IrishCentral*, published March 24, 2010, http://www.irishcentral.com /news/irish-american-zach-bonner-walking-2500-miles-to-help-homeless-children -89079687-237689361.html. (Kate Hickey.)
2. "Hurricane Charley," *National Weather Service Weather Forecast Office*, last modified August 13, 2014, http://www.srh.noaa.gov/mfl/?n=charley.

WANTED: DEAD OR ALIVE

I have faith in my star," wrote Winston Churchill to his mother, on the eve of battle in India, "that I am destined to do something in the world." Perhaps it was this certainty that kept him alive during any number of fights and kept the bullets hitting the horses instead of him. He always emerged from the firefights unscathed. Additionally, he wrote, "Besides, I am so conceited I do not believe the gods would create so potent a being for so prosaic an ending." It could be that with this statement he put the bullets to shame and they dared not hit him.

As the world greeted the new century and 1900 rolled in, England was preparing for war.

The tussle between British imperialism and Afrikaner nationalism had been going on for half a century. The Afrikaners, also known as Boers, had grown in economic power and had built a military strength cheerfully supplied by Germany. Winston, who had participated in recent campaigns, was eager for England to protect its vital interests in South Africa. He surely would not miss this fight. The major disadvantage was that he would be going as a civilian. As a correspondent, his access to important military information would be hampered, and he saw little chance of military glory.

Being a war correspondent is a dangerous career. In the thick of battle, while covering the fighting, many such men have been killed. Winston wrote much of the war, all the time narrowly escaping the bullets. Yet he often ended his correspondence noting his sense of destiny, while he survived one meeting with death after another.

139

Civilians don't carry weapons. Winston had the habit of assisting the soldiers he wrote about, so he often carried a Mauser pistol that he had used at the battle of Omdurman. Now, at Natal, confronted by a mounted horseman with a rifle pointed directly at him, he reached for the weapon. He was surprised to find it not there. He realized that a combatant in civilian clothes could be shot as a spy. To his chagrin, Transvaal Attorney General Jan Smuts assured the Boers that Winston was indeed a combatant and that he should be held as a prisoner of war. Thus began Winston's march to the railhead and eventually to the Boer prison camp in Pretoria.

News of Winston's heroics at the ambush of the train went ahead of him. Even while he was being marched to prison, the natal advisor wrote of Winston's courageous action. Captain Wylie said, "He's as brave a man as could be found." A private, who had been shot in the throat and whom Winston helped climb on the escaping engine said, "He walked about in it all as coolly as if nothing was going on. He called for volunteers to give him a hand to get the wreckage off the tracks. Churchill is a splendid fellow." Even the enemy, the Boers, praised Churchill for his gallantry. On the march, a Boer guard gave Winston a cap to shade him from the sun.

On a final night sharing a blanket with another prisoner on the ground, he began to plan his escape. Those about him did not share his enthusiasm to be free. In fact, they worried. One fellow prisoner was contemptuous of Winston and refused to consider escape possible. When Winston went over the fence, he hid for a long time in the bushes outside the prison compound. He waited in dire peril of being recaptured, for the others who never came. He crept from the cover of the bushes that ringed the prison and began his flight to freedom. Almost immediately, the Boers issued a warrant for his arrest, dead or alive. A twenty-five pound reward was offered for his capture. Winston was insulted. He thought it should be seventy-five at least, considering who he was.

The news of his escape was now spreading across the Transvaal. Every Boer had his description. Winston knew that he should move quickly. He came to a small settlement and skirted around it to take up hiding in a ditch near the railroad tracks. A train halted at the station then moved out slowly. With the agility of a cat, Winston leaped from his hiding place and grabbed a hold on the passing boxcars. He pulled himself onto the couplings between two cars and climbed into one of them. He found himself amid stacks of empty coal sacks. Like a mole, he burrowed in for sleep.

How long he slept he did not know. He needed to leave the train before dawn. Pulling himself from under the coal sacks, he crawled to the open doorway. Into the dark he leaped. He made two running strides and plunged headlong into the ground, shaken but unhurt. Destiny was certainly his companion this night. He hid in a grove of trees where he watched guards ride by. He guessed that they were searching for him. As night turned to day the heat spread over him like a heavy woolen blanket. Thoughts of the cool water in the pond nearby played over him like an ocean tide. To chance a run for it was out of the question, what with the guards still searching the area for him.

Boers stood guard along the road. He had hoped they would not be this far away from the prison. He was wrong. To avoid them required making long detours. Night came again and the moon was too bright. A house came into view. What kind of reception would he receive? His thirst became intense, made worse by the pieces of chocolate that had sustained him for the past thirty hours. Pangs of fear gripped him as he banged on the door. A light came on. A voice called, "Wie is daar?"

"Aah," Winston gasped. "Dutch. All is lost." Gamely he replied in English, "I've had an accident. I need help." The door opened. There stood a man as tall as Goliath, with a pistol in his hand. "What do you want?" he asked in English. Winston lied, "I'm a burgher. I've fallen from the train." As soon as Winston was inside, the man locked the door. *He's going to shoot me,* Winston thought. Instead the man said, "I'm John Howard. I manage the Transvaal Colliery."

Winston had been pulled from the jaws of death once again. Fate was with him. He also knew that for the man to hide him it could mean death as a traitor. Winston offered to move on. "We'll fix up something," Howard said. They settled Winston in a ventilated room deep within the coal mine. This would be his home for the next several days. It didn't last long because Winston soon became sick. No sunshine, no activity, no change of days got to him. Howard brought him to the surface.

Plans were made for him to board a train headed for the border. In the early hours of a December day, Howard led Winston to the boxcars waiting on the tracks beside the coal mine buildings. Winston got aboard and once again burrowed into a tunnel, this time under some cotton bales.

British miners loitered nearby with the idea of distracting the Boers. Instead, they aroused the suspicions of the enemy. The Boer detective confronted the miners. "I know what your game is," he said as he came toward the suspect boxcar. "You might as well give him up." A miner countered, "We've been friends for a long time, but you are not going to stop this business." He ushered the detective away. Saved again.

It was Charles Burnham who owned the wool that was being shipped. When the cars carrying his wool were scheduled to be placed on a siding for an indefinite time, he announced, "That can't be. A sharp fall in wool prices in imminent. We cannot avoid the delay." Burnham got himself a traveling permit to allow the cars to be attached to a passing train. Winston moved with them. At Middleburg another bribe kept his goods moving. Still, they met another crisis; as the train paused at Kaapmuiden, an armed guard approached Winston's car. Burnham came to the rescue again. "How about a cup of coffee at the stall?" he suggested. The guard accepted. He was led away from Winston's hiding place.

At Komatipoort, Burnham persuaded the customs officer to allow the cars to cross without a search. They were placed on a siding for the night. Fears of discovery and return to the prison at Pretoria ran through Winston's mind. Would all that he had endured be for naught? Would his escape end in failure? As morning light spread into his hiding place, he felt the jolt of the cars being moved. Another jolt! The cars rolled forward.

In a short time the train passed through Resana Garcia, and he was across the border and free. Winston Churchill's flight from Pretoria prison was one of the great escapes of all time.

NOTES

1. David Buckerfield, "Churchill's Capture, Imprisonment & Escape," *The British Empire*, http://www.britishempire.co.uk/article/churchillscapture.htm.

2. Ben Draper and Jak Brown, "Sir Winston Churchill," *gov.uk*, http://www.gov.uk/government/history/past-prime-ministers/winston-churchill.

3. "Winston Churchill Biography: Sword and Pen," *National Churchill Museum*, https://www.nationalchurchillmuseum.org/winston-churchill-sword-and-pen.html.

4. Brian Kaighin, "British Boer War Deaths," *Boer War Deaths and Ladysmith*, http://www.boerwardeaths.com/#!boer-war-deaths/c5ia. (Brian Kaighin.)

5. http://www.ladysmith.com.

6. Martin Edwards, "The Boer War: Winston Churchill (1874–1965)," *Roll of Honour*, http://www.roll-of-honour.com/Boer/BoerWarChurchillWinston.html. (MartinEdwards.)

HOUSTON: WE'VE HAD A PROBLEM

James Lovell, commander of *Apollo 13* spaceflight, was in the lower equipment bay, halfway between Fred Haise in the lunar module and Jack Swigert in the command module. James was wrestling with TV wires and cameras, watching Fred come down. All three heard a loud bang—the explosion of a liquid oxygen tank two in the service module. Haise said, "I felt a vibration." About two seconds elapsed before the master alarm warned that the main Bus B lost power. The center engine shut down early. This caused the other four engines to burn half a minute longer, using up vital fuel necessary for reentry.

Calmly, Command Module Pilot Jack Swigert radioed NASA. "Houston, we've had a problem." Boy, did they have a problem. Thus began the most gripping episode in man's venture into space. Only American ingenuity would tell whether the men would return alive.

At times like this, feelings explode just like the tank. Lovell looked out the window. "Something is venting," he said, his fears growing. Privately he was thinking, *I wonder what this is going to do to the landing. I wonder if we can get back home again.* When he saw both oxygen pressures, one actually at zero and the other going down, it dawned on him that they were in very serious trouble.

Several omens should have alerted the crew and NASA to the possible dangers of the mission. When they began the chill down system in the rocket, the launch crew poured nearly forty thousand liters of liquid oxygen (LOX) into a nearby ditch. The fuel itself is pale blue and can function as an igniter. Materials will burn rapidly and wildly in liquid oxygen.

Weather conditions prevented the liquid from evaporating, turning it into a soupy fog. Once the crew had filled the rocket tanks and dumped the excess in the ditch, three of the workers went to their cars. When one of the men turned the ignition switch, his car burst into flames. Like timed explosions, each of the other cars also burst into flames. Luckily, the three escaped unharmed, but the cars were completely consumed by the fires.

Next, during ground tests, they discovered a poorly insulated critical helium tank. This would jeopardize the reentry. Finally, the number two tank, which was a transfer from the Apollo 10 flight, was dropped in the transfer to *Apollo 13*. After much testing, officials decided that it would be okay, so they installed it in the spacecraft. They made a fatal mistake.

At the time Lovell thought, *Hold it. Wait a minute. I'm riding in this spacecraft. Just go out and replace the tank. I should make them install a new tank.* Instead, he went along with it. On nearly every spaceflight, NASA had some kind of failure. In the case of *Apollo 13*, the failure was one human error added to another.

Yet both the *Apollo 13* crew and mission control remained cool in the present crisis. "We'd like you to attempt to reconnect fuel cell 1 to main A and fuel cell 3 to main B."

"Okay, Houston. I tried to reset, and both fuel cells are showing zip on the flows." No response. "Houston, are you still reading?" Swigert asked with doubt in his voice.

"That's affirmative. We're trying to come up with some good ideas for you."

With oxygen tank two blown, and oxygen tank one losing pressure, the command module's normal supply of electricity, light, and water were lost, and they were still two hundred thousand miles from earth.

Lovell looked out the window and reported, "We're venting something into space."

NASA casually replied, "Roger, we copy you."

Lovell said, "It's gas of some sort." NASA knew but did not admit that the gas was the oxygen from the last tank. Disaster in the making!

Mission control reported to the world: "*Apollo 13* is 207,000 miles from earth and moving away at 2100 miles an hour." Moving away with no oxygen to sustain the crew! "We're looking to an alternative mission, swinging around the moon and using lunar power system because a problem has developed here this evening." What an understatement!

Right after the bang, the crew tried to close the hatch between the command module and the lunar module. They had reacted on impulse, just as a submarine crew acts in an emergency to stop flooding in the submarine. Frustrated because the hatch would not stay closed, they strapped it to the command module couch: American ingenuity at work.

Pressure in oxygen tank one continued to drift down. Commander Lovell and his crew, as well as mission control, knew that they would lose all oxygen, which meant the last fuel cell would die. The system was built for a forty-five-hour return; ninety hours remained.

From mission control came another suggestion. "We figure you've got about fifteen minutes worth of power left in the command module. So we want you to start getting over to the lunar module (LM) and getting some power on that." Imagine! Only fifteen minutes of electricity under normal conditions, and they were three days from home. "We'd like you to start making your way over to the LM now." Lovell and Haise quickly floated through the tunnel into the LM, leaving Swigert to complete the last chores in the command module.

Ground controllers carefully worked out a procedure so that the command module batteries were charged with LM power. "I have an alternative procedure," came the announcement. "Turn off all non-critical systems." The main priority was keeping everything aligned, keeping the guidance system on course. That guidance system remembers the spacecraft's position and guides it home.

They learned that they would run out of water—as vital in space as on earth. Not only was water used for drinking, but it was critical in cooling the engines. They had enough to last five hours before earth reentry, or about 150 hours to earth. The crew rationed themselves to six ounces per day. Of course, dehydration set in. Lovell would lose fourteen pounds during the flight.

But how to remove the carbon dioxide? Without some way to clean the air, they would suffocate. They had enough canisters of lithium hydroxide, which would help purify the air, but the square canisters would not fit in the round openings in the LM. Then too, the LM was built to support two men for two days.

Now, it must support three men for four days. Twelve hours later, a warning light flashed telling them that the carbon dioxide had reached the danger level.

American ingenuity was called upon again. Mission control came up with a system using plastic bags, cardboard, and tape, luckily, all these materials were carried on board. The men attached the canisters to the LM system using the plastic bags.

The craft had returned with all parts still attached. They had to get rid of these before landing. It was up to James Lovell, commander of *Apollo 13*, to judge the timing. Lovell yelled, "Fire!" Swigert jettisoned the service module. It went off in a shower of debris. The sound of its departure sent chills through the men before they left the module and closed the hatch. An hour and a half before reentry, they discarded the lunar module, what had been their lifeboat. "Farewell, Aquarius, and we thank you." Lovell's benediction was simple and to the point: "She was a good ship."

On April 7, 1970, at 1:07 p.m. spaceflight *Apollo 13*, landed in the Pacific Ocean near the island of American Samoa, just four miles away from the USS *Iwo Jima*. A helicopter was sent to the landing site. Divers jumped into the Pacific to get the astronauts out of the capsule. They airlifted them back to the waiting ship to be taken to Hawaii. Later, President Richard Nixon and a few thousand friends and family greeted them. *Apollo 13* became the successful failure of manned spaceflight.

"Houston, we've had a problem," was certainly an understatement of the near-fatal flight.

NOTES

1. "Apollo 13," *Apollo Kennedy Space Center*, http://www-pao.ksc.nasa.gov/history /apollo/apollo-13/apollo-13.htm.

2. "Apollo 13 Space Mission," *Century of Flight*, http://www.century-of-flight.net /Aviation%20history/space/Apollo%2013.htm.

3. http://er.jc.nasa.gov/seh/pg3.htm.

4. "Apollo 13: Technical Air-to-Ground Voice Transcription," *National Aeronautics and Space Administration*, http://www.hq.nasa.gov/alsj/a13/AS13_TEC.txt.

5. http://www.hq.nasa.gov/office/pao/History/Sp-350/ch-13-1.html.

6. David R. Williams, "Apollo 13," *National Aeronautics and Space Administration*, http://nssdc.gsfc.nasa.gov/planetary/lunar/apollo13info.html.

7. David R. Williams, "Detailed Chronology of Events Surrounding the Apollo 13 Accident," *National Aeronautics and Space Administration*, http://nssdc.gsfc.nasa.gov /planetary/lunar/ap13chrono.html.

8. Jim Dumoulin, "Apollo-13," *Kennedy Space Center*, http://science.ksc.nasa.gov /history/apollo/apollo-13/apollo-13.html.

HIN-MAH-TOO-YAH-LAT-KEKT

As white settlers spread across North America, they came into conflict with western tribes. One of these tribes was the Nez Perce, led by Hin-mah-too-yah-lat-kekt, better known as Chief Joseph. The tribe's hunting grounds stretched from Idaho through Oregon to northwestern Washington. Chief Joseph's father had signed a treaty with the United States government that allowed the tribe to keep its lands. The tribe had lived in peace ever since Lewis and Clark explored the area. They now trusted the government and did not fear any treachery.

Eight years later the government forced the signing of another treaty that gave the government much of the tribe's lands. At this time on the east coast, the Civil War was in its second year of conflict. Joseph said,

> The treaty was never agreed to by my people. I am not a child, I think for myself. Suppose a white man should come to me and say, "Joseph, I like your horses. I want to buy them." I say to him, "No, my horses suit me; I will not sell them." Then he goes to my neighbor and says, "Pay me money, and I will sell you Joseph's horses." The white man returns to me and says, "Joseph, I have bought your horses, and you must let me have them." If we sold our land to the government, this is how they bought it.

Fighting the Civil War left government officials with little tolerance or willingness to debate tribal land claims. The Nez Perce had to move.

Joseph had his people gathered their belongings. "I have carried a heavy load on my back ever since I was a boy," Joseph said. "I realized that we could not hold our own with the white men. We were like deer. They were like grizzly bears." The tribe began the trek to the reservation in Idaho, but it was not the peaceful trek Joseph anticipated. While marching eastward, some young Nez Perce warriors broke away from the main body and attacked white settlements. They killed some two dozen people. The news spread like wild fire. Reprisal was swift, but the government underestimated the fighting ability of the Nez Perce. The cavalry attacked the tribe in White Bird Canyon. As it turned out, June 17, 1877, was a dark day for the army; the Nez Perce proved to be expert marksmen and strong foes. When it was over, the army had lost thirty-four men. The Nez Perce had lost none. Ultimately, it would be a short victory.

Chief Joseph knew that although he won the battle, he could never win the war. He also knew that he had to find someplace safe for his people. Deciding they could find freedom in Canada, he led seven hundred members of the tribe through the Bitterroot Mountains. Along the trek, the small band fought off the army in the Battle of Clearwater on July 11, Camas Meadows on August 11, and the Battle of Canyon Creek on September 13. They beat the army every time. Americans along the East Coast read stories of their outstanding bravery and amazing skill in battle.

Sadly, just forty miles short of the Canadian border, the tribe was stopped by army attacks. At the Battle of Bear Paw, on a bitter cold October 5, 1877, the war came to an end. The American general whispered to his aide, "The most amazing campaign of my career. This Indian is an absolute genius in the science of warfare."

Joseph said,

> I am tired of fighting. Our chiefs are killed. Chief Looking Glass is dead. Toohulhulsote is dead. The old men are all dead. It is the young men who say yes or no. He who led the young men is dead. It is cold and we have no blankets. The little children are freezing to death. My people, some of them, have run away to the hills and have no blankets, no food. No one knows where they are, perhaps, freezing to death. I want to have time to look for my children and see how many I can find. Maybe I shall find them among the dead. Hear me, my chiefs. I am tired. My heart is sick and sad. From where the sun now stands, I will fight no more forever.

In 1904, Chief Joseph died at the Colville Reservation, according to his doctor, of a broken heart—but the courageous chief lives on through his immortal words.

NOTES

1. "Chief Joseph Surrenders: October 5, 1877," *America's Story from America's Library*, http://www.americaslibrary.gov/jb/recon/jb_recon_chiefjoseph_2.html.
2. Rob Spooner, "Chief Joseph," *United States History*, http://www.u-s-history.com/pages/h3813.html. (Rob Spooner.)
3. "Chief Joseph," *In the Beginning*, http://www.inthebeginning.com/articles/joseph.htm.
4. *JuntoSociety.com*, http://www.juntosociety.com/native/nezperce_chief_joseph.
5. http://learnenglish.voanews.com/content/chief-joseph-1840-1904-great.
6. *New World Encyclopedia*, s.v "Chief Joseph," accessed June 1, 2016, http://www.newworldencyclopedia.org/entry/Chief_Joseph.

PEACEMAKER

Practically unassisted, he captured 132 German soldiers, three of them officers, took thirty-five machine guns, and killed twenty-eight with twenty-eight bullets," said the official report made by officers of the Eighty-Second Division in the battle of the Argonne Forest in France, on October 8, 1917. Patrick Donahue said, "I was guarding the mass of Germans taken prisoner and devoted my attention to watching them during the shooting." Private Michael Sacina reported, "I was so close to those prisoners that the machine gunners could not shoot me without hitting their own men." Private Percy Beardsley added, "I saw Corporal York fire his pistol repeatedly in front of me. I saw Germans who had been hit fall down." George Wells, private in the Eighty-Second said, "When the heavy fire from the machine guns commenced, I was guarding some of the German prisoners." That pretty much left Alvin York alone to fight the enemy forces.

Alvin York had been born in Tennessee some twenty-nine years before. Prior to coming to France, he said, "If a man can make peace by fighting, then he is a peacemaker." At the time he was trying to reconcile his feelings about war and killing. Alvin had found religion after one of his good friends was killed in a barroom brawl. Up until that time, he himself drank heavily and got into fights. Like many young hill-country men, at a young age he became a marksman with a rifle, hunting animals to feed the family. His marksmanship would prove vital in the war.

On the morning of the eighth of October, just before daylight, they started for the hill of Chatel Chéhéry. Before they got there, it got light, and the Germans sent over a heavy barrage of cannon fire, along with poison gas. They put on gas masks and just went right on through those shells and fought their way to the top of the hill.

The Germans gave them another barrage of cannon shells. Then no barrage. They started over the hill. The Germans put their machine guns to work all over the hill in front of the Americans and on the sides. Alvin was support and he could see his pals getting picked off until it looked like there was none left. This was their first offensive battle in the Argonne. They got through the shells, and occupied the hill. They had to charge across a valley several hundred yards wide and rush the machine gun emplacements. So, they were getting it from the front and both flanks. Their losses were heavy.

The Germans got them. They just stopped Alvin and his friends dead in their tracks. It was hilly country covered with brush. The Germans had plenty of machine guns entrenched in the ridges. The Americans went down like the long grass before the lawn mower. Something had happened to their artillery. They had no covering fire, so their attack faded out. There they were lying down halfway across the valley, and no barrage with those German machine guns and big shells hitting them hard.

Alvin knew that they couldn't go on again until those machine guns were mopped up. So they decided to try and get the Germans by a surprise attack from the rear. Alvin and sixteen others went around on the left flank to see if they could put those guns out of action. Without any loss, they were across the valley and on the hill where the machine guns were placed. The brush and hilly country hid them from the Germans. They decided on a rear attack.

The first Germans they saw jumped out of the brush in front of them and bolted like two scared rabbits. The Americans called to them to surrender, but they kept on going. Alvin and his friends wanted to capture them before they gave the alarm because the Americans were well behind the German trenches behind the machine guns. When they jumped across a little stream of water, about fifteen or twenty Germans jumped up and threw up their hands and said, "Kamerad!" It was their headquarters. They were unarmed. The Americans jumped and covered them, and told them to throw up their hands. They did. They must have thought the American army was in their rear. Alvin and his group didn't tell them anything different, just "Put 'em up!"

The Germans got their machine guns turned around and fired on Alvin. They killed six Americans and wounded three; that left eight. Alvin didn't know whether it was the German major, but one yelled something in German. The gun on top of the hill swung around and opened fire. There were thirty of them. They couldn't miss, and they didn't. They killed all of Corporal Savage's squad; they got all of Alvin's but two; they wounded Corporal Cutting and killed two of his squad. The other squad escaped except the squad leader. When he went down, that left Alvin in command. He was right out there in the open. And the machine guns were spitting fire and cutting down the undergrowth all around him. The Germans were yelling orders.

Alvin's other men didn't fire a shot. They were guarding the prisoners. The prisoners were lying down so the Germans could fire over their heads to get Alvin. He exchanged shots with them. He let fly with a bullet every time he saw a German put his head up. He was giving them the best he had.

As soon as he could, Alvin stood up and shot offhand. In the middle of the fight, a German officer and five men jumped out of a trench and charged him with fixed bayonets. They had about twenty-five yards to run. Alvin shot the rear man, then the fifth, then the fourth, then the third. He did it that way because he didn't want the front ones to know that he was shooting the back ones. They keep coming until he get them all. It was like shooting wild turkeys back home.

Then Alvin returned to the machine guns. He knew that if he kept his head and didn't run out of ammunition he'd have them. He hollered to them to come down and give up. He didn't want to kill anymore. The Germans must not have understood English. He had to keep shooting. Then, he'd yell again. Finally, after the German major saw Alvin stop the six soldiers who charged another American soldier, he got up and walked over to him and yelled, "English?"

Alvin said, "No, not English."

The major said, "What?"

Alvin said, "American."

The German said, "Good. If you won't shoot any more of us I will make them give up." Alvin covered the major with his automatic and told him if he didn't make them stop firing, he would take off his head next. The German told Alvin if he didn't kill him, and if Alvin stopped shooting the others in the trench, he would make them surrender. The major blew a little whistle and they came down and began to gather and throw down their guns and belts. All but one of them came down off the hill with their hands up. Just before he got to Alvin he threw a hand grenade that burst in the air in front of him. Alvin had to shoot him. The rest surrendered without any more trouble.

Alvin called to his men that were left. "Let's git these Germans out of here." One of his men said that it was impossible. Alvin said, "No, let's get 'em out."

The German major wanted to know how many men Alvin had and he said, "Plenty." He lined up the Germans in front of him. Alvin marched them straight into those other machine guns and got them. The German major could speak English as well as Alvin could. Alvin told the prisoners to pick up and carry the wounded Americans. He wasn't going to leave any good American boys lying out there to die.

Alvin marched the prisoners straight at the German front line trench. More machine guns swung around to fire at us. Alvin told the major to blow his whistle, so he did and they all surrendered. On the way back they were constantly under heavy shellfire. So, when he got back to American lines the lieutenant of intelligence came out and counted them. He counted 132.

"York, have you captured the whole German army?" he asked.

"I've got a tolerable few," Alvin said.

Alvin's actions had now silenced the German machine guns. He had enabled the regiment to capture the railroad. Although his statement understated the odds he overcame, his fighting got rid of the enemy pressure against the American forces in the Argonne Forest. He was given the French Republic Croix de Guerre and the Legion of Honor. Italy awarded him the Croce di Guerra, and General Pershing hung the Medal of Honor on his chest for his courage.

NOTES

1. "Sergeant York and His People," *Project Gutenberg*, accessed May 23, 2016, http://www.gutenberg.org/ebooks/19117. (Sam Cowan.)

2. "World War I Medal of Honor Recipients: York, Alvin C.," *U.S. Army Center of Military History*, last modified June 3, 2015, http://www.history.army.mil/moh/worldwari.html#WOODFILL.

3. "Alvin York in his own words," Ryan, *Born on SH1*, published January 29, 2010, http://statehighwayone.com/blog/2010/01/29/alvin-york-in-his-own-words/. (Ryan Sproll.)

4. "The Diary of Alvin York," Alvin C. York, *Acacia Vignettes*, accessed May 23, 2016, http://acacia.pair.com/Acacia.Vignettes/The.Diary.of.Alvin.York.html.

COMBAT MEDIC

He must have had some misgivings when he was promoted to sergeant in Korea in 1952. Twenty-year-old David Bruce Bleak from Idaho Falls was being promoted to replace another NCO medic who had been killed. At the time the Fortieth Division was in a holding action at the thirty-eighth parallel. Actually, the American army did a lot of holding. The two opposing armies were stalemated at the thirty-eighth and had been for months. It came down to a situation where American troops were not allowed to engage in combat with the enemy, but North Koreans had every right to kill men on our side. Forays into American and South Korean lines happened regularly.

David was with his outfit in mountain country where the trees had been cut down to be used to reinforce enemy trenches. The only cover was a scattering of low brush and the rugged contour of the land itself. Before things had settled down to a stalemate, both sides set up fields of fire and lobbed in artillery shells. They followed these with patrols to find out what each side was planning. The irony of the situation was usually carried by the media as "quiet times."

On one of these probes, David and his patrol ran into enough enemy resistance to last them a lifetime. The squad was ordered into North Korean territory to capture one of the enemy and bring them back alive, as command wanted to question a prisoner about enemy movements. Giving the order was easy; any stay-behind officer could do it. Making it happen was not easy. It was like solving a Chinese puzzle. The enemy always had surprises waiting—land mines, listening outposts, fields of crossfire, and trip flares. These lit up the night like backyard parties. As some GI joked, "These patrol guys are poor insurance risks." In fact, many times they were like clay pigeons or ducks in a shooting gallery.

To make matters worse, it was the dark of the moon. Not even the stars seemed to glitter. A simple misstep put a man in a hole or tripping over some protruding rock or landform.

The patrol moved out. 4:30 a.m. turned into a gray light. The enemy opened fire with automatic weapons and small arms. Of the twenty men creeping along some trenches, several were hit, and David quickly attended to their wounds. He joined his surviving men and ran into heavy fire again. He thought of his purpose as a combat medic.

While under heavy hostile fire, David entered the trench from where the fire was coming. He disabled the enemy soldiers who had been shooting at them from the trench. Moving from the emplacement, he saw a grenade fall in front of a buddy. He quickly placed himself to shield the man from the blast. His Goliath-like frame made an adequate cover.

Moments later he was tending other wounded and was struck by an enemy bullet. Despite the aching hole in his leg and the blood that soaked his fatigues, he carried a wounded buddy to safety. As he moved down the hill with his buddy on his back, he was attacked by two enemy soldiers who came at him with fixed bayonets like horns on charging rhinos. Closing with the aggressors, he grabbed them and smacked their heads together. He had no time to think about it. He and his men were outnumbered, yet he had a wounded buddy to get to safety. Seeking what little shelter a narrow ravine could give, he carried his helpless friend down the hill out of harm's way.

David's six feet six inch frame and 250 pounds served him well. In talking about his courageous actions and saving his wounded buddies, he made light of the peril and danger. Of the enemy in the trenches that he easily dispatched, he said, "A couple of 'em got in the way."

Someone might ask, "Was the mission successful?" The answer is, yes, Sergeant David Bleak and his patrol did bring prisoners back alive to question. The patrol came back safely, a third of them walking wounded, but, they succeeded courageously.

NOTES

1. "A Couple of 'Em Got Too Close," *The Official Newsletter of the Idaho Military Historical Society and Museum*, (2000), http://museum.mil.idaho.gov/Newsletters/3rdQtr2000 .pdf.

2. "Medal Recipients," *Charles H. Coolidge Medal of Honor Heritage Center*, accessed May 23, 2016, http://www.mohm.org/medal-recipients.html.

3. "Korean War Medal of Honor Recipients: Bleak, David B., *U.S. Army Center of Military History*, last modified May 7, 2015, http://www.history.army.mil/moh /koreanwar.html#BLEAK.

4. "Soldier David Bleak; Won Medal of Honor," Adam Bernstein, *The Washington Post*, published March 27, 2006, http://www.washingtonpost.com/wp-dyn/content /article/2006/03/26/AR2006032601081.html.

DR. LIVINGSTONE,
I PRESUME

Have you ever tromped through a jungle as hot and humid as a boiler room? Hacked your way through dense undergrowth that tore at your skin like razor blades? Come face-to-face with a spider as large as your hand? Been menaced by a snake that could swallow you? Welsh-born American journalist Henry Stanley did. He trekked through the uncharted wilds of Africa in 1872. While he was a famous explorer, he was also a journalist who went in search of a great story. Great stories sold newspapers and his editor of the *New York Herald*, Gordon Bennett, knew that too. Great stories were the bread and butter of journalism, and editors searched for them as much as they searched for lost persons. When celebrated missionary and African explorer, David Livingstone, disappeared in the African jungles, Bennett said to Stanley, "Go and find Livingstone."

Henry Stanley left with the promise of a full-expense account. The year was 1871, just two years after the Transcontinental Railroad joined in Utah.

Henry had been born as John Rowland. He grew up in a workhouse before leaving for New Orleans in 1859. There he met and befriended Henry Morton Stanley. Because he had no parents he adopted Stanley's name.

The reports on Livingstone that Henry sent back from Africa were printed one after the other. The stories sold well, so well in fact, that public interest was aroused to a fever. The *Herald*'s enthusiasm in printing the Livingstone story built the man into a legend. It also fostered public interest in exploring Africa. This contributed to the eventual conquest of the continent by Europeans.

Stanley hacked his way toward Lake Tanganyika in Ujiji, the last place that anyone had ever heard of Livingstone. The explorer had reported upon his last departure into the jungles that he was going in search of the source of the Nile River. He believed that Lake Tanganyika was that source.

In following Livingstone's path, Stanley encountered poisonous reptiles, dangerous animals, disease, and bad water. Mosquitoes as large as silver dollars ate him alive. On top of all the natural dangers, he awoke one morning to find that his native bearers had run away. Pushing on, he fought through the jungles another seven hundred miles for one hundred days short of a year.

Near Tanganyika, he found Livingstone. His impulse was to rush forward and embrace the lost man. He might even have turned somersaults, vented his joy by biting his hand, or leaped into the air. His feelings were almost uncontrollable—he was overjoyed that he had actually found the man. He was not distracted by the mass of natives who lined his approach to the man he had come seven hundred miles to see. He walked between them as down a narrow alley lined by tall dark trees. At the end of the alley stood a white man with a gray beard. Stanley could see that he was also pale, somewhat stooped with a weary, sad look on his face.

He wanted to run, but protocol said no. He did not want to detract from the attention that was now focused on the man at the end of the line. He thought himself a coward for not acting on his impulses. Instead, he took off his hat and walked blindly forward. He extended his hand. "Dr. Livingstone, I presume?"

He thought, *What a pompous thing to say.*

They shook hands and replaced their hats. Stanley said, "I thank God, Doctor, I have been permitted to see you." The doctor replied, "I feel thankful that I am still here to welcome you."

Since Livingstone had traveled much in the area, he could act as guide while they explored the northern regions of the lake together. Stanley returned to America. In 1873, he learned of his fellow explorer's death. Saddened by the news, he decided to complete some of the work Livingstone had begun. He sailed to Africa, crossed the continent again to reach the Congo and Zaire. Here he explored the Nile system. Editors published his diary, *How I Found Livingstone,* and his journey through the Dark Continent several times. Stanley was a courageous, world-class explorer.

NOTES

1. Henry M. Stanley, *How I Found Livingstone*, (Project Gutenberg), e-book, http://www.gutenberg.org/ebooks/5157.

2. Henry Morton Stanley, *How I Found Livingstone*, performed by LibriVox volunteers, 2008, ebook, https://librivox.org/how-i-found-livingstone-by-sir-henry-m-stanley/.

THIRTEEN STARS

At twenty-one, Elizabeth Griscom became Mrs. John Ross when she eloped with him in 1773, but everyone called her Betsy. A few months later she became a widow when John was killed by an exploding powder keg. Betsy inherited her husband's upholstery business. One day, in 1776, three men quietly entered the shop. Betsy looked up to see chief of the Continental army in the colonies, George Washington, with George Ross and Robert Morris. Ross was a respected, well-liked businessman, the uncle of her late husband. Morris was a wealthy landowner. Betsy smiled warmly and rose to greet her visitors.

Since she had been married to his nephew, Ross was first to greet her. She was further acquainted with the general—wasn't her pew next to his at the church where they both gathered on Sundays? She and Martha always exchanged pleasant chitchat. Also, the general had come to her shop a few times to place orders for sewing. It was because of this mutual friendship that the men had chosen her to do some sewing for them. She could also be trusted to be discreet.

Washington pulled a folded piece of paper from his shirt pocket. He unfolded it and spread it on the table before Betsy. She saw a rough drawing of a flag with thirteen red and white stripes and a field of blue in the upper left corner with thirteen white, six-pointed stars, like the stars on his headquarters flag. He asked, "Could you make a flag from this design?" Betsy thought *A flag?* but said nothing except, "I will try." She added, "Perhaps the stars could have only five points rather than six?" Washington did not agree. Quickly, she carefully folded a paper and

160

with one snip, produced a five-pointed star. Somewhat mystified by her seeming magic, the three men agreed that her five-point star was indeed more pleasing to the eye.

Since Betsy was struggling to support her child, she was glad to obtain any work that came her way. The business barely provided income for the both of them, so extra work was welcome. Why not a flag, a new American flag? She smiled at the idea. She would set about obtaining the necessary cloth. Privately she thought, *It will be a welcome change from the heavy tents, uniforms, and shirts I make for the soldiers.* Those took time and required hand-sewn seams.

One flag for all the colonies was a novel idea. Until now, each colony had its own flag that flew over its state capital. At the battle of Concord, Nathaniel Page carried the Bedford flag. It was designed with an arm— that represented the arm of God—coming out of a cloud on a field of red. The Bunker Hill flag was blue with a white square in the upper left corner. It had a red cross with a green pine tree in the very upper left. The First Virginia Regiment of 1775 displayed a coiled rattlesnake on a field of white. The words "Liberty or Death" were emblazoned across the middle and the words "Don't Tread on Me" printed across the bottom. The navy's flag had three alternating red and white stripes with a rattle-snake sprawled across it, again with the words "Don't Tread on Me" at the bottom. The Grand Union flag looked much like the British Union Jack.

Revolution had been coming for some time. With the making of the flag, full rebellion was breaking wide open. Betsy worked for several weeks on the project. She kept it hidden when callers came because a third of the colonists were still loyal to England. She finished it sometime in early June. It was about three weeks later, on July 4, 1776, that someone read aloud the Declaration of Independence at Independence Hall, and Betsy presented her finished flag.

The colonists would win the war, but as in all wars, much property was lost, stolen, or destroyed. Many men lost their lives. Men of great fortune lost everything they owned. Betsy Ross remarried, but lost her second husband to the war also. During the war, British troops were quartered in her house. Her secret project with its seven red stripes, six white stripes, and thirteen white stars on a field of blue was adopted as the flag of the new United States of America, June 14, 1777. It became a symbol of freedom for the world.

NOTES

1. "Betsy Ross Did She or Didn't She?" Donald N. Moran, accessed May 23, 2016, http://www.revolutionarywararchives.org/betsyross.html.

2. "Betsy Ross," *usflag.com*, accessed May 23, 2016, http://www.usflag.org/about.betsy.ross.html.

3. "Betsy Ross and the American Flag," *USHistory.org*, accessed May 23, 2016, http://www.ushistory.org/betsy/flagtale.html. (Doug Heller.)

HEROES AND HUMOR IN AMERICAN HISTORY

TEA PARTY MEMBERS

Any child who pays attention to his history lessons knows that thirty or forty Sons of Liberty dressed themselves up as Native Americans to protest the British tea tax. The tax was only three cents, but it was the principle that they were protesting. They boarded a ship in Boston Harbor to toss bales of the popular drink into the water. It was December 16, 1773. Hardly anyone knows about the second tea party protest. Politically incorrect Bostonians climbed aboard another ship March 7, 1774, and dumped more tea into the harbor. In today's money it cost the British three million pounds.

HARRY BURN

Twenty years into the nineteenth century, the Tennessee legislature met to debate the Anthony Amendment. The amendment was big deal, because it proposed to give women the right to vote. Thirty-five other states had already ratified the change. If Tennessee bowed to public sentiment, the Nineteenth Amendment would become part of the US Constitution. After two votes by his fellow legislators, twenty-four-year-old Harry Burn, the youngest member of the body, changed his vote. Women's suffrage had become the law of the land. The young legislator admitted that he changed his vote because he had received a telegram from his mother: "Don't forget to be a good boy," it read, "Hurrah, and vote for suffrage!" Angry anti-suffrage members lit into young Harry and chased him around the chamber. He dashed out of the room and climbed onto a third-floor ledge in the Capitol attic. He stayed there until quitting time.

GEORGE WASHINGTON

Unknown double agents carried false troop strengths during the Revolutionary War. They risked being caught and shot as spies. They were part of dozens of Washington's network of espionage rings. For the man who could not tell a lie, he was good at spreading false information.

OLD IRONSIDES

The USS *Constitution*, known as Old Ironsides, was a combat vessel. It carried 48,600 gallons of fresh water in addition to 475 crewmembers. It sailed from Boston on July 27, 1798, with the water, 7,400 cannon shot, 11,600 pounds of black powder, and 79,400 gallons of rum. Its mission was to destroy and harass English shipping. At Jamaica, Old Ironsides took on 825 pounds of flour and 68,300 gallons of rum. At the Azores, it took on 350 pounds of beef and 64,300 gallons of Portuguese wine. On November 18, it sailed for England. There it defeated five British men-of-war and captured, or scuttled, twelve English merchant ships. Crew salvaged only the rum from the ships. By January, its powder and shot were exhausted. Unarmed, it made a night raid up the Firth of Clyde in Scotland. The brave crew captured a whiskey distillery and loaded forty thousand gallons of rum aboard. Old Ironsides headed home, arriving in Boston February 20, 1799, with no food, no cannon shot, no powder, no rum, no wine, no whiskey, and thirty-eight thousand gallons of stale water.

THE JERSEY GIRL

The Battle of Monmouth was fought on a very hot day in New Jersey on June 28, 1778. This was a time when women occasionally accompanied their husbands to war. A woman by the name of Mary Hays McCauley had gone with her husband to the battlefield. She was distributing water to the thirsty troops, carrying the water in a pitcher, which quickly earned her the nickname "Molly Pitcher." Across the bullet-swept wastes, a striped skirt darted here and there. Mary was earning her nickname. After one trip around the battlefield, she saw her husband get shot. Instead of panicking or fainting, she dropped the pitcher, picked up his rammer staff and took his place with the gun crew. No one messes around with a Jersey girl. She also tended the wounded and hefted one badly wounded young soldier onto her sturdy back and carried him from the field. For her courage and bravery General Washington made her a commissioned officer in the army.

ABRAHAM LINCOLN AND PETER CARTWRIGHT

As a Whig, Abraham Lincoln ran for Congress in 1864 against Methodist minister Peter Cartwright. During the campaign Lincoln decided to attend a meeting conducted by the minister. After a stirring welcome, Cartwright asked everyone who was going to heaven to stand. A few stood up. "Now, all those who do not wish to go to hell stand." Everyone stood up except one person. Cartwright was annoyed. He was used to having his congregation do as he bid. "May I ask, Mr. Lincoln, where you are going?"

"I came here as a respectful listener," Lincoln said calmly. "I did not know I was to be singled out by Brother Cartwright. I believe in treating religious matters with solemnity. I admit that the question asked by Brother Cartwright is of great importance. I did not feel called upon to answer as the others. Brother Cartwright asks me directly where I am going. I desire to reply with equal directness: I am going to Congress."

CLARA BARTON

Clara Barton, founder and president of the American Red Cross was once prominent but has since faded into obscurity. She began teaching at age fifteen without salary if tuition were waived. She was proud of the fact that she never bore a grudge. A friend reminded her, "Don't you remember the wrong done to you years ago?" She replied, "No, I distinctly remember forgetting it."

CECIL B. DEMILLE

I once met Cecil B. DeMille in Hollywood at a private showing of his film *The Ten Commandments.* I asked how he made the parting-of-the-sea scene, but he smiled and avoided the question. When making his *The Ten Commandments,* he received word that investors were worried about the rising cost of the film. He replied, "What do they want me to do? Stop now and release it as the Five Commandments? Money should not be an issue when crafting a Bible epic." Cecil was one of the most successful filmmakers of all time. Through his daring, he championed the change from short subject pictures to feature-length films.

ROSS PEROT

It takes a certain kind of courage to be Ross Perot. Looking for a suitable way of serving the community, Mr. Perot decided that he would give a Christmas gift to every American prisoner of war in Vietnam. Accordingly, thousands of parcels were packaged and a fleet of Boeing 707s chartered to deliver them to Hanoi. The Communists rejected the offer. "No such gesture could be considered during the course of the bloody war," which was at its height. Perot argued back. The Viet Cong replied that such charity was impossible while American B-25s were devastating Viet Cong villages. "No problem," Perot said. He would hire an expert American construction company to rebuild anything the Americans knocked down. The puzzled Viet Cong became inscrutable and declined to talk to him. Christmas drew near. In desperation, Perot took off in his chartered fleet and flew to Moscow where he posted the parcels, one at a time at the Moscow Central Post Office. All the parcels were delivered intact.

JOHN HANCOCK AND BEN FRANKLIN

Great courage was required by the signers of the Declaration of Independence. John Hancock, one of the signers said, "We must all hang together." Ben Franklin replied, "We must indeed all hang together, or most assuredly, we shall all hang separately."

NOTES

1. Author originally received these vignettes in the 1950s as uncopyrighted mimeographed sheets.

2. "The History of Boston Harbour Tea and The Boston Tea Parties," *Boston Harbour Tea*, http://bostonharbortea.com/history.

3. "Little Known Tidbit of Naval History," *NATO Veterans Org*, http://natovetorg.blogspot.com/.

4. http://www.navy.mil/navy-data/people/secnav/dalton/speeches/aapa1008.txt.

5. John H. Dalton, http://mt.goodpoliticsradio.com/?page_id=40.

6. "Clara Barton," *Paw Prints*, http://pawprints.kashalinka.com/anecdotes/clara-barton.

7. "Showdown in Nashville," *Tennessee4me*, http://www.tn4me.org/article.cfm/era_id/6/major_id/20/minor_id/56/a_id/136. "Welcome *Teach Tennessee History*, http://www.teachtnhistory.org/.

8. "Spy System 1777," *Historic Valley Forge*, http://www.ushistory.org/valleyforge/history/spies.html. (Doug Heller.)

9. "Molly Pitcher," *Historic Valley Forge*, http://www.ushistory.org/valleyforge/youasked/070.htm. (Doug Heller.)

10. Fremont P. Wirth, *The Development of America* (Boston: American Book Co., 1946).

EARTH KEEPER

The young protesters picked their way through the undergrowth and around the giant fir trees.

They were climbing toward the loggers farther up the mountainside. The loggers shouted vile and obscene words at them. The protesters tried to reason with the men sawing the trees, but they could not get the workers to listen. One logger shouted, "This is a tall one. It's gonna fall in your direction!" Among the protesters was twenty-four-year-old David Chain, nicknamed Gypsy. He was farther down the hill making his way through the brush. He never saw the tree coming.

Many people worry about the earth. One of the biggest problems is the loss of wilderness and forests. As the forests disappear, oxygen disappears. Wildlife habitats are destroyed when the trees are cut, but as the population expands, the need for natural resources also grows.

Some people believe that the demand for trees and population growth must be balanced. Yet logging companies overcut the forests. As a result, in 1979, Earth First! was formed. This conservationist group faced violence from the start. Still, the group works to save the earth. They do this at great personal expense and danger to themselves. One of the areas the group hopes to save is the Headwaters Forest in Northern California. David was there with the Earth First! group on September 7, 1998.

In the past, loggers had threatened or attacked protesters many times. Only the day before a logger said, "I wouldn't hesitate to cut a tree down with an activist in it." During the second week of August, loggers ran down activists and treed some by cutting all the lower limbs so that the activists could not get down. The previous May, a logger kicked an activist in the head, which resulted in a concussion and a trip to the hospital.

Gypsy's tree sitting had already enraged corporate interests. He had swung from tree to tree like Tarzan on a vine. The boys made a video of their meeting with the logger the previous day, which was a smart thing to do, because the sheriff sided with the loggers. Once deputies had poured pepper spray into protesters' eyes as they lay chained on the ground. A company called Maxxam bought Pacific Lumber and began clear-cutting the forests. A clear-cut above the town of Stafford resulted in a mudslide that wiped out many houses.

On this fateful day, a logger chased the group down the hill. "You better leave!" The young men scrambled out of the way as a tree crashed to earth, exploding like a bombed house. Before the boys arrived, trees had been felled downhill, but this one was purposely aimed in their direction. One of the protesters hid himself as the logger began to cut another tree. There was no warning. He only yelled, "This can easily reach you." What would they do next?

The boys heard the next tree crack. It sounded like a distant rifle shot, followed by a brief silence before it crashed through the trees in its fall line. They froze where they stood. Some of them heard the tree coming. They dove for cover behind tall standing growth that could protect them. The falling fir sounded like a thundering train crash as it shattered only feet from them. They decided to try one more time to reason with the loggers. The boys kept shouting for the loggers to stop, that representatives of the Forestry Department were coming. No luck.

One of the activists stepped out into the clearing made by the tree. He shouted, "You could have killed us." At the same moment, the protesters and the loggers gathered by the fallen tree. Someone was shouting, "I can't find Gypsy." He called for his friend. "Gypsy! Gypsy! Where's Gypsy? He was right behind me. Where is he?" There was no answer. At that moment, they found David Nathan Chain, "Gypsy," farther down the slope, crushed under the giant fallen tree. They discovered that he had a massive injury to the head. Gypsy died trying to save the earth.

Soon after David's death, the public learned that the California Department of Forestry & Fire Protection had charged Pacific Lumber with 250 violations of the Forest Practice Act from 1995 to 1997. Violations continued into 1998; the company was the first ever to lose its logging license in California.

NOTES

1. http://civilliberties.org/pattern.html.

2. http://www.albionmonitor.com/011a/davidchainsettle.html.

3. "How Gypsy Really Died," *Jail Hurwitz*, http://www.jailhurwitz.com/media/death_of_david_gypsy_chain_done/33_media.htm.

4. http://slingshot.tao.ca.displaybi.php?0063022.

5. Richard Widick, *Trouble in the Forest: California's Redwood Timber Wars* (Minneapolis: University of Minnesota Press, 2009).

NIGHT OF TERROR

The court sentence was seven months in the District of Columbia jail. What was the offense?

Obstructing traffic on sidewalks. Even in 1917, the sentence was harsh and unusual punishment. Alice Paul and other suffragists had been picketing at the White House for the right to vote. For several months, women continued to protest and get arrested on similar charges. Judges sent Alice to the DC jail for several days. They sent others to the dreaded, infamous Occoquan Workhouse for women in Virginia.

Alice Paul was a very comely woman with a voice for the right of women to vote. While in England, she and Emmeline Pankhurst took part in more radical protests for woman suffrage. They went on hunger strikes, but guards force-fed them. She and Lucy Burns worked together to further woman suffrage. In the fall of 1912, twenty-six-year-old Alice and thirty-three-year-old Lucy talked with the National American Woman Suffrage Association to get a constitutional amendment through Congress. Major problems stood in their way. They had no office, no money, few supporters, and the public sentiment wasn't with them at this time.

Alice organized the largest and longest parade Washington, DC ever witnessed. She staged it for the eve of Democrat Woodrow Wilson's inauguration as president, as Wilson was anti-woman suffrage. More than eight thousand working-class, college, professional, and middle-class women dressed in white and marched. They carried flags and banners and rode on dozens of floats down Pennsylvania Avenue from the Capitol to the White House. They intended to end the march at the Daughters of the

American Revolution Hall. Some half a million people lined the streets to shout vulgar words and throw garbage at the women while the police, who sided with the crowd, did nothing. The parade lasted six hours before the state finally ordered troops to bring the mob under control.

Alice and the woman suffrage movement received much attention. For weeks, newspaper writers wrote about the parade. Republican politicians wanted to know why the police did nothing about the conduct of the crowd. The politicians met with the president, but he would do nothing. His actions brought about more parades, demonstrations, arrests, and hunger strikes. Suffragists laid the liability on the party in power, the Democrats, who fought against the vote for women.

The first jail sentences were for a few days. As arrests continued, the sentences grew in length, days turning into weeks, weeks turning into months. Now Alice was in jail for a seven-month prison sentence. Not only that, guards put her in solitary confinement where she spent her time alone in the dark cell. She went on a hunger strike. When time came for her release, she could not walk. She was placed in a prison hospital. Prison officials transferred her to a psychopathic ward. They wanted to prove that she was insane so she could be put where she could not protest.

Guards placed an electric light over her face night and day. This deprived her of sleep. They tried to break her spirit. Officials threatened to transfer her to the insane asylum, noted for its mistreatment of inmates. Attendants there treated people as less than human. She still refused to eat. During the last twenty-one days of her stay, doctors pushed a tube down her throat to force-feed her. They poured liquids into her stomach three times a day. Suffering from pain and illness, Alice still refused to end her hunger strike. One doctor finally admitted, "She has a spirit like Joan of Arc."

The courts moved Alice and thirty-two others to the infamous Occoquan Workhouse. Describing the food was like describing a dung heap or pig trough. The beans, hominy, rice, and cornmeal all had worms in them and smelled of rot. Sometimes the worms floated to the top of the slop. The Night of Terror took place on November 15, 1917.

W. H. Whittaker, superintendent of the Occoquan Workhouse, sent more than forty guards, with clubs and baseball bats, on a rampage, brutalizing the jailed suffragists. They beat Lucy Burns, pulled her arms above her head and chained her wrists to the cell bar and left her all night. They threw Dora Lewis into a dark cell and smashed her head against an iron bed and knocked her out cold. Her cellmate, Alice Cosu, who believed that Lewis was dead, suffered a heart attack. The other women were grabbed in vice-like holds until their skin bruised and turned purple. They were dragged like sacks of potatoes across splintered floors. They were beaten, slammed against brick walls, pinched, kicked until their ribs cracked, and choked until they passed out.

Newspapers got hold of the truth. They ran stories about the vicious treatment. Americans, angered by what they learned, demanded change. On November 27, 1917, the court of appeals had no choice but to overturn all convictions.

A week later, Congress met to vote on the Susan B. Anthony Amendment. By now, President Wilson had seen the writing on the wall. The Democrats could no longer hold out. The very next day, the House narrowly passed the bill on a vote of 274 to 136. It failed in the Senate. The women's movement kept up pressure on Congress. They burned Wilson's speeches in front of the White House and called them "watchfires." Police continued to arrest the women.

In 1918, voters swarmed to the polls like angry hornets and turned away the Democrats who had fought against woman suffrage. Voters replaced these men with pro-suffrage members. The Senate revoted and passed the Nineteenth Amendment by one vote.

The new year brought new laws, and women, including Florence Harding, the next First Lady, voted for the first time—thanks to Alice Paul and thousands of other brave women.

NOTES

1. *American Civil War*, http://americancivilwar.com/womens/Womens_Suffrage/Alice_Paul.html.
2. *American Civil War*, http://americancivilwar.com/womens/Womens_Suffrage/Dora_Lewis.html.
3. *American Civil War*, http://americancivilwar.com/womens/Womens_Suffrage/Lucy_Burns.html.
4. "Women of Protest: Photographs from the Records of the National Woman's Party," *Library of Congress*, http://memory.loc.gov/ammem/collections/suffrage/nwp/profiles.html.
5. http://www.keepandshare.com/doc2/5768/night-of-terror-1917-against-suffragists.
6. Barbara Leaming, *Katherine Hepburn* (New York: Crown Publishers, 1995), 182.

MALAY SCOUTS

He was drafted and sent to Cherry Tree Camp for jungle training. The training was conducted in a thicket, but what he was taught would prove to be of little value when faced with the real thing in Malaya. After training, he embarked on a troop ship. It was quite a thrill for nineteen-year-old Roy Russell, who had never traveled farther than the next city from where he had grown up. Watching the flying fish land on the deck and porpoises spring from the waves was a new experience. Then there was the excitement of knowing he was headed for danger.

As the ship entered a foreign harbor, it rammed into a sunken wreck. This was the first event of many that should have been an omen to Roy as he headed for Malaya. He wiled away three months in Egypt until his ship was repaired. He was with the 799th Company that went to the aid of HMS *Amethyst*. The ship had been blockaded by the Chinese in the Yangtze River. The Chinese took the supplies that were sailing in two Sunderland flying boats. The following day, while under heavy cannon fire, the *Amethyst* made a run for it.

Roy became a member of the Malay Scouts. "Mad" Mike Calvert, a man famous for his exploits with the British India Special Forces in the recent war, formed the unit some time ago. The outfit would soon be fighting the Communists in Malaya. Communist party leader, Chin-Peng, had control over most of the area. His terror campaign was to raid villages and kill a child in front of the entire village. Chin-Peng used these and other kinds of terror tactics to keep the people obeying his will.

Mad Mike ordered a month of intensive jungle training. In this training, Roy was taught to use plastic explosives, lay booby traps, and handle various weapons. In one exercise he and the other men put on fencing masks and fired darts at one another using air rifles. "A man could get hurt doing this sort of crazy thing!" Mad Mike had everyone stand at attention twice a week. He'd walk up and down the lines of men and without warning, he'd punch a guy in the gut. If the man went down, Mad Mike would have the guy returned to his unit. There was one nice thing about being at the camp at Kuala: they got to swim and bathe in the hot springs.

Sometime later, Roy was on patrol with a squad and came upon a Chinese terrorist camp in the jungle. *The Malay jungles are a far cry from the woods back home,* he thought. In the camp, they found food still cooking on an open fire. It smelled like dirty, hot grease. One of the guys picked up a pot of rice and it blew his hand off: the whole camp was booby trapped. The most innocent object might hide an explosive. They had to evacuate the injured man before they could continue their patrol.

The thing he hated most on these patrols, besides being shot at, were the leeches. They would suck a man's blood and swell up like giant slugs. They were like suction cups, and when the men pulled them off, they came out like fishing barbs.

Another thing that got to the men in the jungle was the dampness. They were never dry. Their boots lasted about two or three weeks. "They just rotted away," Roy said. "Right on our feet."

On another patrol, the squad had just dropped off three Chinese terrorists they had captured. An urgent message crackled over the radio. They were to proceed to Bentong Gap in the Cameron Highlands to aid a convoy that was under attack. Off they raced but arrived too late. Roy was somber as he surveyed the tragic scene. All the men were dead. The Chinese had done a complete job on them. With sadness, the rescue team loaded the bodies on a truck to haul them back.

Sometime later Roy was riding in a train from Sungai Petani to Kuala Lumpur. The train was ambushed and came under fire from enemy hidden in the jungle. The engine was derailed and crashed off the tracks. Roy immediately took command. The women were screaming, and the children were crying hysterically. "Lie down!" he yelled. "You men, lie beside them. Protect them as much as you can."

Quickly, he jumped from the train and ran along the teetering cars. "All military personnel muster at the engine. Quickly! Keep your heads down. Don't make yourself a target!" He didn't know it, but he was playing out the same scene that Winston Churchill had in the Boer War. As loudly as he could, he ordered, "Spread out along the tracks, every ten feet." He whispered, "Ignore my next order." He yelled as loudly as he could in Malayan, "You ten men. Go into the jungle." He knew that the Chinese heard him. He knew they would think there were more men than just the five Malay and three Gurkha riflemen. "Open fire!" he shouted. The men fired into the jungle. After about five or six rounds, Roy shouted, "Cease fire! Hold your positions."

When the relief squad arrived, they discovered several dead bodies in the jungle. Not one of the lads firing from along the tracks was injured. Although the passengers' cars were full of bullet holes, none of the passengers were hurt. The relief squad found Roy lying beside the tracks. At first they thought he had been shot but it turned out he had stumbled on the rough ground and fallen, injuring his spine and preventing him from moving.

Although Roy had survived all the previous death encounters and even the notorious tree jumps out of planes, he was now to spend nearly two years in hospitals before receiving a medical discharge in 1954. His time in the Malay Scouts won him a medal for bravery.

NOTE

1. http://www.nmbva.co.uk/Roy%20Russell%20Story.htm.

RIDE LIKE THE WIND

Wanted: Young, skinny, wiry fellows. Not over eighteen.
Must be expert riders. Willing to face death daily. Orphans preferred.

That's the ad Johnson William Richardson, William "Sam" Hamilton, Johnny Frye, and others answered in May 1860. They were the first to sign with the Pony Express, the brainchild of Russell, Majors, and Waddell. They planned to carry the mail from St. Joseph, Missouri, to Sacramento, California, and do it in ten days! In 1860, it took more than a month for mail to reach the west coast. The owners' plan was a daring one, but the three men had courage and vision beyond their time. Mail would be carried twice a week by a relay of riders. The men would carry the mail both day and night, summer and winter.

Russell, Majors, and Waddell built relay stations along the two-thousand-mile route, about twenty-five miles apart. They hired station keepers to care for the ponies in these remote, lonely outposts.

For riders, they hired the best young men America could provide—men with courage, who were small (about 125 pounds), who showed no fear, were efficient, cool-headed men, expert at keeping themselves alive. Very few were orphans. Most were around twenty; the oldest was forty. They were all proud to serve their country. With their shiny black leather boots, deerskin jackets, and red flannel shirts tucked into their deep blue trousers, they made a handsome sight as they galloped across the country. The best riders earned one hundred dollars a month—quite good money for the time. The high pay was to compensate for the risk involved, at least that's what they were told. At the time, regular guys were lucky to be paid one dollar a day or about thirty dollars a month.

The *St. Joseph Daily West* reported that twenty-six-year-old Johnson "Billy" Richardson was the first pony rider out of the pony barn on April 3, 1860. His sister, Delaware Richardson, was among the cheering crowd at the Pike's Peak Stables to watch her brother ride out on his sleek, shiny, black horse with the leather *mochila* (saddle pouch) and its four mail pouches covering the saddle.

Being a skinny, wiry fellow, Billy Richardson fit the physical needs of his bosses. He was orphaned when Native Americans killed his parents while they were crossing the plains. When he was just a lad, he had been shanghaied by impressment gangs and forced to serve on a freighter. He'd survived raging storms, putrid food, rancid water, and had seen men beaten with leather strips. When an opportunity came along, he escaped. Just after he signed on with the Pony Express, he posed for a picture with Johnny Frye and the Cliff brothers, Gus and Chuck. He was still wearing his sailor suit, the only clothes he owned in the world. He had long, uncombed hair and an ample mustache.

Billy had the heart of a lion and the constitution of an iron man. He rode through hail, snow, wind, and ice storms. He urged his pony across raging rivers and waterless stretches. If his bosses needed a poster boy, Billy was him. "Ride light," said Russell, Majors, and Waddell. "Pounds tire the horses and slow delivery."

Johnny Frye was another who fit the Pony Express rider needs. He weighed 120 pounds but was every inch a man with a handsome face. He had signed up with Billy Richardson. Known as the "Cowboy-Knight," he became one of the most familiar figures between St. Joseph and Seneca, Kansas. As he passed through each town, the women ran out to hand him cookies and cakes. It is believed that this is where the idea for the doughnut was born. Women made cakes with holes in the middle so that Johnny could spear them as he galloped by.

One young lass asked, "Johnny, may I have your red neckerchief to sew into my log-cabin quilt?" Johnny declined the request. On his next pass through town, he was not surprised to see her waiting for him, but he was surprised to see her on a horse! She spurred her steed into a gallop and rode along side him. The two of them rode at breakneck speed through town and out onto the trail again. She tried to tear his neckerchief from around his neck but missed. Not to return without a memento, she grabbed at his shirt and was able to tear a piece of it away. She returned home with her trophy and promptly sewed her prize into her log cabin quilt.

Young Charlie Miller and his older brother, Walter Henry, were often in trouble. Their father arranged for them to work on a ship as cabin boys. When the ship pulled dockside in San Francisco, both boys jumped ship and ran away. Walter was caught and sent back to New York, but Charlie was hired on at a ranch where he learned to ride like the wind. Spanish vaqueros nicknamed him "Bronco Carlos." Of course, this Spanish variation would later change to Bronco Charlie. To avoid being sent back east, he told people that he was born in a covered wagon and his parents had been killed by Native Americans. It was with his newly learned skill at horse riding that he hijacked a riderless pony at a relay station then dashed out of Sacramento with the mail on his way to Placerville to become the youngest Pony Express rider.

A rider named Bob Haslam rode 370 miles to set the record for longest ride.

Eighteen-year-old William "Bill" James, one of the best Pony Express riders in the service, rode between Simpson Rock Port and Cole Springs, Nevada, in the Smokey Mountains. Crossing two mountain summits while riding through Shoshone territory, he traveled a lonely, dangerous trail. He never thought about the danger as he rode the 120 miles in twelve hours.

It was Abraham Lincoln's inaugural address of March 4, 1861, that was carried in a record seven days and seventeen hours from Washington, DC to Sacramento. The message was telegraphed from Washington to Kearney, Nebraska, then taken by Pony Express to Folsom, California. From there, it was telegraphed to Sacramento and finally published. Jim Morse carried important government messages over 280 miles in fourteen hours at eighteen miles an hour.

The Pony Express route stretched from St. Joseph, Missouri, through the present-day states of Kansas, Nebraska, Colorado, Wyoming, Utah, Nevada, and all the way to Sacramento, California. Mail was carried from both east and west. Delivery was once a week from April 3 to mid-June 1860, and twice a week from mid-June to late October 1861. Russell, Majors, and Waddell kept their promise of ten-day delivery in summer. It took a little longer in winter.

Russell, Majors, and Waddell had hired the best men they could find, but as swift as they could ride, they could not outride the telegraph. The brave Pony Express riders were replaced by this new invention. Electricity had come and the lines of the Western Pacific Telegraph were strung across America. Regular Pony Express service was ended in October 1861, a mere eighteen months after it began. The three men of vision and courage were forced out of business and into bankruptcy, but not before the Pony Express had ridden its way into the hearts and history of America. It is one of America's finest hours.

NOTES

1. "Photographs of the American West: 1861–1912," *National Archives*, http://www.archives.gov/research/american-west.
2. Kate B. Carter, *Utah and the Pony Express* (Salt Lake City, Utah: Utah Printing Co., 1960).
3. G. B. Dobson, "About Wyoming Tales and Trails," *Wyoming Tales and Trails*, http://www.wyomingtalesandtrails.com/about.html.
4. "Johnson William Richardson," *Wikipedia*, https://en.wikipedia.org/wiki/Johnson_William_Richardson.
5. Ernie and Elaine Hartnagle, "The Correct Identity of Billy Richardson: The Pony Express Rider," *HistoryReference.org*, http://www.historyreference.org/library/refrichardson.html.
6. Jeanne Joy Hartnagle-Taylor, "Billy Richardson—Stolen Identity," *Billy Richardson: Pony Express Rider and the Pony Express Mystery*, https://billyrichardson.wordpress.com/.
7. Jackie Lewin, http://www.xphomestation.com/names.html.
8. G. B. Dobson, "The Oregon Trail," *Wyoming Tales and Trails*, http://www.wyomingtalesandtrails.com/OregonTrail4.html.

DOWN TO THE
SEA IN SHIPS

In 1837, people traveled in ships with sails. The ships were not as safe as they are today. At this time, Joshua James was only ten, the ninth of twelve children. He was saddened when he lost his mother and baby sister in the sinking of the one of these ships, sunk by one of the hidden reefs that lurk along the shores of the Atlantic coast. He was secretly angered by their deaths, but he did not shed one tear. Instead, at this moment, he promised himself that he would devote his life to saving the passengers from other sinking ships.

Immediately, he began his career as a lifesaver. He knew that he could not succeed without mastering the skill of sailing, but he must have been born a seaman because he always seemed to know what to do. He also applied himself to his books and charts and learned quickly. On regular voyages to sea and along the treacherous rivers with his father and brothers, Joshua learned what he needed to know about handling a ship. By age fifteen, he joined the lifesaving crews of the Massachusetts Humane Society. By charting the stars and sounds of the sea, he learned to navigate through the dangerous underwater reefs and ledges.

One night, when the helmsman lost his bearing, the crew rousted Joshua out of bed. Yawning and with eyes half-closed, he looked at the heavens, laid down a course, and said, "You will see a light in two hours. Now I am going back to bed." The crew sighted the light one hour and fifty-five minutes later. On another sailing, a ship's officer asked, "Where are we?" Joshua replied, "We are just off the coast of Long Island." The officer doubted it. "How can you tell?" Joshua, as calm as a summer evening, replied, "I can hear the land talk."

With each venture into danger, he grew more skilled. A list of his lifesaving efforts is as long as a man's arm. He was awarded a bronze medal for the rescue of the crew of the Delaware. He guided the rescue of the crew from the brig Odessa. When the crews of the *Nellie Walker* and the *Helene* were about to drown with their sinking ships, Joshua pushed his lifesaving boat into the wild surf to row out to rescue them.

The greatest storm in local history roared along the coast in 1888. Joshua and his men rescued twenty-nine people from five sinking ships. Another rescue took place at midnight, December 1, with a northeastern wind blowing heavy snow, blinding them in their efforts. They could lower only one man at a time into the lifeboat, which could hold only five people. Joshua worked quickly, but the operation was painfully slow. He agonized over the possibility that he might not save all aboard. On the trip to the beach, a huge wave smashed over the boat and they nearly capsized. He knew that a plunge into the icy water could be fatal. Yet he had to make another trip for those still on the stricken ship. The snow continued to blind him and his men as they pulled on the oars.

During the second trip, which was even more dangerous, they lost the steering oar. Wreckage carried by the angry waves, crashed against the boat, yet they steered for shore where people gathered to witness the rescue and offer food and lodging to the survivors.

Some years later, a hurricane, with its yawning mouth, swallowed everything on land, then ripped along the Atlantic coast pushing a ship toward shore. The pilothouse, torn loose from the decks, crashed on the rocks, tossing the people inside into the waves. Joshua rushed to pluck survivors from the clutches of the boiling sea.

Joshua had been saving lives nearly fifty years. For his bravery, he received dozens of medals. In the face of advancing years, he continued as captain of the Allerton Lifesaving Station—saving some six hundred lives. It was on March 19, 1902, that Joshua James was returning from a drill. A friendly smile softened his grizzled face as he reached shore. The bearded, seventy-five-year-old Joshua sprang onto the damp sand, glanced at the wind-swept sea, and said, "The tide is ebbing." He dropped dead on the beach.

NOTES

1. Richard A. Boning, *Getting the Facts: Book E* (Barnell Loft Books, 1997).

2. file://D/WEB%20REDESIGN/Station/Point_Allerton.html.

3. http://www.rips.gov/nr/travel/maritime/poi.htm.

4. http://www.rips.gov/nr/travel/maritime/text.htm.

5. "Station Point Allerton: Captain Joshua James, USLSS (1826–1902)," *United States Coast Guard*, http://www.uscg.mil/d1/staPointAllerton/joshua_james.asp.

6. "Captain Joshua James, USLSS: 22 November 1826–19 March 1902," *United States Coast Guard*, http://www.uscg.mil/HISTORY/people/Joshua_James.asp.

DEFENSE OF THE ALAMO

He disliked the nickname Davy and thought it a childish name for a man who was described as the backwoodsman. He was always moving like a buffalo driven before a western wind, not wanting a neighbor nearer than ten miles. When he couldn't cut down a tree that fell within ten rods of his log house, he knew it was time to sell out and be off. Add to this the fact that Davy Crockett was not reelected in 1835 to Congress, he had little reason to stay where he was. He decided that he could restart his political career and get rich in Texas.

In March of 1836, the Texans were fighting the Mexicans for independence. With a dozen of his Tennessee volunteers, Davy joined young officer James Bonham, frontiersman Jim Bouie, and Commander Colonel William Travis in the Alamo. The men in the mission fort now numbered 187. They watched as General Santa Anna's Mexican army—shortly to number four thousand when reinforcements arrived—moved toward them. In the bell tower, young Daniel Cloud rang the church bell loudly. The battle of the Alamo was about to begin.

The Mexicans carried a bloodred flag, which meant that any survivors would not be spared. The defenders knew they could not win; they continued to hope for reinforcements, but none came. Knowing full well that to stay meant certain death, they took up their rifles in defiance of the greater numbers. In temperatures near freezing, Santa Anna sent a courier to demand that the men in the Alamo surrender. Commander Travis replied by firing a cannonball. There would be no misunderstanding of the meaning of his response.

Santa Anna's artillery set about smashing the mission walls. Davy knew the mission could be easily overrun, so to protect his back, he took up a position in a corner. His Tennessee volunteers targeted advancing soldiers at great distances and stopped dozens of Mexicans in their tracks.

Ex-congressman Davy Crockett; courageous, young Jim Bonham; and powerful Colonel William Travis took crack shots at the advancing troops. Others manned the walls, firing away as fast as they could reload. Jim Bowie, sick in bed, lay on his cot with his trusty pistols and large bowie knife across his chest. Santa Anna stubbornly insisted on storming the fort. Wave after wave of Mexicans threw themselves into the hail of bullets coming from the defenders.

The Texans held out for twelve days. On the thirteenth day, in the chilly predawn hours of March 6, a wave of Mexicans clamored over the crumbling walls. They attacked from all sides, pouring through the crumbling north wall. Travis chose how he would die. He faced his attackers to fire his pistol, took a few short steps back, turned and fired, stepped back, turned and fired again. Finally, he was shot through the head. He fell across his cannon.

Some Texans took refuge in the church. With cannons pointed at the great doors, the Mexicans lit the fuse. Cannonballs blasted the doors away. Soldiers poured into the chapel with grapeshots, muskets, and bayonets—anything they could use—wiping out all those inside. When the Mexicans came to the room where Bowie lay, the first to enter were shot down as they came through the door, but Bowie was overpowered by sheer numbers and slaughtered like a helpless calf.

Seven men survived the general carnage, Davy Crockett among them. One Mexican officer tried to save Davy, but Santa Anna answered his plea with a gesture of indignation then ordered the execution of all seven men. The troops thrust themselves forward, to flatter their commander, and with swords in hand, fell upon the seven just as wild dogs attack their prey.

Though tortured before they were killed, these courageous defenders died without complaint and without humiliating themselves before their executioners. The battle took a terrible toll—1,600 Mexicans and 187 Americans. The delay allowed Sam Houston to gather an army and win the war with the cry, "Remember the Alamo!"

NOTES

1. "The Battle of the Alamo," *Lone Star Internet*, http://www.lone-star.net/mall/texasinfo/alamo-battle.htm.

2. "Remembering the Alamo," *The Library of Congress*, http://memory.loc.gov/ammem/today/mar06.html.

3. Joaquin Miller, "The Defence of the Alamo," in *Poems of American Patriotism, 1776–1898*, ed. R. L. Paget (Boston: Colonial Press, 1906), 101.

4. www.tennesseehistory.com/.../DavyCrockett.html.

5. "The Battle of the Alamo," *Texas State Library and Archives Commission*, https://www.tsl.texas.gov/treasures/republic/alamo-01.html.

6. usa.gov/David_Crockett_Tennessee_myths_and_legends.

RESCUE ON THE RIVER

Ordinarily, rafting a river on an inner tube is a reasonably safe float. On Labor Day of 2012, fifty-year-old, Mike Hoer and his wife Laurie were kayaking the Weber River that empties from a canyon to flow past Ogden, Utah. There are a couple rapids along the float, with one being an especially large, rough run. They can be avoided by staying on the far side of the river. The current, however, takes most river rats through them. Laurie had dumped her kayak at the spot before—today was no different.

This time she was unable to keep a hold on her paddle or the kayak. Mike caught the kayak farther downstream. He pulled it to shore, but the paddle had disappeared. Laurie knew she would not be able to complete the run down the river without it because it was are needed to maintain balance. She now knew what it meant to be up a creek without a paddle. They walked back along the bank in search of it.

Despite the rushing water, Mike swam to the large boulder mostly submerged in the river where Laurie had taken her spill. He dove under to find a rather huge tree caught in front of the rock. It was extremely dangerous, both to swimmers who might get caught in its branches and pulled under, as well as rafters who could be thrown into the swift current. After a couple tries, he came up. "I can feel a paddle." Down he went again to rise with it in his hand.

"That's not mine," Laurie called above the noise of the rapid. On this second try he brought up another paddle, which also turned out not to be Laurie's. On another dip under the wild water, he found yet a third paddle. Again, it was not Laurie's. By now they were both laughing. "This is hilarious," Laurie said. Because it was a holiday, the additional people on the river added to the comedy—kayakers, inner tube rafters—some laughing, but many screaming as they rushed toward the huge rock. Many tipped as Laurie had. Luckily, they were able swimmers and made their way to shore. Anyone less able could be swept away by the current.

The hilarious scene was about to change. Mike and Laurie watched as a couple of women with very young children came floating past on tubes. The current swept them through the larger rapid straight toward the rock. Bounced off their floating devices, they were thrown into the rushing water, powerless to save themselves. The kids were screaming. The mothers had the look of terror on their faces. Any chance they had of grabbing the tubes as life rafts was gone when the tubes stuck against the rock. The families were being dragged under the water.

Screaming for help, they begged Mike to save them. He swam out to reach the women who clutched at their children. Fear drives a drowning person to grasp onto anything that offers a chance at safety and drowning people often pull their lifesaver under with them. Mike knew this, but he was able to secure a hold on the mothers, to pull them to shore. Others floating by, but unable to help, hooted their approval.

The women, looking like half-drowned puppies, hugged Mike. "You saved our lives."

The kids, who were still terrified, refused to go back in the water. Mike assured them that the worst was past. "You've gone through the bad part. The rest should be smooth sailing. You shouldn't have any trouble."

He explained how Laurie had just taken a spill at the same spot. They were trying to find her paddle, but the women continued to thank him. "We're just grateful that you were here."

Suddenly, as if by magic, or by providence, Laurie's paddle miraculously popped to the surface. Somehow it had become unstuck, but only after Mike had helped rescue the families. After he retrieved it, they continued downstream, finding an owner for one of the paddles.

NOTE

1. Laurie Hoer, "Rescue on the River," *Newsletter* (September 2012).

MOOD INDIGO

Albert Ryder sat with veiled eyes without saying anything. His mother looked at him from across the room. "What is going to happen to him?" she asked. "What is going to become of him? He seems to be in a dream world." He did not return his mother's gaze. He acted as if she were not even in the room. Since the infection that affected his eyes, he had undergone a serious change. He was withdrawn and silent. "I worry about him," she said. Albert's dad was concerned for his wife, so the next day he acted on his feelings and stopped at the local craft store. He selected a set of paints and canvases and brought them home. "Maybe these will spur him into action," he suggested.

The boy ignored the box for a long time. Finally, he opened it. For months he had not shown this much interest in anything. Still, hours passed and he did nothing. It was as if he did not know what they were or what do to with them. As the day waned, he picked up a brush and daubed it into some yellow paint. He drew his first strokes across the canvas. More days passed, and Albert became more and more interested in his new hobby.

Mr. Ryder began to change his opinion and doubted his choice of materials for his son who had been drawn into another world. He knew that a lot of would-be painters were starving and living poorly. He knew that people bought very few artists' paintings. Even if an artist were lucky enough to sell a painting or two, he did not earn much from the sale.

The Ryders lived in New Bedford, Massachusetts, but Mr. Ryder decided to move his family, so he picked up and left for busy New York.

The change did not hinder Albert from his new pursuit in painting. The boy decided to take lessons from William E. Marshall. To do this, he enrolled at the National Academy of Design. Afterward, he told his parents, "It's time for me to move out. I should be living on my own." He rented a space in an attic on Fifteenth Street in New York City. The place was like an abandoned hayloft with a skylight.

The move also ended his formal training, but even so, he began to paint nonstop. He was never satisfied with what he painted. He worked all day and long into the night hurrying to finish a canvas with broad strokes of a boat bathed in yellow moonlight, a sea in deep shadow, a wharf jutting into a yellow sunset—these were his subjects, always an eerie seascape of dark indigo and blacks. He painted small people in a vast landscape of nature. Nothing he painted satisfied him. Although he exhibited his paintings, he received little attention for his work.

As the years passed, Albert gave less and less care to his cluttered loft. Dust covered everything. Wooden crates, opened tin cans, dried food scraps, dirty glass jars, broken picture frames, and discarded trash littered the room. Dirt and grime blocked any view through the window. Dead mice lay in filthy traps, and live ones played at will under his feet. He could hardly make his way through the clutter to greet the few visitors who came. When asked about his living conditions, he said, "An artist needs only a crust of bread, a roof over his head, an easel, and all else God gives in abundance." He lived on twenty cents a day.

Carelessly, Albert spread his paints heavily across the canvases. Sometimes he worked on a painting for ten years, always adding new layers of paint over old ones with a varnish coat over everything. He often painted into wet vanish or applied fast-drying paint over slow-drying paint. The result made his paintings unstable; they began to crack and yellow, and even after decades, they never dried. Some completely disintegrated and fell apart. He never signed his work.

Today, Albert Ryder's paintings are housed in private art collections and in art museums around the world. They sold for only pennies in his time, but today, they bring prices that reach hundreds of thousands of dollars.

In the end, Albert Ryder rose courageously above his physical disability. His mother need not have worried about "What will become of poor Albert?"

NOTES

1. Richard A. Boning, *Getting the Facts: Book D* (Barnell Loft Books, 1997).

2. "Albert Pinkham Ryder," *Wikipedia*, http://en.wikipedia.org/wiki/Albert_Pinkham_Ryder.

3. http://www.nps.gov/wefa/historyculture/albertryder.htm.

PATRIOT, WARRIOR, PRESIDENT

Washington and his army left bloody footprints in the snow as they marched toward the Delaware River on Christmas Day of 1776. When they arrived at about four in the afternoon, large, flat-bottom Durham boats were waiting for them, each about forty to sixty feet long and eight feet wide. They were built with high sides, tapered at both ends and could be outfitted with a mast or long oars. They were capable of carrying seventeen tons of mounted artillery, horses, and military equipment. The men, 2,400 strong, began to load the guns, muskets, horses, and food into the boats, then crowded themselves into any space that was left. The river was swollen with broken chunks of ice and choppy whitecaps. Washington secretly looked at his men and saw the worry in their faces. They worked quickly and as quietly as they could, but not without the booming voice of Colonel Knox shouting orders above the sound of oars thrashing the icy water. Washington wished he could silence them. White puffs of vapor gushed from the nostrils of the nervous horses. A frightened neigh could reveal their presence and thwart their surprise attack.

There were 1,400 Hessians (Germans hired by the British to fight in the Revolutionary War) with six light guns facing them on the far side of the Delaware. Their uniforms were blue wool with traditional grenadier miter with brass front—quite visible but warm. In the American boats, the men wore whatever they brought from home, some without shoes.

Foremost in Washington's mind was hope of eventual success. The men, too, thought mostly about getting safely across. They knew a night

191

crossing was dangerous, but the element of surprise was on their side. They thought too, about families, loved ones left at home, but Washington needed a victory. How many would die winning it?

The Hessians had set up an outpost in a cooper shop, a noisy, wood-making place where workers tore about hammering, pulling, and twisting iron straps around oak casks. The shop was about a quarter mile northwest of Trenton on Pennington Road. Once across the Delaware, Washington mounted his white horse to lead the main body as the men marched up the road. He ordered Edward Hand and his men to block the road to Princeton. General John Sullivan led another American column and entered Trenton along the abandoned river road from the south.

In the north, Nathanael Greene drove the Hessians from their outpost. The enemy pulled back to their barracks. Washington moved to the high ground at the head of King Street and Queen Street to command the assault. Like a giant crab with mighty pincers, the Americans closed in on the bewildered Hessians while American artillery blasted the Hessians' position. Aside from the two units that did not cross as planned, the attack was flawless.

In desperation, the Germans formed and marched up the street like little wooden soldiers all in a row. The Americans, firing guerilla-style from houses along the approach, broke the Hessian march. Washington blocked their escape; Sullivan pushed his forces into the thick of battle. He overwhelmed the enemy forces who were taking fire from the Americans from three sides. The hired, mercenary troops fell back in confusion. During the exchange of rifle fire, the Hessian leader was mortally wounded, and the enemy suffered losses. The Americans captured a thousand men, but lost one man who froze to death crossing the Delaware River.

The Battle of Trenton was a turning point in the Revolutionary War. American defeats to this time had been demoralizing. Trenton gave them new hope. Of course, the Americans did win their independence. Patriot Washington, who led the country as a warrior, was rewarded by being elected as president at the birth of a new nation—the United States of America.

NOTES

1. http://www.americanhistory.gov/aa/wash/aa_wash_subj.html.

2. *AmericanRevolution.org*, http://www.americanrevolution.org/delxone.php.

3. "George Washington," *Conservapedia*, http://www.conservapedia.com/George _Washington.

4. General W. W. H. Davis, "Washington on the West Bank of the Delaware, 1776," *The Pennsylvania Magazine*, 4, no. 2 (1880).

5. http://www.ushistory.org/washingtononcrossing. (Doug Heller.)

6. "George Washington," *The White House*, http://www.whitehouse.gov/about/presidents /georgewashington.

BATTLE AT CHOSIN RESERVOIR

Lieutenant Colonel Don C. Faith, age thirty-two, earned the Medal of Honor at the Battle of Chosin Reservoir in Korea in 1950. The reservoir is a man-made lake located on the central, northeast coast of North Korea and is surrounded by barren mountains. Very few people live around it. The seventeen-day battle raged along the seventy-eight miles of road connecting the reservoir and Hungnam, which was the only escape route for the twelve thousand United States X Corps, now trapped by 67,000 Chinese troops. The 9,675 Americans who died there, and the wounded, were but a few of the thousands of American men who sacrificed their lives in that far away land. They died fighting in what became known as the Forgotten War. Few people today even know that a war took place in Korea.

North Korea had invaded South Korea, prompting America to send troops to fight the invaders. The Americans landed at Inchon Harbor in September 1950. Lieutenant Colonel Faith led the First Battalion, Thirty-Second Infantry Regiment in the Seventh Army. He was instructed to "climb aboard those tanks and head north until you get shot at." So Lieutenant Colonel Faith and his men obediently did just that.

The Americans pretty much had it their way with the North Korean army for a few months, but the tide of the war was about to change. In late October, Chinese forces came screaming across the border from China like a swarm of murderous army ants, devouring everything in their path. The Americans found themselves in the enemy's direct line.

In a month, the enemy drove the Americans and their few allies down the peninsula. With them was Lieutenant Colonel Faith and his men. At Chosin Reservoir, on November 27, the Americans were ambushed and met the Chinese head-on.

They were fighting beside the First Marine Division. At the reservoir they became surrounded by the greater numbers of Chinese soldiers. One of the men said, "They're attacking us on three sides, Colonel. They're beating the dickens out of us. They're not all that good as soldiers, but it's just that there's so darned many of them." The Chinese weren't the only enemy they had to fight. It was freezing—the worst winter in a hundred years—and they were not equipped for it. They were sleeping on the ground in flimsy sleeping bags, and many froze to death.

As the battle of Chosin Reservoir raged, Lieutenant Colonel Faith did not take cover. He led his men in counterattacks to try to win back their position. Hundreds were wounded. Faith found a way to escape across the frozen water. In a hail of enemy fire, he directed the movement of his large army trucks, now loaded with hundreds of wounded men, across the reservoir. They began to make their way south through the hills and shallow rivers. They came around a blind curve in the road and right into a Chinese blockade.

"On your feet!" Faith shouted as he led the attack on the roadblock, firing his pistol and tossing hand grenades. Faith was hit several times by enemy rifle fire. Just thirty yards from the enemy position, he was hit by an exploding grenade. Shrapnel peppered his body like hot splinters. He continued to lead the attack, but Lieutenant Colonel Faith's wounds were mortal. A major picked him up to carry him to safety.

"Just put me down, Major," Faith whispered, his blood nearly gone, "I'm dying."

His platoon commander, Joe Clark, wept when he finally died. "He was a great man," Clark said. "If anyone ever deserved the Medal of Honor, he did."

Chosin Reservoir was a battle where bravery was as common as bullets and ice. Very few survived. Of the platoon that Joe Clark led, only two lived. The enemy had sent 120,000 against the Americans' 12,000. The odds were against the Americans from the beginning, but Lieutenant Colonel Don Faith was a gallant and noble example of courage. His sacrifice was worthy of America's highest award, the Medal of Honor. The combat at the Chosin Reservoir surpassed both the Alamo and Iwo Jima in violence and small unit fighting in the history of American warfare.

NOTES

1. *Chosin Reservoir,* http://www.chosinreservoir.com/index.php.
2. T. R. Fehrenbach, *This Kind of War: The Classic Korean War History* (Washington, DC: Brassey's, 1963).
3. Russell A. Gugeler, *Combat Actions in Korea.* (Washington, DC: U.S. Government Printing Office, 1954).
4. Lee N. Mead, "*Newsweek* Magazine Article," *Chosin Resevoir* (April 11, 1999), http://www.chosinreservoir.com/newsweek_magazine_article.htm.
5. "Korean War Medal of Honor Recipients: Faith, Don C. Jr.," *U.S. Army Center of Military History,* last modified May 7, 2015, http://www.history.army.mil/moh/koreanwar.html#FAITH.

HERO ON THE HUDSON

I t was winter, bitter cold, and the Hudson River that separates New Jersey and New York for seventeen miles, was full of chunks of ice. A northwest wind had blown the ice that was now floating in the river into a hard pack along the New York shore. On January 30, 1870, a ferry boat was slowly churning its way through the cakes of ice until the thickness of the ice choked the paddles and halted the ferry in mid-river. As hard as the captain tried, he could not get the ferry to move forward.

It was early morning and the decks were swarming with workers and their teams of horses, prancing about like nervous dancers. A solid mass of women and children, in their heavy woolen clothes, crowded against the doors. While the captain tried to gather steam for a further effort, he could not get his boat to move as an ocean tugboat loomed out of the fog. The tug captain, unable to steer his boat away, rammed into the side of the ferry, cutting a V-shaped gash below the waterline. Water rushed into the helpless ferry, and it pitched to the side, plunging the hapless horses, neighing like wild banshees, into the icy water. Men, women, and children screamed and ran about the decks like blind mice. A plunge into the ice-choked river meant death.

Captain Thomas A. Scott, a renounced seaman, happened to be passing in his wrecking tug. He quickly steered up to the sinking ship and sprang like an agile athlete onto the ferry's tilting deck. His appearance could not have been more welcome. Men crowded to shake his hand; women fell on their knees crying. A chilling silence fell over everyone, all thinking silently, *What will he do now?* He ordered everyone to,

"Stand clear! Move to the starboard!" People stood in dumb confusion not understanding. "That way!" he yelled pointing to the right side of the failing boat. The increased starboard weight gradually began to right the stricken ferry until it gained an almost even keel. Still, it pitched somewhat to the leeward side, the side sheltered from the wind.

"Stay where you are! I'll throw overboard any man who stirs!" With that said, Captain Scott slid down the handrails to the engine room. He met the engineer, who was trying to abandon his post, halfway down and pulled the frightened man down with him.

Wading through ankle-deep water, they quickly dragged the mattresses from the crew's bunks, stripped blankets, racks of clothes, coveralls, carpets, rags and anything that could be stuffed into the gash. They pushed until the space of each splintered plank of the ship's side was replaced. Still, one space remained through which the icy water spurted like a fire hose.

"Another mattress," Scott said. "Quick! None?" It was useless. They had even gathered the oily rags from the engine room and stuffed them into the hole. "Your coat then! Think of them babies, man, do you hear me?" Quickly, they took off their coats and vests to use as stuffing. Captain Scott forced the garments into the splintered opening, but water poured though a small space.

For a moment he stood as if paralyzed, his eyes searching the engine room for something, anything! He saw nothing that could help him. Suddenly, he forced his own body into the gap with his bare arm outside, which was immediately pounded by the floating ice. The damaged ferry was pushed into the Hoboken docks with every child, woman, and man still on board. When some men pulled Captain Scott from the wreckage, they found him unconscious and barely alive.

The icy water had frozen his blood; the jagged ice had torn the flesh on his arm from shoulder to fingertips. Workers warmed his body. As color returned to his face, he opened his eyes. His first concern was, "Were any of them babies hurt?"

The valor of men is often understated. So it was with Captain Thomas A. Scott. When the newspapers later reported the story of his heroics, the editors merely printed, "Captain Scott stopped a leak in the ferryboat."

NOTES

1. Richard A. Boning, *Getting the Facts: Book E* (Barnell Loft Books, 1997).

2. "Taking the Sea: Perilous Waters, Sunken Ships, and the True Story of the Legendary Wrecker Captains," *Dennis M. Powers*, http://dennispowersbooks.com/taking_the_sea _excerpt.html.

3. http://www.lighthousesociety.org/historicalcollections/masterdiver. (Carol House.)

4. Dennis Powers, *Taking the Sea: Perilous Waters, Sunken Ships, and the True Story of the Legendary Wrecker Captains* (New York: AMACOM, 2009).

5. F. Hopkinson Smith, *Captain Thomas A. Scott: Master Diver* (Cambridge: Cambridge University Press, 1908).

PEACE PILGRIM

Police threatened to arrest her for vagrancy. Thinking that she had money, thugs sometimes attacked her. Interviewers sneered at her because their outlook on life would not allow them to believe that she was sincere. Many people did not understand what she was doing, or why. She even fought off a couple of psychopaths. In Arizona, she nearly froze to death in a snowstorm. Yet she walked with sparkle and enthusiasm and boundless energy.

When the world was moving through the Cold War of the 1950s, Mildred Norman hoped for peace. She thought, *What can one person do?* She came to the conclusion that she should become a wanderer until mankind learned the ways of peace. She gave away all her possessions, including her name calling herself Peace Pilgrim. The name had a meaning everyone could understand. A pilgrim is a wanderer and she would wander for peace. She "walked the talk." She walked in complete fearlessness.

She carried only a few things: the clothing she wore, a comb, a toothbrush, a pen, and some postal stamps. No one backed her with money, and she carried none of her own. She never asked for food or shelter. When she began her pilgrimage, she took a vow to wander without food until given, and without shelter until offered, and to wander until mankind learned the way of peace. She believed that no one should discriminate against any human being, that everyone should have tolerance for others.

Peace Pilgrim gave everyone she met a printed folder explaining the reason for her walk. It stated a simple message: *The way to peace is to overcome evil with good, falsehood with truth, and hatred with love.* Everyone who met Peace Pilgrim thought that she was witty, intelligent, sincere, and loving. Those who opened their homes to her also opened their hearts to her. They said, "Peace Pilgrim changed our lives." She taught them a different way to live.

Her purpose to spread the idea of peace over the world was stronger than ever. Publishers printed her booklet in thirteen languages. People found it at Bedouin hostels, in Central America, in the shadows of the pyramids, in African villages, in Thailand, in libraries in the Himalayas, in an English class in China. Stories continue to filter in from those who met her and from those moved by her words of wisdom and the life she lived.

"I first met Peace Pilgrim some years ago when she spoke before my college classes. It was such a moving experience for all of us to be in the presence of someone who was truly living her beliefs and faith," said a college professor. "I have never heard anyone express it in a more beautiful way what it means to be a human being. And what is possible for each of us."

A Texas newspaper article reported, "She brought heaven onto earth. She brought the divine qualities into her life here. She changed lives all over America." Early in her wanderings, she joined Richard Lamb in 1952, as war raged in Korea. He noted that she was the first woman to walk the entire 2,500-mile Appalachian Trail. A friend said, " I followed her for two weeks in Hawaii, sleeping on the ground. Mosquitoes were so bad at one time I was on my third spraying, trying to sleep. She was sound asleep, not one mosquito touched her, and she never used anything to stop them!"

People loved her, and it is easy to understand why. She was a fountain of love. "There is great freedom in simplicity of living. Never think of any right effect as being fruitless. All right effort bears fruit, whether we see the result or not. Spiritual truth should never be sold; it need never be bought. The way of peace is to overcome hatred with love."

At forty thousand miles, Peace Pilgrim stopped counting. She walked the United States for twenty-eight years. She began her journey at the Pasadena Rose Parade January 1, 1953. She ended it on July 7, 1981 in a car crash in Indiana. Her mission is immortal, and she lives through the power of her message.

NOTES

1. *Friends of Peace Pilgrim Newsletter,* no. 49 (Winter 2007), http://www.peacepilgrim.com/FoPP/newsletter/nl49/index49.htm.

2. "Modern Heroes," Donna Henes, *Creations Magazine,* accessed May 23, 2016, http://www.creationsmagazine.com/articles/C90/Heroes.html.

3. www.trailtherapy.com.

4. "Peace Pilgrim's 1952 Appalachian Trail Journey," comp. Bruce Nichols, *Peace Pilgrim,* http://www.peacepilgrim.com/ap_trail.htm.

5. Marta Daniels, Mildred Norman Ryder, AKA Peace Pilgrim: July 18, 1908–July 7, 1981, *Friends of Peace Pilgrim,* http://www.peacepilgrim.com/htmfiles/mdppbio.htm.

6. "Peace Pilgrim: 1908–1981, *Peace Pilgrim,* http://www.peacepilgrim.com/index.htm.

7. Ann Rush, "Peace Pilgrim: An Extraordinary Life," *Peace Pilgrim,* http://www.peacepilgrim.org/peacep.htm. (Bruce Nochols.)

8. Bruce Nichols, *Friends of Peace Pilgrim Newsletter,* no. 54 (Summer 2010), http://www.peacepilgrim.org/FoPP/newsletter/pdf/nl54.pdf.

SPIES, SPIES, SPIES

The most famous spy known to the world is probably James Bond, but there are other spies—less well known but more true to life. Spying is one of the oldest and most well-recorded arts known. Ancient civilizations, some six thousand years ago, trained and used spies. Records in Mesopotamia, Egypt, Greece, and Rome speak of spies and acts of spying.

Egyptian pharaohs had court spies to find people who were not loyal to the pharaoh. The Greeks used spies to deceive their enemies. The Byzantine Empire had a large army of spies to protect itself. In later times, in America's Revolutionary War and the Civil War, both sides used spies. Most people think of spies as being men—yet even from ancient times, many spies were women. Being a woman aroused less suspicion and was better cover for her spying.

At the time of the American Revolution, a famous spy ring was in use around New York. A member of this ring—known only as #355—carried information to General Washington. The British captured her, and she was held prisoner on the prison ship *Jersey*. Many stories tell of women who spied for the North or the South in the Civil War. Pauline Cushman was an actress who joined the Secret Service. She was sent to St. Louis, Missouri, to find Confederate spies and end their spying, and from there she went to Tennessee to gather information on the strength and location of enemy troops. Pauline was captured and sentenced to hang on the spot. But the Confederate troops had to leave in a hurry, and Pauline was left behind. News of her capture spread like wildfire through the country, so she was unable to continue as a spy for the North.

The work of Elizabeth Van Lew and Mary Bower was so useful that General Grant gave them special praise. Mary Walker did not act like other women of the time. She spied for the Union Army and wore men's clothing. Crossing enemy lines was dangerous, and there was always the chance that she would be caught. On April 10, 1864, she was captured by the Confederates and arrested as a spy. She was sent to Richmond prison until she was let go in a prisoner exchange. She continued to work in the army and won the right to be an army surgeon.

Harriet Tubman is famous for her work in the Underground Railroad. She formed a spy network and led many raids into the South to find information for the North.

Dozens of women were also spies for the South. Emeline Pigott gathered information about the enemy while gathering food, clothing, and supplies for troops. She hid her loot in hollow trees for soldiers to pick up later. While entertaining Union troops, she learned much information, which she then gave to the South. She went to her death without ever telling any of her secrets.

One of the most renowned spies of the Civil War was Rose O'Neal Greenhow. A secret note she sent to General Beauregard helped him to win the Battle of Bull Run. Her spying was so good that Confederate President Jefferson Davis gave her credit for winning the Battle of Manassas. Even after her capture, she was able to send secret notes using codes. They were carried inside women's hair buns and other secret places.

Sarah Edmonds dressed as a man and spied for the North. Madame La Force was a man dressed as a woman who spied for the South. On June 28, 1861, the liner *St. Nicholas* left the docks at Baltimore, Maryland. On board was a rather strange, showy French woman known as Madame La Force. She kept the crew's attention while other men traveling with her carried toolboxes and army trunks onto the ship unnoticed. Once the ship sailed, she went below to her cabin. When she came out, she was no longer Madame La Force, but Richard Thomas, a Zouave colonel from Maryland. He wore a uniform with sword and pistol. He and his men took over the ship and sailed to Virginia with arms for the South.

Men and women who are spies must be very courageous. They have to be able to keep a cool head. If they are caught by the enemy, their reward for what they do is often death.

Margaretha Zelle, better known as Mata Hari, was such a person. As a Dutch subject, she was able to cross international borders easily.

To avoid battlefields, she traveled between France and the Netherlands through Spain. It was a rather roundabout way, but it was safer. With the outbreak of World War I, her many border crossings made the French secret police curious. They watched her closely and finally brought her in to question her. They got her to travel to Spain to contact German officers and report what she learned. In the dark world of the spy, the French suspected her of being a double agent.

In January of 1917, Mata Hari was arrested in her hotel room in Paris. She was put on trial and accused of spying for the Germans. She was found guilty and sentenced to be executed. The French based their suspicions on a message sent by the Germans in code that the Germans knew had been broken by the French. Experts believe that the message was a fake, but Mata Hari was put before a firing squad anyway. Later, writers said that Mata Hari was never a double agent. They say that she was used as a scapegoat by the head of French counterespionage, George Ladoux. He was later arrested for being a double agent himself. He had tried to use Mata Hari's activities as a cover for his own treason.

Another famous spy from World War I was Edith Cavel. She worked as a nurse in Belgium. When war broke out, she worked undercover to help soldiers from France, England, and Belgium escape from the Germans. When the enemy found out what was happening, they put her on trial for harboring foreign soldiers rather than for spying. The trial was a sham. Edith was taken out and killed by a firing squad in October 1915. Later, Hollywood made a movie about her.

Princess Noor-un-Nisa Inayat Khan worked with the French Resistance in 1943. The princess evaded the brutal Gestapo for many months. She rode her bike and carried a small radio from one safe house to another. Her code name was Madeleine. She was the only link between the French Resistance and home base across the channel. Sadly, she was captured and killed.

Virginia Hall was from Baltimore, Maryland. She went to work for the French as an agent and was so successful that the Nazis began an all out hunt for her. By the winter of 1941, the Nazis were about to arrest her, but she escaped on foot over the Pyrenees Mountains into Spain. This was no easy trek for Virginia, as she had lost a leg in a hunting accident. The Gestapo sent out wanted posters with a warning: "The woman with the limp is one of the most valuable agents in France, and we must find and destroy her." Her smart disguise fooled the Germans; she gathered information that she sent to the allies and helped direct air drops in support of D-Day.

On her first mission, Violette Szabo was parachuted into German-held France. Using the code name Corinne Reine LeRoy, she found that a friendly spy ring had been infiltrated by the Nazis. She returned a heroine. Her second mission was to parachute in, find the traitor, shut down the sub circuit, and get home alive. After shutting down the sub circuit, she asked to go to Paris for a couple of days. She bought new clothes, chocolates, and perfume. Then she met Philippe, who would drive her out of France. She insisted on taking some Sten guns. He felt a foreboding, since searches at checkpoints were all too common.

They arrived at the checkpoint, and they were stopped. The guards found the guns. Violette was arrested and put in prison. She died there only days before the camp was liberated by Americans.

NOTES

1. http://www.aboutfamouspeople.com/article.html. (John Marck.)
2. "The Civil War," *National Park Service*, http://www.nps.gov/civilwar/spies.htm.
3. http://civilwartalk.com?Resource_Center/General_Resource_Women/emeline-pigot.
4. http://www.denisebotsford.com/.../Violette_Szabo_The_Bravest_of_Us-All.pdf.
5. "Mata Hari," *Wikipedia*, https://en.wikipedia.org/wiki/Mata_Hari.
6. Virginia Hall, *Wikipedia*, https://en.wikipedia.org/wiki/Virginia_Hall.
7. "Female Civil War Soldiers and Spies," *Fold3*, http://www.fold3.com/page/778_female_civil_war_soldiers_spies/. (Ned Jackson.)
8. Robert Heldman, http://voices.yahoo.com/executed-a-spy-mata-hari-may-have-been-innocent.html.
9. "Pauline Cushman 1833–1893: Union Spy," *AmericanCivilWar.com*, http://americancivilwar.com/women/pauline_cushman.html.
10. http://userpages.aug.com/capbarb/spies.html.

SURVIVOR

The Nazis built about twenty thousand concentration camps between 1933 and 1945. Into these camps they forced millions of "enemies of the state." Some camps were for transit of prisoners; others housed slave labor. The most vicious were the extermination camps. Into Mauthausen, a slave labor camp, the Nazis sent thirteen-year-old Tibor Rubin. It was here that Tibor learned the meaning of torture and despair. The Nazi guards told him, "You Jews, none of you will make it out of here alive." Many of his relatives died there. He was just a teen when he lost his mother and two sisters at one of the infamous extermination camps.

"Every day so many people were killed." They were led like lambs to the slaughterhouse. "We had nothing to look forward to but dying. It was a most terrible thing, like a horror movie." Of the Nazis, Tibor remains confused by their ability to kill without feeling. Among such cruelty and horror, Tibor learned lessons of bravery, courage, and survival. He was a survivor.

In 1945, American soldiers swept into the camp to free the prisoners. It was a miracle to Tibor, a day he promised to remember. The memory of it is imprinted in his heart: "The American soldiers had great feeling for us even though we were filthy. We stunk and had diseases. Lice crawled over our bodies. The Americans just picked us up and brought us back to life." Tibor made a vow that he would join that army. Three years later, when he arrived in New York, he kept that promise.

"I wanted to express my thanks," he added. Two years later he passed the English language test—after two tries and with "More than a little help," he joked. When the war broke out in Korea that year, Tibor was called into the commander's office. "The Twentieth Infantry Regiment is getting ready for combat. You are not a citizen, so we can't take you. A lot of us are going to get killed. We'll send you to Japan or Germany," Tibor was told.

"I can't just leave my unit for some safe zone," he replied. "I've been with these guys in basic training. They're like my family now. Even though I'm not a citizen, America is my home." By now his buddies called him Ted. He got his wish and headed for Korea to the good fortune of many buddies and other soldiers who found themselves in his unit.

In June 1950, the North Koreans, like a swarm of locusts, had surged across the South Korean border. They spread out across the thirty-eighth parallel and swept south toward Taegu. Tibor and his unit helped stop the forward move of the invaders by pushing them back north to the mountains near the China border. Thousands of Chinese were hiding in the hills. They covered themselves with brush to blend with the surroundings then set up smoke screens to conceal their movement and position. When the American forces were spread thin across the battle area, Tibor saw the whole mountainside open up and begin to crawl with enemy soldiers and rifle fire.

Under the constant barrage of bullets and grenades from the Chinese, the American firepower dropped to one machine gun. The three infantry-men who tried to man the gun were killed. Nobody wanted to take over, but somebody had to. That job fell to Tibor. He ran to the gun and pulled the trigger. From this machine gun emplacement, Tibor and the remaining men of his unit struggled to stop the Chinese advance and stay alive. They fought savagely, returning fire. The battle was furious and violent. The men began to feel that it was hopeless.

At the end of the third day, their feelings were confirmed. The Chinese overwhelmed the American forces and they were forced to withdraw. Yet in the face of this disaster, Tibor argued with his sergeant to go back for a fallen friend. The sergeant issued orders that the man be left behind. "But we don't know if he is dead," Tibor pleaded. All he could think of was that somebody was waiting for the man back home. Then he remembered the American soldiers who poured into the concentration camp to save his life.

So back he went to carry his buddy out. He became pinned down by sniper fire. For several hundred yards, he crawled on his belly, careful to keep his head below rifle fire. He discovered his buddy lying with his body so full of shrapnel that he could not lift his arm. Hefting the wounded soldier onto his back, Tibor dodged bullets all the way. Sweat poured from his brow and thoughts of getting hit by enemy fire made him hurry a little faster. When they returned to their lines, the buddy said, "Ted not only saved my life but kept the snipers off us."

While his unit was retreating to the Pusan Perimeter, Corporal Tibor Rubin was assigned to stay behind to keep the vital Taegu-Pusan road open. Thousands of enemy troops attacked the hill defended solely by Corporal Rubin. He was facing a hail of enemy fire that came at him like a swarm of angry bees, buzzing past him in deadly pursuit of each other. Bullets buzzed past millimeters from his head.

The retreating men had dug foxholes in the hillside. Tibor ran from one foxhole to the next, throwing grenades so that the enemy would believe they were fighting more than just one man. He could not think straight. In a situation like this, he became hysterical trying to save his life. While firing the machine gun, he continued to fight like a cornered tiger. With true aim, he inflicted a great number of casualties on the attacking forces. For twenty-four hours he single-handedly slowed the advance, allowing the Eighth Cavalry Regiment to complete its withdrawal successfully.

Eventually, he ran out of ammo, but he had delayed the enemy advance to give his retreating unit time to regroup. They could now mount a new assault.

As courageous as he was, with no ammo, and hordes of enemy soldiers at bay, Tibor was struck by enemy fire. Severely wounded, he was captured. Once again, he found himself as a prisoner in a camp. The camp was like a pigsty. The little food the guards fed them was mostly slop filled with maggots. Most of Tibor's buddies simply gave up. *No one wants to help anyone,* he thought. *These guys are a little different from the ones who liberated me from the Nazi concentration camp.* Nevertheless, he knew what he must do if they were to stay alive. Since he had survived a Nazi concentration camp, his past experiences made him most qualified for what had to be done. He had learned how to scrounge for food and nurse the sick.

To survive, he would sneak out at night to steal whatever he could find. He broke into enemy food storehouses and gardens. He brought back barley, millet, and even animal food. He found medical supplies, which he used to save the lives of several. He called on his survival skills learned in the German camp. He had endured beatings, torture, starvation—he also knew that if he were caught, he would suffer certain torture or death. He was used to torture.

"We share alike," he said to his fellow prisoners. He even carried those unable to walk to the latrine. He sloughed off the compliments by saying, "These are *mitzvahs* (commandments) in the Jewish tradition," and helping his fellow man was important to him. He knew he owed his very life to guys like these, the guys who had stormed into the camp in 1945 and nursed him to health.

More than 1,600 Americans died in the Chinese prisoner of war camp. Tibor Rubin continued to be an example of courage and honor by refusing repatriation to his native Hungary by his captors. His brave selfless actions were directly credited to saving the lives of many. He was a courageous survivor. Not until 2005 did America repay him for his service and courage. At the time, the president draped the Medal of Honor about his shoulders in a ceremony at the White House. He was proud to receive the honor but humbled by his memories of camps, torture, fallen buddies, and death.

NOTES

1. Army Corporal Tibor "Ted" Rubin, "USCIS Oakland Park, Florida Field Office and Application Support Center," *U.S. Citizenship and Immigration Services*, https://www.uscis.gov/about-us/find-uscis-office/immigrant-medal-honor-recipients/uscis-oakland-park-florida-field-office-and-application-support-center.
2. old.nationalreview.com/robbins/robbins/2000509190836.asp. (Am. Foreign Policy Council.)
3. http://blockyourid.com/gbpprorg/judicial-inc/tibor_rubin_supplement.htm.
4. "An American Hero," Beth Reese, *Corporal Tibor Rubin Medal of Honor Korean War*, accessed May 24, 2016, https://www.army.mil/medalofhonor/rubin/citation/printable.html.
5. "Citation," *Corporal Tibor Rubin: Medal of Honor Korean War*, https://www.army.mil/medalofhonor/rubin/citation/index.html.
6. usa.gov.http://www.defense.gov/news/newsarticle.aspz?id=17224.
7. www.veteranteam.com/files/VET-Advisory.pdf.

A BRITISH SPY
IN THE REVOLUTION

On a Thursday evening in 1781, a woman dressed in a Levite (a dress with a snug bodice, long, tight sleeves, and a fairly full skirt), dainty shoes that matched her outfit, and an enormous headdress, stepped out of the camp of German mercenary Baron Ottendorf, headed for Kingsbridge. The baron had recently been dismissed by George Washington only to join the British against the American Revolutionaries. At Kingsbridge, the woman slept the night. The following morning, she walked some three or four miles only to meet some refugees who stopped her. They brought her back to the Kingsbridge camp of Colonel Warner, who issued her a passport.

After leaving Colonel Warner's camp, she followed the main road, this time to be met by a French soldier coming from the woods. She asked, "Monsieur, would you show me the French camp?" He answered her, "Why? Are you French?" She replied, "Yes, Monsieur." To this he said, "Come with me, I'll take you there." The officer led her to the outermost guard post of the camp, which was situated near White Plains.

"I have come from the direction of York. I've learned that my father is here in your camp. I would be delighted to see him." She added, "I am a seamstress, my mother is a good wife. We have found out that my father has returned from France with the troops. It's been six years since he went to France from Canada."

The captain did not believe her story. "That's a lie. You are a spy for the British, aren't you?"

She denied his accusation. "We are trying to find my father. That's the truth."

The captain said, "You are Miss Jenny, a loyalist for the British."

"No!" she cried.

In the end, the French learned nothing. They sent her to General Washington's headquarters, where Monsieur de Rochambeau was camped with Washington, the French having joined the Americans in their fight for independence. They questioned Miss Jenny for two days, but still they learned nothing. Washington sent her back to the French, who cut her hair short as punishment and led her from the camp. "You are to leave here and never return," they ordered.

In the eighteenth century, it was rare to punish women by hanging or by putting them in prison. Women were thought to be more of a nuisance than a threat to the army. Women did not cut their hair short, so it was believed that women with short hair were ill or had been disgraced. By cutting her hair short, the French were able to disgrace Miss Jenny, but she got through her ordeal. She moved boldly through the French and American camps picking up information that she was able to return and report to the British. "The American troops are ready to advance. They are planning to meet up with Rochambeau's troops, cross the Hudson, and attack the British. General Washington is planning to attack New York in two places," she said.

Miss Jenny's report caused British Commander Clinton to keep his troops in New York. News arrived in the French camp news arrived that twenty-nine ships would dock in Chesapeake Bay. The commander of the French and American armies decided to use the ships to transport their men from the Chesapeake Bay to attack General Cornwallis at Yorktown. The British general had put his men at the end of the peninsula. When Washington and Rochambeau placed themselves across the head of the peninsula, they cut off any way of escape for the British.

The surrender of Cornwallis in Yorktown, while British Commander Clinton remained in New York, led to the disgrace of Henry Clinton. Of course, he had acted on the strength of the information that he had. The irony of the whole affair was that Miss Jenny's information caused Clinton to stay in New York, ultimately leading to the end of the Revolution. It turned out to be fatal news for the British. While the bravery and courage of the British spy in the red Levite may have served the Americans better than it served the British, it was still courage.

NOTES

1. https://www.si.umich.edu/spies/stories/women-1.html.
2. "Miss Jenny," *Wikipedia*, http://en.wikipedia.org/wiki/Miss_Jenny.

PSYCHIC DETECTIVE

Some people close their eyes, place their thumbs against their lower jaw, and press two fingers against their temples and think they are going to experience ESP (extrasensory perception). Actually there are only a few people who are able to predict the future. The power to predict the future is called a sixth sense. It is an ability beyond our regular five senses and comes from spiritual energy.

There are also those who are able to help the police find criminals using similar methods. In the case of Peter Hurkos, his ability to find people and help the police came only after he fell from a ladder in 1941. He lay in a coma three days in Zuidwal Hospital. Medical records show that he suffered a brain injury, but when he awoke, he was surprised that he could see in three dimensions—present, past, future. It was like being able to diagram all the tenses of a sentence at once. Peter's ability is called psychometrics. Pictures flashed through his brain so that he could see into the unknown.

The pictures that he saw were of people and places he'd never seen before. Those who believe in Peter's abilities say that he is a great psychic detective. He was called in to help on cases of murder and missing persons and planes. His most notable cases were the Stone of Scone case in England, the Boston Strangler Murders in Massachusetts, the Ann Arbor Coed Murders in Michigan, and the Sharon Tate Murders in Los Angeles. By 1969 he was credited with solving twenty-seven murders in seventeen countries.

"I see pictures in my mind like a television screen. When I touch something that belongs to another person, I can then tell what I see," Peter said. It can be anything—a picture, a shoe, or a piece of clothing can start his mental mirror going. He proved his mirror powers on TV. In his mind he could see the private lives of members of the audience. He was able to reveal information that he would not otherwise have known. He was on *The Tonight Show* three times with Johnny Carson. His story was told on *One Step Beyond* and TV shows in Japan, Holland, and Canada. When a Dutch millionaire was kidnapped and escaped, he asked Peter to help find his kidnappers.

For the good of all, Peter Hurkos chose to use his talent within the law. This is probably because he was a courageous patriot working in the underground in Holland during World War II. After the war, Queen Juliana decorated him for his bravery. He came to the United States to become a consultant for every president from Eisenhower to Reagan. Just think of what he could do if he had decided to be a thief. His abilities would have made committing crimes all too easy.

Of course, sometimes police chiefs were too proud to accept Peter's help, even though some of his more important work was helping police departments. "They don't like to admit they need my help," he said. One police officer said, "I don't believe in this kind of hocus pocus," yet later admitted, "but this time I'm stumped." In one case, Peter was able to identify the guilty parties when the police had given up. His description of the criminals led police right to their doorstep.

Doctors do not know why Peter Hurkos sees these pictures that nobody else does. Soon after coming to the United States, Peter allowed himself to be tested at the Glen Cove, Maine, medical research laboratory under strict control. After two years, his ability to pass their tests 90 percent of the time convinced the doctors of his powers. There are people who would like to be able to do what Peter does. Others say that he's just lucky. Of course, nobody could be correct 90 percent of the time and just be lucky.

Some go so far as to say that he achieved success through suggestion. Peter always said the test of a true psychic is whether he can predict without questions or prior information. Peter always found his suspect the honest way. Anyway, being right 90 percent of the time was good enough.

Since Peter Hurkos, many people have been identified with similar abilities.

ROY RUSSELL

NOTES

1. Richard A. Boning, *Getting the Facts: Book F* (Barnell Loft Books, 1997).
2. www.archive.org.
3. *One Step Beyond: The Peter Hurkos Story*, episode 1 (1960).
4. *One Step Beyond: The Peter Hurkos Story*, episode 2 (1960).
5. www.peterhurkos.com/images/biography/peterbio.pdf.
6. http://www.peterhurkos.com/peter_biography.htm. (Stephany Hurkos.)

RESCUE OF
THE SQUALUS

He was a navy officer who usually had navy officials wondering what he was up to. They never knew what to make of him. His quiet nature hid his extraordinary vision of the future. He was a man of action who dreamed about things that nobody else did. At the time, the navy was run by battleship admirals who could not begin to envision what he did. One navy officer said, "Who does he think he is, Jules Verne?"

He was Charles "Swede" Momsen. But he might as well have been Jules Verne. Growing up in Minnesota, he had read Verne's book, *Twenty Thousand Leagues Under the Sea*. He had been enchanted by what he had read; it is what inspired him to enter the Naval Academy in the first place. He wanted to live what Verne wrote: to be in submarines, "to live within the ocean." At this time, the depths of the ocean were still an unknown. No one knew how being down there for a long time might affect a man. If a submarine sank to the bottom—and they often did—the crew was doomed.

Swede decided that things had to change. On his own, fighting scoffers in the navy and government red tape, he set about to invent an escape lung, an underwater breathing apparatus, so that trapped seamen could rise to the ocean surface. Next came a submarine rescue chamber, also known as a diving bell, that could be lowered deeper into the depths of the ocean. Today's deep-sea diving methods, artificial lungs, and rescue chambers can be traced to the efforts of Swede Momsen. They were the result of his active mind and willpower. The first to try his own inventions, he always put his own life on the line. Today, at the core of the navy is its nuclear-powered submarines. They were really just surface ships until Swede Momsen gave them the fish-shaped USS *Albacore* that ran on a new helium-oxygen mixture. With this they could stay down for months. Swede's perilous mission to save the crew of the sunken *Squalus* submarine in 1939, remains the greatest undersea rescue in history to this day.

It was 8:41 a.m. on May 23, 1939. The board in the *Squalus* control room was dotted with red and green lights, each connected to an important point in the sub's conning tower. Green meant closed. Red meant open. The last two lights—connected to the two big valves in the side of the tower—turned green. The chief glanced at the board; everything was green. A yeoman manning the control room phone looked at the board to see only green lights. The seaman who held the lever that closed the valves saw that the board was green. The test officer looked at the board: green. They were about to make their nineteenth crash dive, trying to reach a depth of fifty feet in sixty seconds. Crash dives were a way to avoid enemy destroyers.

The Klaxon horn was honking loudly as Captain Naquin stepped from the ladder that led to the conning tower. He was always careful to check the board before any dive. The lights registered green. The sleek sub slipped into the depths of the ocean like a giant blue whale. At twenty-eight feet, the *Squalus* stalled briefly, allowing the batteries to kick in and take over the running of the sub. It was but only a moment of hesitation, and the sub plunged down again.

At thirty feet, the test officer said to Captain Naquin, "Good, good."

Captain Naquin replied, "This is going to be a beauty."

The depth gauge pointer read thirty-five feet, then forty, then forty-five feet. A seaman in the conning tower saw the ocean wash over the eyepiece. At fifty feet, Captain Naquin and the test officer called, "Mark!" telling the crew to record the time.

Both men pushed the stop on their watches. They compared readings to discover that the time was only a few seconds over the desired sixty. Naquin grinned. He was happy with the dive results. Only a few more dives before the *Squalus* passed her final tests and joined the fleet. Satisfied with the sub's performance, he stepped to the periscope. He gripped the rubber-covered handles. As he did, he heard a strange fluttering sound, something he had never heard before in any of the previous dives. A moment later, the yeoman manning the control room phone was startled at what he heard. The sound was not showing on the board. In a terrified voice he cried out, "Sir! Water flooding the engine room!"

The *Squalus* began to float down like a dying leaf falling from a tree. As water filled the aft (the back) part of the submarine, it began to sink faster. Naval architect Harold Preble knew that they needed more high pressure than two air banks, so he tried to cut in another bank. He wedged himself between the chart desk and the high-pressure air manifold to reach the handle for opening the air banks. He felt a sudden terrific increase in pressure and was struck on the back by a force of water coming in the air ventilation line. The flow knocked down a trim manifold seaman, who crashed onto Preble. At the same time, he saw the door to the aft battery room close.

When the water reached the electrical wiring, it shorted the system. The sub lost all power and lights. Sparks burst like a shorted electrical wire from the battery room. Smoke began to fill the sub. Seaman Gainor, noting the high rate of discharge, dashed into the battery tank and pulled the switches to prevent fire in the forward battery. Amazingly, during the emergency, the entire crew—officers and men—remained cool under the pressure.

There was no communication once word came that the engine room was flooding. When the *Squalus* struck bottom at 247 feet, they were in total darkness. Captain Naquin said, "Send a red dye to the surface; it can be seen for miles. Wrap blankets around yourselves and be still."

Harry Preble said, "We have nothing to worry about. Just wait and help will be at hand. In five hours we will know that help is above us and in thirty-five hours we will be on the surface." He knew that their sister submarine *Sculpin* was nearby, and Preble learned from one of the men who served on the rescue ship *Falcon* that it would take fourteen hours for it to arrive over the sunken *Squalus*. Nevertheless, the men secretly wondered.

True to predictions, the men in the *Squalus* heard the propellers of the *Sculpin* as the sub circled their marker buoy and the sounds of its being hauled on deck. The voice of the captain of the *Sculpin* came over the telephone. Lieutenant Nichols told him that the thirty-three survivors in the *Squalus* were okay, but while they were talking, the telephone line broke. Shortly, the *Falcon* arrived. Aboard were divers and Swede Momsen with the latest in rescue bell equipment. Calling orders, he directed operations aboard the ship. The luck of the crew of the *Squalus* was changing.

The *Falcon* was positioned and anchored directly over the sunken sub. One of the most able and skilled divers, Martin Sabitsky, was picked to go down first. Navy divers are tough by nature—healthy and unafraid— but none of them had worked at such depths in such cold water. At these depths, they were in danger of nitrogen narcosis, where their speech becomes blurred, their ability hampered, and the possibility of death.

More than luck was with Sabitsky as he landed right on the deck of the *Squalus*. His boots made clanking sounds as he moved about. The crew members shouted and beat metal objects against the inside of the sub. Working desperately, Sabitsky bolted the cable in place. Twenty-five minutes later, surface crew hauled him up even as time ran out for the men below.

They lowered the diving bell, modeled after Momsen's early designs, and attached it to the escape hatch. They helped the crew one at a time into the bell. The climb out seemed to take forever. On the first ascent, they brought seven to the surface. On the second and third ascents, nine men crowded into the bell. On the final trip, eight men came up. The entire operation took forty hours. During his naval career, Charles Momsen never boasted of what he had done or the lives he had saved. Navy brass had scoffed at him, "But seeing the first survivors from the *Squalus* come out of the rescue bell made it all worthwhile."

NOTES

1. Richard A. Boning, *Getting the Facts: Book E* (Barnell Loft Books, 1997).
2. www.hampton.lib.nh.us/hampton/.../usssqualus/lossofsqualus.htm.
3. Charles B. Momsen, "Lecture: Rescue and Salvage of USS Squalus," *Naval History and Heritage Command*, http://www.history.navy.mil/research/histories/ship-histories /danfs/s/squalus-ss-192/squalus-ss-192-sinking-rescure-of-survivors-and-salvage /lecture_squalus_rescue.html.
4. "Report of Rescue Operations," *Naval History and Heritage Center*, http://www .history.navy.mil/research/histories/ship-histories/danfs/s/squalus-ss-192/squalus-ss -192-sinking-rescure-of-survivors-and-salvage/rescue_ops_report.html.

LIVING IN FEAR

Anne Frank was born in Frankfurt, Germany, in 1929 where she lived with her parents and sister, Margot. They attended the Jewish synagogue until she was four. When the Nazis rose to power in Germany, her family moved to Amsterdam, Holland, to escape the persecution of Jews. In Amsterdam, her parents wanted their children to live normal lives, so the girls went to a Montessori school, played at the ocean side, and ate ice cream. What could be more normal? Anne liked to sit in a chair on the flat roof of the house where she lived. It was like having her own private beach.

For a while, the Frank family lived a somewhat trouble-free life. During this time, Adolph Hitler, dictator of Germany, was invading the countries bordering Germany. All Jewish people were ordered to wear a yellow Star of David with the word "Jew" written on it. Eventually, these people were hauled like cattle in boxcars and taken to concentration camps. When she turned twelve, she received a diary from her father. Not long after, the Germans invaded Holland, and the family was forced to go into hiding to avoid the Nazis.

Their friends owned a shop with a hidden annex above it. The Franks went into hiding. The door to the secret place could not be seen because it was behind a small bookcase on the third floor. Another family, Mr. and Mrs. van Pels and their son, Peter, who was barely older than Anne, were also brought to live in the annex with Anne's family. For the two years they lived there, Anne wrote in her red-checkered diary. The two families had to be very quiet during the daytime. At night, they could take baths, flush the toilet, and talk.

One summer day, the Nazis came to order them out. They were taken first to the Westerbork transit camp, then to the Auschwitz death camp in Poland. Here they received very little food—many prisoners starved to death. Of the thousands of Jews hidden by non-Jews, half ended up being sent to a death camp. Nazis didn't find these hidden Jews by chance; they were betrayed by other people.

Camp life was like living a nightmare but knowing that it was real. Anne and her sister slept in unheated chicken coops crammed with other women. It was at these camps that prisoners were ordered into the showers, which had been converted to gas chambers. Those who died in this camp were children, not yet fifteen. As luck would have it, Anne had passed her fifteenth birthday, and for the present, was spared.

Mr. van Pels died in a gas chamber only a few weeks after he arrived there. Anne and Margot were moved to Bergen-Belsen camp in October 1944; they never saw their parents again. Their mother lived a few more months then died at Auschwitz. Peter died in Mauthausen camp in Austria in May 1945, just one month before the Americans freed the prisoners from all the death camps. Margot died in March 1945 to be followed by Anne a few weeks later. Sadly, the camp was liberated just weeks after her death. Of the original seven who had shared the hidden annex, only Anne's father survived.

When he returned to look at what had been their home for two years, he found Anne's diary. He made some spelling corrections, removed some of the private entries, and had it published. Not only is it read in fifty-five languages around the world, the book is required reading in many American schools. It is a grim story of living in fear.

Anne never wrote about hate. "Despite everything, I believe people are really good at heart." She also wrote, "Think of the beauty still left around you and be happy." She was positive, always upbeat. "The best remedy for those who are afraid, lonely, or unhappy is to find a place where they can be quiet, alone with nature, the heavens, and God. Only then does one feel that all is as it should be." Anne's diary is a legacy not so much for the past as it is a signal fire that lights the way to the future.

NOTES

1. Anne Frank, *Anne Frank: The Diary of a Young Girl* (New York: Doubleday, 1967).
2. http://www.ushmm.org/wic/en/article.php?Moduled.
3. http://www.ushmm.org/research/library/bibliography/index.php?content_anne
_frank.

TWINS FOREVER

Chang and Eng were born joined at the chest. Their birth in 1811 caused a sensation; in fact, they might easily have lost their lives soon after. Siam at the time was a feudal land, full of superstition, and the king's rule was the only rule. He actually owned the people. When the twins were born, none of the midwives would touch them for fear of becoming cursed. People saw them as a bad omen. When the king heard of their birth, he ordered the infants to be killed. Another threat came from doctors. They wanted to separate the boys with everything from saws to red-hot wires. Because their mother refused to abandon them, they were allowed to live.

One day, Captain Abel Coffin had his ship anchored in the bay. He saw two boys swimming in the muddy water. As the boys each moved one arm at a time, they pretty much looked like a small paddleboat. The captain stared harder. He wondered why the boys were swimming that way. As he watched, he decided that he must have a closer look, so he signaled for the boys to come aboard his ship. They climbed up the rope ladder and jumped onto the wooden deck. Coffin saw that they were joined at the chest by a band of flesh. Dripping wet and clad in black cutoffs, they smiled at Coffin. Captain Coffin touched their connected skin. "Yes, we can both feel it," they said.

The boys had adapted to their dual life. Not only could they swim, but they could run and jump quite easily. They were about five feet tall. They said, "We are most comfortable when we are standing with our arms around each other. Yet, when one of us is sick, the other may continue to feel well."

By doing physical things, they had stretched the connecting flesh from four to six inches. By the time they were fourteen, their father had died, and the boys were selling duck eggs to support the family. Now they had been discovered. Captain Coffin and a partner, Robert Hunter, told the boys' mother that their future and fortune were with them. It took another three years to talk the king into letting his vassals—the boys— leave Siam. Whether she realized it or not, Chang and Eng's mother all but sold the boys to Hunter and Coffin for $3,000.

Hunter and Coffin knew they would get rich showing the boys in exhibits. They became the twins' managers for the next few years and showed them to curious crowds in America and England. The boys got very little rest since the greedy managers worked the pair as if they were pack mules. An exhibit lasted four hours but was held every day. At first, the twins simply stood on stage or walked and ran about or answered questions.

Admission was fifty cents. The shows did improve over the years. Soon the twins wowed the audiences with somersaults, backflips, and shows of strength. In this last trick, the twins would carry the largest member of the audience. At one time, the man they toted weighed 180 pounds. Audiences ate it up and to show their approval, they clapped, whistled, and stomped their feet.

While touring, the Siamese Twins, as they came to be known, were treated with respect, for the most part. Their connected life aroused much attention and rumor. Sometimes people were rude and asked stupid questions, but the twins tried to remain polite and in good humor.

Chang and Eng got only ten dollars a month for all their work. After two years, they got fifty dollars a month—still a very small amount of money when the managers were getting $1,000. When the twins turned twenty-one, they freed themselves to live their own lives.

After they became independent in 1832, the twins went on tour for about seven years, visiting city after city. People never tired of seeing them. They became wealthy with the pay that they received, but they had changed. They were no longer just foreign boys with no knowledge of English or the outside world. They had become men of the world. They had gained culture, but were unhappy with the life that they were living.

They began to quarrel more often. They looked for a place where they could just be themselves.

Their search took them to a small town in North Carolina where they took up an interest in two sisters, Adelaide and Sarah Yates. The people were shocked. How could two of the county's most sought-after belles think of marrying the twins? Their parents said no at first, but when they learned that the foursome intended to elope, they gave in to the marriages.

In 1839, North Carolina had been in the Union for about fifty years but had grown very little. It remained an agricultural state where farmers grew cotton, tobacco, and made moonshine. Schools, health care, and printed newspapers were poor—mostly incomplete. Disputes were still settled with pistols. It was this kind of backwards place that drew the twins. They had some money, but not enough to stop working, so they took up farming to become eligible to marry the sisters.

After the weddings, which were held at the Yates's farm in 1843, the married couples moved to a house Chang and Eng had built. A year later, a child was born to Eng and Sarah. Six years later, a child was born to Chang and Addie. By 1860, Chang and Addie had seven children; Eng and Sarah had nine. With so many children to feed, the twins had to return to show business. They toured California, raising enough money along the way to care for their needs. Back home they continued to quarrel. Something had to be done.

The twins wanted to be separated. By this time, the wives were living in separate houses. This caused even more quarrels. One argument ended with the twins pounding each other with their fists. In another fight, one twin threatened the other with a knife. They went to England and Europe on a tour, mainly to find a doctor who would separate them, but war in Europe prevented their further search, forcing them to return home where the quarrels continued. They went to their family doctor. "We want to be separated," they said. "Now!" The doctor laid out his instruments and turned to the two men.

Calmly he asked, "Which would you prefer, that I sever the flesh that connects you, or cut off your heads? Doing one will bring about the same result as the other." That was enough to cool the twins' tempers. The good doctor did promise to perform the separation upon the death of either of the brothers; however, he was not there when that time came.

The debate was settled for them. On the night of January 17, 1874, a scream split the silence. It raised no alarm in the large house outside

Mount Airy, North Carolina. Just a dream, everyone thought, maybe a nightmare. A few hours later, the winter stillness was broken again. This time it was a different voice, but it was the same kind of scream. Eng had awakened and seeing his twin brother dead beside him, knew his fate.

Chang and Eng, the world's most famous connected twins, the ones who gave us the term Siamese twins, had died. They left the world the same way they entered it sixty-three years before: together. They had raised not only eyebrows, but many medical questions. One question was, would the death of one twin cause the death of the other? Even with their passing, that question was never really answered.

The cause of death, half of it anyway, remains a riddle. Chang had suffered with ill health for some time, ever since he had been injured in a carriage accident. Eng, on the other hand, was in top health and seemed not to be affected by his brother's condition; yet, on this cold January night, he, too, had died. Had he died of shock? Of fright? The townspeople thought as much, as did many doctors. Believing that the death of his brother would cause his own death, Eng was literally scared to death.

Another theory held that the band of flesh was a lifeline and would pass death from one to the other. Doctors did learn that the twins might have been separated as children but could not be later. As courageously as they had lived, fate bound them together in death.

NOTES

1. "Reader Favorites: Eng & Chang Bunker: A Hyphenated Life," Page Chichester, *Blue Ridge Country*, http://blueridgecountry.com/newtwins/twins.html. (Kurt Rheinheimer.)
2. "Chang and Eng Bunker—The Siamese Twins," http://www.phreeque.com/chang _eng.html.
3. Irving and Amy Wallace, *The Two: A Biography of Chang and Eng—the Original Siamese Twins* (New York: Simon & Schuster, 1975).

KATIE'S KROPS FOR NEEDY KIDS

In 2008, a little nine-year-old girl named Katie Stagliano, who lived in South Carolina, brought a very tiny cabbage seed home from her third grade class. She was taking part in the Bonnie Plants Third Grade Cabbage Program. With tender loving care, she poked the seed into the ground, watered it when needed, and was thrilled when the first green leaves popped up through the dirt. She watched the cabbage grow, and grow, and grow. When her cabbage was three feet across—weighing an amazing forty pounds—Katie knew that she had something special. That was a lot of cabbage for one family.

At dinner one night, her father talked about being grateful for the healthful meal that they were eating. He explained, "There are families who are not able to put food on their tables. They go to bed hungry." An idea struck Katie so hard that she actually moved in her chair. She thought, *I can donate my cabbage to a soup kitchen.* She was so thankful that she had she decided to help someone else.

When the day came to take her cabbage to a charity, she arrived to find many people standing in the food line. Her huge vegetable drew a lot of attention. "Did you grow that?" someone asked. "How big is it? How much does it weigh?" Finally, someone asked, "Is it for us?" Katie said, "Yes." At that moment it was no longer her cabbage, but their cabbage.

"Thank you," they said all together. The words made her happy because Katie knew the power of words especially "please" and "thank you." She thought these words were some of the most important words in any language.

From this point on, Katie was set on a course to help those in need. Through Katie's Krops and the help of others, thousands of pounds of fresh produce were donated to feed needy people.

Katie has many gardens tended by her many friends. People call her a hero. She says the real heroes are those who support her dream. She gives credit to Miss Lisa, her master gardener, who taught her much of what it takes to grow a productive garden. Mr. Bob, Miss Linda, and people of the Summerville Baptist Church were especially helpful. She says that her Pinewood Prep School deserved many thanks because they let her use a plot of land the length of a football field.

Four years later, with the help of friends, Katie's Krops produced an abundant harvest of food for the community. Kids ages nine to sixteen joined her in planting vegetable gardens in their own communities. The items grown were strawberries, tomatoes, broccoli, cucumbers, eggplant, squash, greens, celery, okra, and, of course, cabbage. Others who are unable to tend gardens make donations—as few as five dollars. Katie is especially thankful for them because they help pay for seeds and the cost of water.

To her surprise, Katie learned something she hadn't thought about. "I did not know that there were so many people who liked to garden." Luckily, their interest in gardening helped Katie's Krops change the world.

NOTES

1. "The Two Most Important Words: Thank You," *Katie's Krops*, http://www.katieskrops .com/katies-blog.html.

2. "Welcome to Katie's Krops," *Katie's Krops*, http://www.katieskrops.com.

UP FROM THE FIELDS

He learned about justice—or rather injustice—early in life. César Estrada Chávez was born and grew up in a small adobe on uncleared land in Arizona. When César was a small child, his father agreed to clear eighty acres of land for a large landowner. In exchange, the landowner agreed to deed forty acres that adjoined the house property to César's father. When it came time to transfer the land, the owner sold it to a man named Justice Jackson.

César's dad went to a lawyer who advised him to borrow money and buy the land. Later, when César's father could not pay the interest on the loan, the lawyer took back the land and sold it to the original owner. César learned a lesson that he never forgot. He said, "The love for justice that is in us is not only the best part of our being, but it is also the most true to our nature." He would soon put that belief to work.

When César's family moved to California, they lived in the La Colonia Barrio, in Oxnard, for a brief time. Eventually, they moved to San Jose and lived in the *barrio* (neighborhood) called *Sal Si Puedes*, or "get out if you can." César thought the only way out of his poverty was to work his way up. He disliked the schools he attended. "I feel like a monkey in a cage," he said. He attended segregated schools but felt that his education had nothing to do with his migrant-farmworker life. Since his father moved up and down the state to harvest the crops as they ripened, he and his brother, Richard, attended thirty-seven different schools. He did graduate from eighth grade.

An injury accident to his father forced his mother into the fields. Because he did not want his mother to labor in the fields, César skipped high school to earn money. That meant laboring as a migrant farmworker. Although he missed part of his education, later in life, he made education his passion. He believed that the end of all education should be service to others. He practiced this belief all his life. In 1944, at age seventeen, he joined the navy. He served two years, as the war was about over. He married soon after he returned from service. The couple motored through California, visiting all the missions from Sonoma to San Diego. Because he loved education, he wanted to learn more about the Mexican history of California.

César Chávez became an organizer for the rights of farmworkers. These are the laborers who move from farm to farm and town to town or to where they're needed. They work hard for minimum pay. The work can be dangerous because of the use of pesticides. Farm machinery is also some of the most dangerous to use.

Prior to this, he had met with Father McDonnell and Fred Ross, and had read about St. Francis and Gandhi. All of these men spoke in support of nonviolence. César adopted these nonviolent ways to fight for the rights of migrant farmworkers. Although the workers were not citizens of the United States, the country did allow them some civil rights.

César held meetings to tell the people of their rights. He found it hard to talk the workers into changing their lives; they were afraid of losing their jobs. They knew that even a job in the fields was better than what they had left in Mexico. By 1962, César could no longer stand to see the owners treat his parents and friends like serfs. He resented the filthy huts they lived in that were without modern features such as indoor toilets, and sometimes, running water.

He founded the National Farm Workers Association, later to become the United Farm Workers (UFW). A fellow worker, Dolores Huerta, joined him, and together they created a union. His brother designed the UFW eagle, which became the union symbol.

"I asked Richard to design the flag, but he could not make an eagle that I liked." Finally, he sketched one on a piece of a brown paper bag. He squared off the wing edges so that the eagle would be easier for union members to draw on the handmade red flags that would give courage to them as their own powerful symbol. He said of the flag, "A symbol is an important thing.

That is why I chose an Aztec eagle. It gives hope. When people see it they know that it means dignity." César was very proud of what he had done.

Everyone agreed to nonviolent protests. They also approved their flag *La Causa* (the cause). With a strong leader to represent them, the workers began to demand fair pay and better working conditions. In the past, millions of people in the United States and other countries had fought for these same rights.

In the beginning, not many workers joined the union. Those who did said, "Without these rights, no one will work in the fields." In 1965, the owners of the grape vineyards would not listen to the union demands. The farmworkers went on strike and walked out of the fields.

"The strike is good," César said to them. "Men standing side by side and telling the growers we will no longer work for low wages. We want a union contract that will guarantee us our jobs. We must be strong if we are to win decent wages and decent living conditions and a better life for our wives and children." To the growers, he said, "We do the work and you make most of the money. We are showing our unity in our strike. Our strike is stopping the work in the fields, stopping ships that would carry grapes, and stopping the trucks that would carry the grapes. We are making this sacrifice because we know our only hope is in a strong union."

César believed that "A nonviolent protest is the best way to teach people about the struggles that the farmworkers are living. It also is a good way to gain support for social change. The way we think about other people. Nonviolent protests are protests that do not hurt anyone." To this end he went on fasts, going without food for long periods of time. He said, "A fast is first and foremost personal. It is a heartfelt prayer for all those who work beside me." His first fast lasted nearly a month. Only Christ had fasted longer. A second fast lasted twenty-four days. A final fast lasted thirty-six days. He was willing to sacrifice his own life to change the terrible suffering.

César's hope that he could accomplish his dream with nonviolence was not always the way events happened. In his five-year grape boycott, he urged people to stop buying California grapes until farmworkers had contracts insuring better pay and safer work conditions. His organized *huelgas* (strikes) often turned into bloody fights. They erupted between union members and grape growers in the vineyards. The courts did not side with César, and he and others found themselves in jail more than once.

César Chávez organized strikes, boycotts, fasts, marches, and won a victory for the workers. Finally, grape growers and union members came to an agreement.

Who is César Chavez? César Chávez is a heroic figure who helped migrant farmworkers. He died peacefully in his sleep on April 23, 1993, near Yuma, Arizona—a very short distance from his small family farm in San Luis, in the Gila River Valley, where he was born sixty-six years before. He became an American folk hero.

César Chávez is remembered as the courageous, migrant farmworker who rose up from the fields to become a force for human rights.

NOTES

1. "Activists and Reformers: Cesar Chavez," *America's Story from America's Library*, http://www.americaslibrary.gov/aa/chavez/aa_chavez_subj.html.
2. http://chavez.cde.ca.gov/ModelCurriculum/Teachers/Lessons/Resources/Biographic/High.
3. http://chavez.cde.ca.gov/ModelCurriculum/Teachers/Lesson/Resources/Biographic/Middle.
4. "Cesar Chavez, 1927–1993: He Organized the First Successful Farm Workers Union in America," *ManyThings.org*, http://www.manythings.org/voa/people/Cesar_Chavez.html.
5. David Seidman, *Cesar Chavez: Labor Leader* (New York: Franklin Watts, 2004).
6. Mercedes Silveira-Gouveia, "Cesar Chavez: The Story of a Giant," *San Joaquin County Deomocratic Party*, https://sjcdems.wordpress.com/2011/04/04/cesar-chavez-the-story-of-a-giant.

THE LADY AND
THE TIGERS

She was as agile as the cats she handled. With deft, skilled moves, she led the big cats through a routine. Using what circus people call the gentling method—speaking to them softly but firmly and giving them rewards and friendship—Mabel Stark got the tigers to perform without using threats and fear. At age eight, watching the tiger act from her first circus, she thought, *I'll train tigers someday.* From that moment on she wanted to do nothing else.

She stayed true to her desire. When a circus came to town, she was always there. Finally, she felt she had waited long enough. She asked the owner to let her show her stuff. "You've got to be kidding," the circus owner laughed. Mabel kept after him. "It's the only thing I want to do."

"Those are wild animals," he chided, trying to keep Mabel from entering the cage. "They're not tabby cats you play with at home." She persisted and at last he agreed. He swung the iron door open, and Mabel stepped in with the wild tigers.

Their roars ceased when Mabel gently talked to them. Amazed, the owner asked, "Would you like to join the show?" Mabel adopted a tiger cub named Rajah and played with him at the beach. She actually kept the tiger in her home. She made up an act with Rajah. He would run straight toward her. Up he would go on his hind legs, his forefeet around her neck. They would waltz around a couple times; she'd throw him to the ground, and they'd roll three or four times. She would open his mouth and put her head inside. People shuddered and screamed with fright. Then, she would jump up and wave to the crowd.

When she wasn't performing with Rajah, she was in the cage with the other cats. People cheered loudly as Mabel worked with them. The owner of the circus filled one cage with eighteen wild tigers. Mabel made some leap through hoops. She had others sit up on their hind legs and told others to roll over. She even got one tiger to ride bareback on a horse. Unlike other wild animal acts, in which owners had removed the cat's claws, Mabel's tigers had all their teeth and claws. Her act was clearly the greatest wild animal act of all the circuses.

While performing in Bangor, Maine, she lost her footing in a muddy area and fell. At this moment she did not have control over her cats. As if thrown from a catapult, the tigers leaped from their platforms and attacked her as she lay on the ground. When attacking, tigers go for the head and throat. Mabel found her head in the mouth of one animal. Another had her shoulders in a vice-like grip. Two others were tearing at her legs. One tiger punched a hole in her side. All the while, the beasts were in a frenzy, roaring, growling, snarling, and tearing at the helpless woman.

A fellow trainer, Terrell Jacobs, ran into the cage with whip in hand. He snapped the long leather strip and commanded the animals to return to their places. He had saved Mabel from sure death. The tigers would have eaten her alive, but the mauling did not stop her from performing her act. She came back to the ring in a matter of weeks, wrapped in bandages and walking with a cane. During the time she spent in the hospital, she was wrapped in bandages and looked pretty much like an Egyptian mummy. This was not the only time that Mabel was mauled by her cats; in all, she survived more than a dozen attacks.

She always came back to her act with Rajah. She and Rajah had a special relationship, an understanding in which they trusted one another. Audiences loved seeing the girl in the jaws of a tiger, but shuddered with fear as well. To prevent Rajah's claws from hurting her, Mabel wore a white, heavy leather suit that covered her body from neck to feet.

Back in 1938, Mabel made Jungleland in Thousand Oaks her home base. She was asked to be grand marshal of the Conejo Valley Days Parade, and the town elected her as its first honorary mayor. She lived a remarkable life, one that all of us can only dream about. With courage she faced danger almost every day of her life with truly wild and hungry tigers in a steel cage.

NOTES

1. Richard A. Boning, *Getting the Facts: Book C* (Barnell Loft Books, 1997).

2. http://www.stagecoactmuseum.org/people_link/mabel_stark.htm.

3. "Mabel Stark—Cat Woman Extraordinaire," Robert Hough, *The Infinite Cat Project*, accessed May 25, 2016, http://infinitecat.com/cat-tales/mabel-stark.html. (Mike Stanfill.)

ROW, ROW, ROW YOUR BOAT

R ow, Row, Row Your Boat" is a little song they never sang, a dream
they never fully realized. It's a fame that came too late for Frank
Samuelson and George Harbo. They decided that they had little
future as clam diggers supplying fish for the Fulton Fish Market in New
York City, so the two Norwegian immigrants cooked up a plan to set a
record. They would become the first men to row across the Atlantic to
Europe. To family, friends, and other observers familiar with the seas,
they thought the plan to be suicidal. For Samuelson and Harbo, the trip
was their ticket to fame and fortune.

To their surprise, no one volunteered to back them. They finally won
the support of Richard Fox, editor of the *Police Gazette*. With only an
open, ordinary, eighteen-foot rowboat with water-resistant sides and a
couple of watertight float compartments, the two men were ready. The
boat had no sail, no motor, no rudder, but it did have an oil stove that
didn't work. They named the boat the *Richard Fox*—what else?

On June 7, 1896, the tide was ebbing and just right for rowing out
to sea. The pair rowed for nine hours steady and then rested for an hour.
They kept alternate three-hour watches at night. Day after day they rowed.
The blisters on their hands were replaced by more blisters.

Danger sailed with them all the way. Their double-ended rowboat
was like a tiny piece of driftwood on the giant sea. As they rowed in the
shipping lanes between America and Europe, they could not be seen by
captains of large cargo ships. Many times they narrowly escaped being
crushed like walnuts under the screws of a passing freighter. At one time,

they were surrounded by a school of migrating whales that surfaced like volcanic domes. Floating icebergs loomed like tall skyscrapers, presenting a constant danger.

They had been at sea nearly a month by now. Even though it was June, the Atlantic Ocean was rarely calm or peaceful. It was especially rough in the North Atlantic where the two men were crossing. In seas everywhere, rogue waves come up suddenly that swamp boats, sweep people from shores, and bury anything in their paths. Even large oceangoing ships are in peril. The two men were about to experience this danger. A giant wave rose from the ocean and swept across the surface. It slammed against the tiny rowboat. The helpless craft was turned upside down and the men were pitched into the ice-filled water.

Luckily, the compass, sextant, and extra oars had been safely lashed in place. They did lose part of their food supply and all the loose equipment, but their life belts kept them afloat. Short lifelines held them close to their boat, although anyone thrown into such icy water lives about fifteen minutes. Since they had special rails fitted to keep the boat balanced, they were able to turn it right side up again. They climbed back in and rowed the rest of the crossing soaking wet, but the rails had saved their lives.

Rowing all day every day, the courageous pair finally saw land ahead. A month and twenty days after rowing out of New York Harbor, they arrived at the Isles of Scilly off southwest England. They had averaged fifty-six miles of rowing each day. Their intent was to row to France, and that they did, rowing up the Seine to Paris for a total of 3,200 miles. The partners cabled their success to Fox and loaded their rowboat on a steamer for the return trip.

The steamer ran out of coal off Cape Cod, so the captain ordered all wooden objects to be broken up and fed into the furnaces. The intrepid two refused. No way were they going to feed what had been their home for more than a month into the hungry mouth of a steamer's furnaces. They tossed their boat, the *Fox*, overboard and rowed into New York. Sadly, they never received the fortune they dreamed of. Only now have they achieved some fame.

NOTES

1. Richard A. Boning, *Getting the Facts: Book D* (Barnell Loft Books, 1997).

2. http://hildringstimen.no.

3. "Logs and Stories by/about Oceanrowers," *The Ocean Rowing Society: International*, http://www.oceanrowing.com/logs/index.htm.

4. "From the Morgue," *The National Police Gazette*, http://policegazette.us/FromTheMorgue _8-22-1896_Harbo.html.

DEFENDING THE RADIO STATION

was twenty-six at the time. I was also 4F, which meant that the Army would take my mother before they'd take me," said Sergeant Jon Cavaiani.

I kinda had a doctor that knew a couple of guys that were 1A that he had claimed were 4F. I had a talk with him about it, and he decided I wasn't 4F anymore. I went to heavy weapons in basic training and advanced to individual training. A gentleman in an officer's uniform walks up to me with his beret pulled to one side and slightly down over one eye and says, "Are you man enough to be in Special Forces?" Well, question anything about me you want, but don't question my masculinity! So I had to prove it.

Jon was sent to Vietnam in 1970. One of his first encounters with the enemy took place when he and a Vietnamese sergeant major were walking down a trail. Some enemy troops ran from the jungle and fatally wounded the sergeant. The following year, in 1971, Jon was serving as a leader of a security platoon. The platoon was to provide security for an isolated radio station located inside enemy territory. One morning the entire radio camp came under attack from enemy rifle and rocket fire from a large enemy force.

Without thinking of himself, Jon darted from position to position to direct return fire. The whole time he was open to rifle fire from the enemy. In their desperate fight for survival, Jon urged the men by returning heavy fire to keep the enemy away, pinning them down so that they could not advance. The odds were against him. Darkness settled over the jungle.

During the night, Jon directed the men in strengthening the defenses. They would try to defend the radio station with the few men and little ammo they had. A much larger enemy force had quietly moved into position under the cover of night. They began a major attack, throwing hand grenades and opening fire with rifles. Bullets buzzed through the camp like swarms of angry hornets. Hand grenades exploded like overheated potatoes among the men in the camp. The purpose was to wipe out the American unit completely. Jon found a machine gun, stood up powerful like a mechanical robot, and began firing the weapon in a sweeping motion. He looked like he had been staged by a Hollywood director with the kind of daring bravado you'd expect to see in movies. With complete disregard for his personal safety, time and time again he dared the heavy enemy fire in order to move about to direct his platoon's return fire. He rallied the men in a desperate fight for survival.

The enemy kept up a steady fire until Jon could not slow the advance of the Viet Cong. He called in helicopter support. He ordered what was left of the platoon to try to escape. As soon as the men were lifted aboard, the helicopters flew away to safety while Jon stayed on the ground to provide cover fire. Through his daring and courage, most of the remaining platoon members got away.

While causing great losses in the enemy numbers, Jon was wounded several times. With so many bullet holes in him, he looked like he had been used for target practice on a gunnery range. He could not walk and was taken prisoner.

As a prisoner of war in Vietnam, he spent time in Plantation Garden camp—the Viet Cong's interrogation prison where the enemy questioned prisoners about their army units. He was moved to Hanoi Hilton where he was held for twenty-three months. During that time, the Viet Cong's starvation diet brought on pounding headaches. He dropped from 198 to 92 pounds.

Although the war in Vietnam was grinding down, Jon remained a prisoner until the last bullet was fired. Only then did the Cong allow him to go home. On December 12, 1974, in a ceremony at the White House, President Ford greeted him with the nation's highest military honor. Like thousands of others, he showed great courage and bravery while fighting in Vietnam, but with just enough edge to elevate him to Medal of Honor status.

NOTES

1. http://www.pbs.orgWETA/americanvalor/stories/cavaiani_interview.html. (Sarah Amron.)
2. http://pownetwork.org/bios./c139.htm.
3. http://www.pritzkermilitarylibrary.org/events/2010-20-jon-cvaiani-sp. (Mark Heiden.)

HUMAN CANNONBALLS

As children grow, they dream of what they will become. Some want to be actors. Some want to be doctors, pilots, or auto mechanics. Most want to be firefighters or police officers. For Hugo Zacchini the choice was made for him. His father had built a huge cannon. He did not intend to sell it to the army for use in a war or for it to be used as a weapon against soldiers. He did not even intend to fire a cannonball out of it.

He had designed it for something much larger, something about the size of Hugo. At this time, people went to circuses. Hugo's father thought the cannon would be a great new act for the circus.

With the long, silver cannon in the back, Hugo's father drove a huge truck to the center of the circus ring. Hugo worked his way to the mouth of the long silver barrel, then slowly slid down into the belly of the cannon. While raising it, his father aimed it at a net at the far side of the circus ring. Deep in the barrel, Hugo could no longer hear the oohs and aahs. The crowd had become as still as death. His father had designed the air-powered cannon to play to the danger-seeking crowd.

The crowd knew that if aimed a little too far, he would fly beyond the net, too short, he would smash into the ground at one hundred miles per hour. Because he trusted his father, he drew his courage and tried not to think about it. Those were not the only dangers Hugo faced. If the cannon fired on idle, if he scraped against the barrel on his way out, he could end up with some really nasty road rash.

With a loud bang, Hugo shot out in clouds of white smoke. Like a comet with its white tail of stellar dust, he rose thirty feet toward the top of the tent, traveling at a hundred miles per hour.

Mixed thoughts raced through his mind as he felt the thrill of free flight. He knew that great harm could come to him if anything went wrong. He bent his body like an Olympic diver and plunged toward the net. Seconds later, he landed on his back in the net at the far end of the circus tent. He bounced up and down a few times, leapt to his feet and waved to the crowd. They roared their approval. He somersaulted off the net and strode out of the tent. In the following years, Hugo was injured many times because of failures of the cannon. He also served in the French Foreign Legion in World War I and was one of twelve in his battalion to survive. For his courage in the line of fire, Italy awarded him a gold medal.

NOTES

1. Richard A. Boning, *Getting the Facts: Book D* (Barnell Loft Books, 1997).
2. http://cannon-mania.com/human-cannon.htm.
3. John Kobler, "The Zacchinis," *Life Magazine*, 24, No. 17 (April 26, 1948) 111–16.
4. https://books.google.com/books?id=dOEEAAAMBAJ.

"THE TRUTH WILL MAKE YOU FREE"

One of the very basic beliefs of the CIA is to find the truth. This is most often accomplished through covert operations, spying out the enemy.

In 2005, following a successful meeting to do just that in the Middle East, CIA agent Greg Wright was returning with several other agents to base in a two-car caravan. A large group of local rebels ambushed them on the main highway, firing at the vehicles. Greg steered a zigzag course to avoid being an easy target. The ambushers kept after them for more than twenty-five miles, all the while firing at the fleeing cars, more than a hundred bullets, but luckily none of the agents were hit.

Enemy fire pierced the engine compartment, causing the motor to sputter and fail. It burst into flames, and smoke began to seep from under the dashboard. The men tumbled from the car into the open line of fire, taking a defensive position, but one was shot. Greg's real job was to protect employees; that is what he did by placing himself to shield the wounded man who quickly bandaged his own wound. They ran for a safer location.

In the dash for better cover, a bullet struck Greg in the leg. They hid behind a wall until a team from headquarters arrived, evening the odds. The rebels fled. The team transported the two wounded men to a base hospital for treatment. The friend survived, but Greg did not. The bullet struck an artery, and he bled to death before treatment could be administered.

Handsome Greg Wright was born in the Naval Hospital on the Marine Corps base in Quantico, Virginia. His dad was a military man, which required moving often as assignments changed. Greg lived in fifteen places in the first thirteen years of his life. Keeping up in school wasn't a problem, and he became highly skilled at making new friends. The family ended up back in Quantico, where his dad opened an Irish pub to sell the famous Irish ale. It was working in his father's pub that Greg developed his ability to meet and connect with people.

During that time, he also reconnected with his former school friends. Following graduation in 1990, he entered the Virginia Military Institute (VMI), played football, and was chief of the VMI Emergency Response Team. He served as a volunteer with the firefighters and rescue squad. He loved his time working as an ambulance driver. Upon graduation from the Virginia Military Institute, he signed on for a tour of duty with the US Marines and became an officer. From here he was assigned to advanced infantry in scouting for the troops. Four years later, he mustered out of the US Marines and launched a career as a special security officer. Eventually he ended up working for the CIA. His life with the CIA included traveling all over the world. Here he began his job of protecting the important people in US government—the Steve Case family, Secretary of State Albright, and Director of Central Intelligence George Tenet. He was also assigned to protect the lives of CIA agents, especially in dangerous times. He did his job well—always reliable, resourceful, and friendly. Other agents enjoyed working with him.

His final mission was in the Middle East. He died a hero. His courage and sound judgment under fire saved the lives of those whom he was assigned to protect. They, in turn, recognized his sacrifice as he worked and died while protecting them. Greg's star on the CIA Wall of Honor was carved in 2006. Through his example, he taught others what it means to have courage.

NOTES

1. "History of the CIA," *Central Intelligence Agency*, https://www.cia.gov/about-cia/history-of-the-cia.
2. "Remembering CIA's Heroes: Greg Wright," *Central Intelligence Agency*, https://www.cia.gov/news-information/featured-story-archive/2015-features-greg-wright.

LUCKY LINDY

It was the infancy of air flight. At the time, Charles Lindbergh was working as a mail pilot. He heard of the $25,000 prize for the pilot of the first flight between New York and Paris. With backing from a group of St. Louis businessmen, Lindbergh hired some men to build a special plane. For supplies he packed four sandwiches, two canteens of water, and 451 gallons of gasoline. When he reached New York, he was met with bad weather. He looked at the wet, muddy airfield and thought of all the things that might happen while trying to take off in the water, holes, and mud.

Since he was competing with other pilots, he could not delay his flight. A weather report predicted a break in the stormy conditions—the perfect time to take off. He climbed into his small airplane, the *Spirit of St. Louis*, and taxied down the runway. Because the field was soft from the rain, and the plane was heavily loaded, it gathered speed slowly. After passing the halfway mark, he decided that he would be able to clear the buildings at the end of the runway.

The rain came again and the wind blew, bouncing the small plane around in the air. When he flew into a clearing in the clouds, he could see the inky, purple ocean below. It looked like a huge, thick blanket covering the earth. Sometimes he saw mountains of ice that thrust up through the blanket. He thought mostly of reaching the English coast and then on to France. The hours of flying made him tired, yet he knew he must stay awake. Ice formed on the wings like cement on paper. He had to fly lower at times, barely above the ocean's surface, skimming only ten feet above

ROY RUSSELL

the waves so that the water reached up like groping fingers to splash over the wheels.

Darkness set in at about 8:15 p.m. and a thin, low fog formed over the sea, but the white icebergs showed up through the fog so that Lindbergh could use them to measure altitude. There was no moon, only the palpable darkness. Storm clouds piled thousands of feet above him.

On he flew, guiding his plane toward the European coast. As the second day approached, light began to show like shiny coins strewn across the horizon. As the light grew, he spotted some tiny fishing boats below. He thought, *Land can't be far away.*

He flew over the first boat but saw no signs of life. He circled the second and a man's face appeared in a window. On earlier flights, Lindbergh had talked to people on the ground by flying low and shouting a question to them. The people usually answered with a signal. He decided to try it with the man in the boat. "Which way is Ireland?" Lindbergh shouted. He hoped the man would point the way, but the man did nothing. He suddenly realized that he might not speak English.

In the distance, he saw some small mountains. "The coastline should be appearing soon," he said. At 150 feet he was well above the water. The coast came down from the north and curved to the east. *It's the southwest coast of Ireland,* he thought. For several more hours he continued his flight toward Paris. The sun faded like a dying grass fire shortly after he flew over Cherbourg. Before him the lights came on like glowing embers along the landing strip.

Lindbergh nosed his plane closer to the lights. He could see the roads all jammed with cars and people. He could hear the car horns sending up a clamorous noise. He flew low over the crowd and touched the plane down, bouncing a couple of times on the grassy field. A sudden shout of thousands of voices greeted him. The crowds surged toward him like an ocean surf pulsating with life. When he opened the door, he was lifted down onto the shoulders of the police. They carried him through the crowd. "Vive," many of them shouted.

Charles "Lindy" Lindbergh had achieved what he set out to do: fly solo, nonstop across the Atlantic, some three thousand miles—in a record thirty-three hours. He won the prize and the hearts of Americans and French alike. Lindy was the spirit of adventure and success. He was one of the courageous.

NOTES

1. Richard A. Boning, *Getting the Facts: Book F* (Barnell Loft Books, 1997).
2. http://www.centennialofflight.net/essay/Lindbergh.
3. http://charleslindbergh.com/history/paris/asp. (Robert Ragozzino.)

EXPLORING THE
COLORADO

Having only one arm did not stop thirty-five-year-old John Wesley Powell from exploring the Colorado River. It didn't even stop him from completing his tour of duty in the battles of Champion Hill and Black River Bridge in the American Civil War.

Powell left the army with the rank of major. On trips to the West, he decided to explore the Grand Canyon and the Colorado River. So on May 26, 1869, two weeks after the railroads joined in Utah, he and nine other men began their odyssey. It was to become a truly magnificent journey—unlike any other. He and the men pushed their boats, not much more than huge dugouts, from the shore and paddled down the Green River through Flaming Gorge in Wyoming. Many people lined the river to shout and cheer as the daring men quickly disappeared in the tumbling water. They thought to themselves, *We'll never see them again.*

Running rapids was about as dangerous as anything a man could do. The river was like an angry tiger with a yawning mouth, its submerged boulders like sharp teeth ready to devour anything that came their way. As Powell approached a steep trough at one of the first rapids, one of the boats twisted sideways and crashed on huge boulders. It capsized, tossing men and supplies into the churning water. They bounced like bobbins downstream with the swift current. The others increased their paddling to catch the disappearing men. Only when the men scrambled onto a sandbar could Powell and the others catch them. He had failed to stow his supplies equally in the four boats, so most of them were swept away with the destroyed craft.

In the following days, they raced through more rapids. Fear became a constant companion. After three weeks and the first eighty miles, one of the men told Powell, "I've had more excitement than a man deserves in a lifetime—I'm leaving." He climbed out of the canyon and walked away. He found a Native American settlement in southwestern Utah where he lived for many years with the band of Paiutes who hunted in the area.

Those who remained did not know what to expect day to day, but they finally arrived where the Green River joined the Grand River. Here the two mighty rivers became the magnificent Colorado. The river was made muddy by smaller rivers that flowed into it, carrying the red sand and clay from the mesas. Someone looked at the water. "The river is too thick to drink and too thin to plow," he said. The humor was welcome and everybody laughed.

The rapids became powerful tumblers like washing machines thrashing clothes. Massive boulders barred the way in many channels. Along the sides, sandstone walls looked like ribbon candy that soared a mile high. Royal arches and alcoves bridged eroded gulches. Mounds and monuments greeted them at every bend. More rapids tested their courage and strength. Finally, it became more than some men could endure. At Separation Rapids, three more men decided to throw in the towel. They could see only danger and possible death ahead. Surely, there was danger as there had been behind. But their fear did not infect those who stayed.

Powell left a boat for them in case they decided to return. They could not convince Powell to abandon his quest. He remained as stubborn as a cranky mule. The three men climbed out of the canyon August 28, and headed for the Shivwits camp near St. George, Utah. They were mistaken for miners who had killed a native woman and the Shivwits killed them for it.

It was unfortunate that they had left the expedition because just a day later, Powell and the remaining five men reached the mouth of the Virgin River where it empties into the Colorado. They were met by settlers in the area. Powell had completed his river raft of the dangerous and uncharted river to prove his theory that the river preceded the canyon and cut through the land. His courage had carried him through. He returned to Illinois as a national hero.

NOTES

1. http://www.nps.gov/history/online_books/geology/publications/inf/74-24se.

2. J. W. Powell, *Canyons of the Colorado* (New York: Dover Publications, 1895).

3. Margaret S. Bearnson, "John Wesley Powell," *Utah History Encyclopedia*, http://www.uen.org/utah_history_encyclopedia/p/POWELL_JOHN.html.

4. "John Wesley Powell: Soldier, Explorer, Scientist," *USGS*, https://www.nps.gov/parkhistory/online_books/geology/publications/inf/74-24/sec1.htm.

5. Bob Symon, "Man Who Mapped Grand Canyon Thankful For Long Underwear," *Symon Sez*, http://symonsez.wordpress.com/2010/07/08/man-who-mapped-grand-canyon.

CRASH LANDING

The Chance Vought F4U-1 Corsair fighter circled the downed plane sitting on the mountainside with its injured pilot. The Corsair was one of the 12,251 built with six .50-caliber machine guns and eight five-inch rockets mounted under the fuselage. A carryover from World War II, the Corsair was an outdated flying machine. At the controls was Lieutenant Tom Hudner, graduate of the Naval Academy. On December 4, 1950, he and his seven fellow flyers had zoomed into the air off the USS *Leyte,* anchored off the coast of Inchon in South Korea. The drone of their collective engines sounded like Whistling Death, a nickname the Japanese had given them.

Two months earlier, they had begun close air support for ground troops in Korea. Now they were headed to the Chosin Reservoir where several thousand American troops were surrounded by larger numbers of Chinese. Everything seemed to be going smoothly with the flyers until Tom heard on his radio, "I think I may have been hit. I've lost my oil pressure and I'm going to have to go in." He knew his flying buddy was in serious trouble as he watched his fellow pilot fight to control the Corsair. The engine was dead and there was no place to run to. Below, all were snow-covered mountains and below-zero temperatures. The mountains were crawling with hidden enemy soldiers. Tom knew it would be a wheels-up, dead-stick landing. He watched in horror as the Corsair slammed against the mountainside. Clouds of snow masked the craft, then dropped away. The plane was shattered, the engine ripped away, the fuselage torn apart at the cockpit. Light reflected from the closed cockpit glass. Everyone thought their flying buddy was dead.

Before flying away, Tom made one more pass. His heart leapt and the blood coursed through his body. He flew lower to see his buddy waving from the wreckage. The wing commander pulled away to radio for some helicopter support. All the pilots kept circling like lazy hawks in the sky. Tom could see that his buddy was not trying to get out. Either he was badly injured or he was pinned in the wreckage.

Tom didn't have to think twice. "I'm going in," he radioed to his wing commander. Protecting his flying buddy from the enemy was his single thought. He also knew there was only one way—and that was the same way his buddy had made his crash landing. He decided to crash-land an expensive, perfectly good American fighter plane on a steep, snow-covered, Korean mountainside. The other pilots were stunned by Tom's decision. He made a wheels-up crash landing a few yards uphill from his downed buddy. The plane hit the rock-hard ground and rumbled to a stop like a huge tank that had lost its tread. Out and running, he found his buddy in terrible pain from frozen hands, yet as calm as a spring morning, despite being trapped under the buckled instrument panel. Tom struggled to free his friend, but the wreckage held him pinned like helpless prey in a spider's tangled web. Turning the radio switch in the wrecked Corsair could ignite the gas that leaked around the plane. The radio in his own plane still worked. From the safer wreck, he could call for rescuers to bring axes.

Returning to the wreckage, he found his friend's wool scarf which he wrapped around the injured man's hands and replaced the aviator's cap on his exposed head. He knew that wrapping the scarf around the man's hands was more of a gesture than a remedy, but what else could he do?

The helicopter arrived and a man jumped out with the axes and an extinguisher. It ran out of repellant quickly, and smoke continued to rise. They pounded the mangled instrument panel and crumpled cockpit, but with no success. The sun was setting behind the mountains, and the helicopter was not equipped for night flying. Tom could not release his friend. He was told it was time to go. He said, "One of the worst things when something has happened to you is the feeling that you're alone. Just being with him to give some comfort was worth the effort."

NOTES

1. www.airportjournals.com/display.cgm/vannuys.0501033.

2. Allan Bourdius, "LTJG Thomas J. Hudner, Jr., USN," *Their Finest Hour*, http://theirfinesthour.net/?s=LTJG+Thomas+Hudner.

3. http://www.history.navy.mil/photos/pers-us-uspers-h/t-hudner.htm.

4. "The Brotherhood of Soldiers at War: Thomas Hudner and Jesse LeRoy Brown," *Home of Heroes*, http://www.homeofheroes.com/brotherhood/hudner.html. (Doug Sterner.)

THE JOURNEY IS
THE DESTINATION

Dan had everything going for him. Wise beyond his years, gifted beyond measure, inquisitive to the point of agitation, and multi-talented, he was one of those kids who knew that living life was more exciting than learning it from a book. The son of a British dad and an American mom, Dan Eldon had the gene for travel. By the time he was twenty-one, he had visited forty-six countries. He added to his wanderings by studying seven languages, sometimes in school, but mostly out.

As for that part of his life, he developed a phobia of school at the British school in Kenya. His vicious math teacher attacked him regularly with a sneaker. He was able to talk his parents into letting him transfer to the International School in Kenya. There, he mixed with kids from forty-six countries. He had escaped the suffocating walls of traditional classrooms and could push the limits of his energy. While still in school, he became a journalist like his mother. He took an assignment in Somalia only to discover the country was in the middle of a civil war. He shouldn't have gone. Living in a Masai village was a joy as was the trip to strangely beautiful Lamu Island, and climbing Mount Kenya. He lived through the attempted coup in Kenya and its aftermath. He went with his mother on assignments and published the photos from his trips.

He was only fourteen when he started a fundraiser to gather money to pay for a young Kenyan girl's heart surgery. He seemed to have a native instinct to help others. Fundraising for good causes was a regular part of his young life. At fifteen, he helped support a Masai family by buying their handmade jewelry, which he then sold to friends.

In 1988, Dan graduated as the Most Outstanding Student from the International School. He took a breather from school before entering college and worked as a writer for *Mademoiselle Magazine* in New York. College began at Pasadena City College in California. Six months later, he and a friend drove a Land Rover across Africa. The safest place to sleep at night was in jails, to the amusement of jail keepers.

Armed with new knowledge from his trip, Dan enrolled at UCLA in Los Angeles. The first thing he did was organize a charity. With friends, he raised thousands of dollars to buy three vehicles. They traveled to a refugee camp in Malawi where they donated one of their vehicles, some money for needed water wells, and blankets. He returned with handmade jewelry that he sold to merchants on fashionable Rodeo Drive in Beverly Hills.

College did not hold his attention like adventure did. The semester back at UCLA was spent planning his next trip. After several intervening stops for work on a movie, taking photos of a famine, and watching the marines land at Mogadishu, Dan decided to stay there. He was horrified by the violence and tragedy he recorded with his camera. By this time, Dan was an accepted professional photographer.

Pakistani peacekeepers were sent to try to stop the killing but were killed in the attempt. This turned a civil war into an international one. United Nations forces bombed what they thought to be the headquarters of the killers of the peacekeepers, but ended up killing about fifty Somali civilians in the air raid. Local citizens became enraged. In the ensuing confusion, mobs turned their anger on anyone around. Four international photographers became their targets. The mob attacked them with large rocks and heavy clubs, beating them to death in the streets. Among the four was courageous twenty-two-year-old Dan Eldon. His destination was a short journey.

NOTES

1. Dan Eldon, *The Journey is the Destination: The Journals of Dan Eldon*, ed. Kathy Eldon (San Francisco: Chronicle Books, 1997).
2. "Introduction," *Dan Eldon*, accessed May 26, 2016, http://www.daneldon.org/about /introduction/. (Kathy Eldon.)
3. Dan Eldon, "Meeting Ralph: An Essay," *Dan Eldon*, http://www.daneldon.org /twenty-years-on/meeting-ralph-an-essay/.
4. "Dan Eldon," *Wikipedia*, http://en.wikipedia.org/wiki/Dan_Eldon.
5. Mike Eldon, "Being Dan," http://www.daneldon.org/about/family/mike/.

6. Alice Steinbach, "He Gave His Heart, and Life, to Somalia," *The Baltimore Sun* (March 27, 1994). (Permission to use—Editor Andy.)

7. Faiza Elmasry, "Brief Singular Life Inspires Creative Activists," *Voice of America*, http://www.voanews.com/content/extraordinary-short-life-inspires -activists-135945763 /163300.html.

RACING AT THE TOP
OF THE WORLD

Ice storms snap trees and poles, crush buildings and power plants, and freeze vegetation. With one-hundred-mile-per-hour winds howling like a pack of lonely wolves and temperatures below negative seventy degrees, they blister human skin. They can also kill. Susan Butcher knew this, yet she still pushed her dogs through a raging storm and the blinding whiteness of the Alaskan wilderness. She was determined to win the Iditarod sled race this time.

The Inupiaq and Athabaskan peoples used the Iditarod trail hundreds of years ago, before the Russian fur traders came in the 1880s. For many years, the trail served as a supply route to carry materials from the coastal towns to the gold mining camps. Mushers hauled mail and supplies to Iditarod and Nome, then turned around and brought out gold. In 1925, the trail became world-famous when teams of dogs and mushers relayed diphtheria serum to isolated Nome.

In 1973, this trail was changed from a supply route to a modern sports event site. Susan Butcher urged her dogs along this famous trail. The idea was to celebrate the 1925 Last Great Race on Earth. It takes competitors more than one thousand miles from Anchorage to Nome. Mushers and their dog teams are always at the mercy of hungry or enraged wild animals. Susan was enjoying the thrill of holding first place until she came upon a starving moose. She thought that something was wrong; the animal was just skin and bones. Its eyes were sunken bullet holes. Instead of turning and running away, the moose lowered its head, snorted, and charged like a thundering rhino, with horns aimed at the bewildered dogs, plowing like a locomotive into the defenseless team. *She's going to run through me!* Susan thought.

To avoid a clash, Susan threw the sled on its side. She knew the moose had plenty of room to pass, but it came into the team and stomped. She screamed, making as much noise as she could. The dogs scrambled to get out of the way, but they were strapped to the sled. With wild rage, the moose stomped and kicked and gored the cowering dogs. The animal charged at Susan who fought the beast with an ax and her parka.

"Get away!" Susan screamed. "Get away! Get out of here!" She continued to defend herself with the ax and slapping her parka into the animal's face. It was almost like a dream, unreal, yet Susan knew she was fighting for her life and the lives of her dogs. A freezing fear gripped her and she felt her blood surge in her brain. She fought the beast for twenty minutes.

Finally, after what seemed like forever, another musher arrived. Together, Susan and her rescuer fought the moose. "We have to do something," the man said. He grabbed his rifle from his sled and shot the demented moose, but not before it had killed two of Susan's valuable dogs and injured a dozen others.

The tragedy cost Susan the race, but in 1986, she raced to the finish line first. She did it again in 1987 and 1988. She missed 1989, but won again in 1990. She was the only person to win the Iditarod three times in a row. She was named athlete of the year, won many awards, and became world-famous. Governor Sarah Palin declared Susan Butcher Day to be the first day of every March.

NOTES

1. "Iditarod," *Alaska Public Lands Information Centers*, http://www.alaskacenters.gov /iditarod.cfm.
2. Patrick Hughes, *American Weather Stories* (U.S. Dept. of Commerce, 1976).
3. Dominik Mazur, "Susan Butcher Biography—Loved Animals, Hated the City, Began Preparing for the Iditarod, A Dangerous Run-in With A Moose,"
4. http://sports.jrank.org/pages/716/Butcher-Susan.html. (Dominik Mazur.)

BIRD WOMAN

She was fifteen years old when she led the Lewis and Clark expedition through the Pacific Northwest. She was a small woman, if a girl at fifteen can be called a woman. At age twelve, she was taken captive by a Hidatsa war party, enemies of her people, the Shoshones. Taken from her home in the Rockies, she lived in what is today North Dakota. Her life there may have improved when she was sold to Toussaint Charbonneau, a French Canadian fur trader. Of course, during her life with her new husband, she learned French. This knowledge would be a valuable asset when, at age fifteen, she led Lewis and Clark on their intrepid journey through the Pacific Northwest.

In 1803, Meriwether Lewis and William Clark led the Corps of Discovery, a group of forty-five men, to the Mandan and Hidatsa village. Lewis was an army captain, the secretary to President Jefferson, and the party's naturalist. Clark was a lawyer, Native American agent, territorial governor, and explorer soldier. It was here, at the Mandan and Hidatsa village, that they met the Bird Woman, whose real name was Sacagawea. Before the trip was over, they would have written her name into their journals seventeen times and every time in a different spelling.

Clark wrote in his journal that Charbonneau offered to join the expedition to interpret the tribal dialects. Sacagawea also joined them. As it turned out, understanding each other was not easy. Sacagawea spoke Gros Ventre, a Native American dialect, to her husband. Speaking French, he passed what she said to another man who spoke both French and English. He then spoke English in the last translation to Lewis and Clark. Sacagawea also used a lot of sign language.

By the time they were ready to leave the Mandan village, Sacagawea gave birth to a healthy boy on February 11, 1805. She named her son Jean Baptiste Charbonneau. He would become America's youngest explorer. For now, Clark called him Pompey, or Pomp. Along the Yellowstone River, near where the Missouri and Yellowstone flow together, Clark carved "W Clark July 25, 1806," into a huge rock formation. He named the rock Pompey's Pillar. Pomp became Clark's little dancing boy. He rode with Sacagawea in the boats and on her back when she traveled. When they arrived at the Shoshone village, Sacagawea found that the new chief was her brother. Through her efforts, the expedition was able to buy badly needed horses.

Food was not always at hand; Sacagawea quickly made her knowledge of edible plants known. She kept busy in her search for wild artichokes. Picking up a sturdy driftwood stick, she stuck it into the ground to dig for a supply of the roots. Along the way, she gathered and stored wild edibles, gathering the delicious berries that grew along the riverbanks

Raging winds came out of the canyons and gullies along the river. Charbonneau was at the helm in a Cajun pirogue, a boat about sixteen feet long, five feet wide, and three feet deep, with a flat bottom. In addition to various supplies, Lewis and Clark had stored important papers in the boat. A strong gust of wind, like an unseen hand, lifted the boat onto its side. Both Lewis and Clark could only watch in horror at what happened next. "Charbonneau can't swim," Clark cried out. "He's the most timid waterman in the world. He's letting the pirogue lie on its side for too long. Set sail, man!" Lewis yelled from the larger keelboat. The craft began to fill with water. Charbonneau was still crying to his god for mercy and did nothing to right the rudder. "It will capsize!" Clark cried. Not even repeated orders would bring the man to his senses.

The crisis was suddenly solved. A bowman, with muscles to spare, aimed his rifle at Charbonneau. "You useless coward," he bellowed, "Right the pirogue before I shoot you!" The man obeyed as quickly as a whipped dog.

Sacagawea dived into the river and swam as smooth as a dolphin to gather the papers and supplies. Without wasted movements she plucked the valuable documents from a watery grave and pushed them toward the pirogue. The courageous explorers learned that Charbonneau was not the best of helmsmen, and the little boat would continue to be a thorn in their sides.

As a member of the expedition, Sacagawea saved it several times from being attacked by suspicious tribes. Since war parties never traveled with a woman and a baby, bands that they met did not feel threatened and were usually friendly. When the explorers met with tribal chiefs, Sacagawea translated for everyone.

The following spring, they headed for home. Sacagawea remembered the trails from her childhood. Without mistake, like a homing pigeon, she led them along. At the Mandan camp her services ended. For all she had done, she received nothing—the Americans did not even remember to thank her. Sacagawea was one of those rare creatures who comes to earth with bravery as a middle name. She surely had a clear vision of what was before her, glory and danger alike, and went out to meet them. She taught the explorers the meaning of courage.

NOTES

1. http://www.america.gov.
2. "The Story of Sacagawea," *America's Story from America's Library*, http://www .americaslibrary.gov/es/nd/es_nd_sacgwea_1.html.
3. "Sacagawea Biography," *Biography Base*, http://www.biographybase.com/biography /Sacagawea.html.
4. http://www.defense.gov/specials/nativeamerican01/sacagawea.html.
5. Markus Franke, "Sacagawea: Lewis and Clark Interpreter on New Coin," *Kalamalama*, http://www3.hpu.edu/kalamalama/archive/2608/sub/People01.htm.
6. http://www.lewisandclarktrail.org.
7. "Sacagawea," *National Park Service*, http://www.nps.gov/jeff/historyculture/sacagawea .htm.

PLOWING THE EARTH

When the Romans were in power, they had plows more efficient than the Americans had at the time of the Revolution. Somewhere between AD 500 and 1775, the knowledge for making useable plows was forgotten. Farmers sometimes attached rawhide or an iron point to the stick. What was needed was a device to dig deeper furrows, a small ditch, in which farmers would sow seeds. Western American soil was too hard and clay-like for seeds to take root in just a tiny scratch.

Several men tried to invent a workable plow. Thomas Jefferson designed one with the proper curve but never carried through on it. Blacksmiths did make some, but only by special order. Along came Charles Newbold. He got a patent in 1797, just after the Revolutionary War, for the first practical plow: a pointed, curved piece of cast iron. Others followed, but none of their plows really worked in the hard, clay-packed soil of the Midwest and western America. These plows broke easily, and the lumpy clay stuck to the blades like dough in a bread mixer.

Onto the scene came John Deere. When the deep economic recession of 1837 settled over the country, he left his family to seek his fortune in Illinois. He quickly learned that the new pioneers were struggling with the tough soil. Having to stop every few feet to clean their plows was a pain and made tilling the soil and planting crops a nasty chore. They labored for hours but could not produce much.

There is a saying that success is 90 percent inspiration and 10 percent perspiration. So it was with John Deere, who had grown up working in his father's tailor shop in Vermont. Pushing needles through tough leather

264

and rawhide was impossible except for the strongest of men. Since John was built like a gladiator with muscles to spare, he found that he could push the needles through leather more easily than others. He also found that he could push the needles even more easily if he polished them. If he ran the needles through sand many times, he could sharpen them and they became like daggers. This inspiration was all that he needed to solve the problem with the plows. He could easily polish them like the needles, so he invented a highly polished steel and a correctly shaped moldboard. It became known as the self-scouring plow.

John Deere set up a manufacturing plant and made cast steel plows. He sold the first one to a local farmer, Lewis Crandall. The farmer was ecstatic with the success that he had. Of course, he spread the word, and soon two more farmers wanted plows. By 1841, John Deere was making one hundred plows a year. By 1855, he had opened a factory in Moline, Illinois, and was making more than ten thousand plows a year.

Deere insisted on making high-quality farm implements. He said, "I will never put my name on a product that does not have in it the best that is in me." You are as good as the best thing you've ever done.

Certainly, it takes raw courage to walk away from home at seventeen, move west with the settling of the country, and invent useful products like John Deere did.

NOTES

1. Neil M. Clark, "John Deere: He Gave to the World the Steel Plow," *Green Magazine* (September 1986), http://rainbeau.tripod.com/deere.html.
2. David R. Collins, *Pioneer Plowmaker: A Story about John Deere* (New York: Carolrhoda Books, 1990).
3. "Our Company," https://www.deere.com/en_US/corporate/our_company/our _company.page?.
4. "John Deere blog," http://johndeereblog.blogspot.com.

VOYAGE TO THE MOON

All systems go!" came the voice over the public address. "Ten . . . nine . . . eight . . . seven . . . six . . . five . . . four . . . three . . . two . . . one!" Someone in NASA's command center pushed a button. A blast of flame shot out from under the five-story machine and the Saturn V rocket began to lift off.

Jules Verne would have loved to be alive for this event when the United States launched its spaceflight to the moon. The site he chose for his imaginary spacecraft was only a few miles away from where NASA launched Apollo 11 in July 1969. Inside the pod were American astronauts Neil Armstrong, Edwin "Buzz" Aldrin, and Michael Collins. They were the first humans to attempt a landing on the moon.

Armstrong was offered the post of commander of Apollo 11. During the launch his heart rate reached a rate of 109 beats per minute. He would have liked to have covered his ears against the roar of the rocket's engines because they sounded like the roar of a dozen blast furnaces, much louder than his ride in the Gemini 8 launch. The fact that the Apollo had more inside room than the Gemini probably allowed for more shaking and inner turbulence.

As the earth receded beneath them, the astronauts could not help but wonder if they would ever return. The objective was to land safely on the moon. A touchdown in a specific spot would be an ideal landing, but safety was more important. On Earth, millions watched and also wondered if the three brave men would make it back.

Twelve minutes after liftoff, Apollo 11 entered orbit. They orbited the earth one and a half times before the S-IVB engine launched Saturn V into its spaceflight. The craft and its human cargo lurched toward the moon and a date with destiny, immortal fame, and elevation to heroic status.

Following the trans-lunar injection, which moves the rocket from its nearly circular Earth orbit into an elliptical orbit burn, the Command/ Service Module separated from the Saturn V rocket and remained in orbit. It rotated and docked like a ship with the Lunar Module. The United States had successfully landed six moon landers between 1969 and 1972. Apollo 11 was a bridge to the future, as timeless as the pyramids. American space technology had come of age.

On July 19, Apollo 11 passed behind the moon where Armstrong fired its service propulsion engine to enter lunar orbit. Armstrong guided the *Eagle*, the Apollo 11 Lunar Module, around the moon thirty times. Days came and melted away like snowflakes. On each pass, the three men peered through the tiny window at their landing site located in the Sea of Tranquility, a particular place on the moon's surface that was smooth, without rough terrain or ravines. The name seemed to fit the geography of the site. It was a land bleached by the fiery sun and desolate to view.

They were awed by what they saw. Chills rippled through them. The hair stood up on the backs of their necks. Their knuckles turned white as they gripped the controls harder. They began a descent to land. The navigation guidance system set off several program alarms that distracted the crew causing Armstrong to notice that the spaceship was passing landmarks about four seconds early. This would cause them to miss their target by several miles.

The computer had them landing in an area covered with boulders and on the edge of a four-hundred-meter crater. It was the classic moonscape, but not the safest place on the moon to land a fragile spacecraft. Armstrong took manual control of the *Eagle*. He had to find a safer site.

Fuel was running low. The rendezvous radar was not needed for the landing, but Armstrong switched it on in case they had to stop the landing. With fuel to last only a few more seconds, he guided the craft to a friendlier landing surface, before setting it down. They had also been fed the wrong information—premature low fuel warnings. Had they known at the time, lunar gravity—about one-sixth of what is felt on the surface of the earth—allowed much more fuel slosh. One fuel sensor had become naked and failed to perform its needed function.

These were tense moments for the crew. They held their collective breath as the *Eagle* settled into the lunar dust. They were a bit fearful, yet eager, to be on the moon's surface and about the business of exploring its landscapes. The crew could see the bright highlands pitted with dark plains. They had read Galileo's notes on overlapping craters to learn that the moon surface was over 2,200 miles around. As the astronauts landed, they could easily see the curve of the moon's surface. The brilliant light of the sun cut across the surface at an extremely low angle. Shadows seemed to grow endlessly. They were 250,000 miles from home on a space body that has no wind or oxygen. The contact light flashed on. Armstrong, Aldrin, and Collins knew that the Lunar Module had touched ground. As it settled, Aldrin ordered, "Okay. Engine stop." Armstrong ordered the next step, "Shutdown." Then came the words that 450 million people on earth waited for: "Houston, Tranquility Base here. The *Eagle* has landed." If the three men in the module could have heard, they would have rejoiced in the mighty roar from Earth.

Armstrong and Aldrin shook hands and patted each other on the back. After some preparation, Armstrong climbed out and down the few steps to the moon's surface. He described what he saw. "The surface appears to be very fine grain. Very fine grain. Almost like powder." He lifted his foot. Millions of people mentally stepped with him as a single man in a white space suit stepped off the footpad and into history. He stepped onto the moon's surface and onto another world. Since the moon has no atmosphere or erosion, his footprints will be there forever.

For every human who heard his next words, they are like carved granite in the human mind. "One small step for [a] man; one giant leap for mankind."

In addition to fulfilling President Kennedy's desire to land a man on the moon before the end of the decade, Apollo 11 was a positive statement of the Apollo system and the genius and courage of the American mind and will. Armstrong and his Apollo 11 crew are fine examples of that bravery and courage.

NOTES

1. "Who Was Neil Armstrong?," *NASA* (August 28, 2012), http://www.nasa.gov/audience/forstudents/5-8/features/who-was-neil-armstrong-58.html.

2. "Biography of Neil Armstrong," *NASA* (December 18, 2012), http://www.nasa.gov/centers/glenn/about/bios/neilabio.html.

3. "Neil Armstrong: 1930–2012," *NASA*, http://www.nasa.gov/topics/people/features/armstrong_obit.html.

4. "Apollo-11," *Kennedy Space Center*, http://science.ksc.nasa.gov/history/apollo/apollo-11/apollo-11.html.

MAN OF MANY WORDS

As hard as he tried, Noah Webster could not get people to use alphabetic spelling. It would have made spelling and pronouncing words much easier. It was probably too logical for most people. He and Benjamin Franklin lived at the same time, and both agreed that simplified spelling would be a great improvement in language usage. They succeeded in merely getting rid of some useless letters.

Noah was born in Hartford to farmers. At the time, few people ever went to college, but he loved learning so much, his parents let him go to Yale in Connecticut. He left for New Haven in 1774, the year of the Boston Tea Party. When he graduated four years later, the Revolutionary War was over. To earn the money for law school, he taught in public education. Eventually, he graduated from what was the first law school in America.

American schools were not really schools at all. At times, seventy or more children were crammed into one room. They had no desks, the poorest of books, and teachers who just walked in off the streets. What books they had came from England. That was kind of silly, Noah thought. Americans should have their own lesson books. In 1783, he wrote and published his own textbook: *A Grammatical Institute of the English Language.* At the same time, he compiled a speller—a book that teaches spelling.

People called his speller the "Blue-Backed Speller," as it had a blue cover. For one hundred years, teachers used this speller to teach children how to read, spell, and pronounce English words. It was the most popular book in America. People were eager to learn. Before his speller, people spelled words however they could.

Noah never forgot his dream of trying to simplify the English language. With the continued sales of his speller, he had a steady income. Not having to labor or teach, he devoted his time to writing the true and complete dictionary. There was a very good reason for writing a standard dictionary. Travel and communication at the time were slow. People living in different parts of the country spoke, spelled, and pronounced the same words differently. Noah believed that Americans should have a common language that everyone spoke. He did make minor changes that departed from English spellings: "colour" became "color," and "musick" became "music." He added words that were native to America. After twenty-seven years of compiling and writing, in 1806, he was able to publish his book.

Today, we write "catalog" instead of "catalogue," "honor" instead of "honour," "plow" instead of "plough," and many other familiar words that were once spelled with extra letters. Regardless of the quirks, the strange words, the odd meanings, and the language, Noah Webster's work has been a guide for writers trying to navigate the tricky language called English. It has great value especially when navigating the American language. Noah's dictionary is probably one of the most valuable books ever written for Americans, as English is said to be the second most difficult language on the face of the earth.

Two brothers, Charles and George Merriam, purchased the rights to Noah's works after his death. In the deal was Noah's *American Dictionary of the English Language* from 1828 containing seventy thousand words. He left a heritage that lives to this day which is contained in the *Merriam-Webster Dictionary*.

Noah's American dictionary unified the country. When Noah died in 1843, he was considered to be an American hero.

NOTES

1. "Noah Webster's Story," *Noah Webster House and West Hartford Historical Society*, http://noahwebsterhouse.org/discover/noah-webster-biography.htm.
2. Ervin C. Shoemaker, *Noah Webster, Pioneer of Learning* (New York: Columbia University Press, 1936).
3. Patsy Stevens, "Noah Webster: Born in 1758 and Died in 1843," *Garden of Praise* (2001), http://gardenofpraise.com/ibdnoahw.htm.

OVER THE FROZEN SEAS

Before him lay a frozen desert, strangely beautiful in its stark whiteness, like a painting in white, sun bleached like skeleton bones. Everything was dusted with snow, empty, and endless. Ice swells rolled away like ocean waves in every direction. It was a frigid, strange place, where man didn't belong. No greenery, no sound, no life.

Long before the annual Iditarod dog race in Alaska, men were urging their dogs across the frozen ice of North America. In 1909, Robert E. Peary, who had dreamed of making the trip ever since he was six, made his last exploration in search of the North Pole. He called it exploring the roof of the world. He would do it without the benefit of space-age fabrics that keep a man warm in subzero temperatures; no parka, no cell phone, nor advanced navigation device.

He would cross the Greenland ice cap, two million square miles of ice covering most of the land with only snow around him. For weeks, Peary would see only seared sky, brilliant sun, and glare from blinding ice. Sometimes the fog would creep in so dense that even these fragile landmarks could not be seen. He felt entombed.

Risking snow blindness, he dared to make a trip across the cap, which was miles thick, to chart the frozen wastes. On this 1909 trip, he proved that Greenland was an island, not joined to the northern most reaches of the continent. In this region, the temperatures dip to sixty degrees below zero. On a previous try for the North Pole, Peary had lost eight toes. For the rest of his life he would walk without the balance that toes give— shuffling instead of walking.

Each time Peary ventured into the great wilderness of the ice cap, he brought back new information. With increased anticipation, he wanted to reach the North Pole. He and an assistant obtained the help of four Inuits, Egingwah, Ooqueah, Ootah, and Seegloo, who would travel with them. He prepared himself well for his polar odyssey, or epic wanderings over the ice of the frozen seas. He went to learn from the Inuit people who live in the Arctic regions of Canada and Greenland. They taught him how to build an igloo, drive his dog team, and make clothing from skins and furs. He also obtained 133 special dogs, each weighing about seventy pounds. Each dog could pull one hundred pounds of cargo, and each sled was loaded with five hundred pounds of whale meat and supplies.

Peary sat in the basket of the sled and watched the fluid line of dogs run before him, an ever-twisting line of fur against the never-ending field of white. Then the muted yellow and lavender vegetation, snow-dusted evergreens, and craggy hills gave way to endless white snow and ice. Peary felt the loneliness of the place. Were it not for his assistant and the four Inuits, he might even be fearful. Others before him had died on the trails. One expedition was never found. He thought of the possibility of losing his way, of never coming back. He sloughed it off.

From the low vantage point in the sled, Peary saw the dwarf birches with their naked branches painted against the snow. Walls of ice-crusted willows, with their skeletal limbs, passed on either side. The men soon discovered that they were warmer standing behind the basket rather than riding. The excited breathing of the men joined the hiss of the blades through the snow.

Peary chose Cape Columbia, the northernmost point of land in the Canadian Northwest Territories, located on Ellesmere Island, as his jumping-off point. From above, the island looked like a fractured snowflake. It was late March at the time, putting him on the trail in April when night was over, but the winter ice was still strong.

Peary planned to strike straight north over the dangerous, heaving frozen Arctic Ocean. It was a mass of frozen ice floating on the Arctic water. He had traveled at first with twenty-three men on a ship built especially for his needs. The ship could not make it through the thick ice and would be wintered at Cape Sheridan. From there, supplies would be sledged to him along the trail.

They trudged along through endless dunes of ice. Bitter cold came at them from every direction, winds driving temperatures to minus seventy-four degrees. On April 1, the last support team was turned back. They were alone now. The loneliness came rushing back with the isolation and numbing cold.

Only Peary, his assistant, and the four Inuits would make the last leg of the trip. Weary, half frozen, and hungry, Robert E. Peary arrived at the North Pole on April 9, 1909. Peary said, "The Pole at last. The prize of three centuries; my goal for the past twenty years." He raised his arm in a salute to victory.

The dangers and perilous conditions of the polar regions demand a special kind of explorer. He must be willing to risk his life in the pursuit of knowledge. "Nowhere has knowledge been purchased at greater cost or privation and suffering," said a famous Norwegian polar explorer.

In this heroic age of exploration, Robert E. Peary was a courageous and fearless hero.

NOTES

1. http://americanhistory.gov/jb/reform/jb_peary_html.
2. Frederick Cook and Robert E. Peary, *Finding the North Pole* (Washington, DC: W. E. Scull, 1909).
3. http://history.navy.mil/bios/peary_robert.htm.
4. "Northward over the Great Ice," *The Library of Congress*, http://memory.loc.gov /ammem/today/may06.html.
5. Patsy Stevens, "Robert Peary: Arctic Explorer," *Garden of Praise*, http://gardenofpraise .com/bdpeary.htm.
6. Robert E. Peary, *The North Pole* (1910), http://www.gutenberg.org/files/18975/18975 -h/18975-h.htm.

COURAGEOUS TEACHERS

SOCRATES

To the ancient Greeks, thinking was serious business. Greek thinkers applied mathematics and logic to their research. Before then, the human race spent most of its time hunting for food and trying to protect itself. The people were ruled by kings and pharaohs who were tyrants. These rulers made decisions as to who would live and who would die. Society didn't have time for algebra, history, ethics, gravity, math, or social issues.

Among the Greeks were a couple of thinkers, Plato and Socrates, who were part of these wise men. Socrates was Plato's teacher. He was not afraid to think differently or teach new ideas. Change came with the coming of democracy. Socrates questioned everything about the Greek society, from the Athenian government and state religions to the gods themselves.

What he searched for was truth. He believed he could find it by using reason and knowledge. As a teacher, he was able to transfer his ideas to his students. Since he had no classroom, he lectured in public. Anyone could stop to listen. He taught in what became known as the Socratic method. Ask simple questions at first, then move to more complex questions. Using logic and reason, he led the students to a better understanding of the world.

Most governments do not like thinkers; thinkers are dangerous to the forces in power. Socrates questioned everything about the Greek government including its practices, upsetting those in power.

Socrates was put on trial. He was convicted of going against the religion of the state and of corrupting the youth of Athens. He was sentenced to death for his courage to oppose the state. He drank hemlock poison rather than be executed.

ANNE SULLIVAN

Her early life was like a *Grapes of Wrath* story, filled with tragedy. Anne Sullivan was born into a very poor family in 1866, a year after the end of the American Civil War. Her father was mean and had an angry temper. Her mother died of tuberculosis, leaving her to care for her father. Her baby sister and brother were farmed out to some relatives. Eventually, her siblings were sent to the poorhouse where her little brother died as a result of bad treatment.

She later traveled to the Perkins School for the Blind. She hoped to find a cure for the disease that impaired her sight. After many operations, her sight improved enough that she could become a student there. She graduated as valedictorian. To help other children, Anne learned the manual alphabet and worked with a blind and deaf student at the school. This would prepare her for the struggle she would endure with her work with Helen Keller.

Anne got a job in Tuscumbia, Alabama, with the Keller family to help their blind and deaf child, Helen. She and her charge moved into a cottage so that she could work with the child away from her overly protective parents. Helen was as undisciplined as a wild animal. Her parents had never tried to keep her under control. This made Anne's job much harder, but she was able to teach Helen by letting the child touch her throat to feel the vibrations. She spelled letters in Helen's hand, beating them out with her fist. It was kind of like playing "One Potato, Two Potato." Helen learned to read raised letters of the Braille alphabet. She went on to accomplish great things, thanks to her incredible teacher Anne Sullivan.

MRS. ALVEREZ

One day, a mother came to the school to visit with Mrs. Alverez. "You have helped my son, Carlos, this year. Thank you." Tears filled her eyes. "He still cannot read well enough. I worry for him. If you would teach him again, I'm sure he would learn. I think he will be left behind and won't get the help he needs. I beg you. Please stay with him. Teach him to read."

Mrs. Alverez taught in a bad part of the Bronx. Carlos was trying to cope with his parents' breakup. His father ignored him although he lived in the same building. Mrs. Alverez was offered a chance to move to a better school, but now she was faced with a difficult choice. That night she thought about the mother's plea. She knew Carlos's life hinged on his ability to read. Without a teacher to watch out for him, Carlos would fall through the cracks.

The next morning Mrs. Alverez asked her principal to let her move up a grade with Carlos's entire class. When he agreed, she telephoned the new school to turn down her dream job. The year was hard. She struggled with students who didn't care, who didn't want to be there, but she always tried to give Carlos extra help. She was a little sad when his mother did not come back that year.

Carlos moved on. Many years later, Mrs. Alverez, now teaching at another school, left for the day. She dropped a pack of papers that a sudden wind scattered everywhere. Two young men ran to gather them. She smiled at them and said to one of them, "Thank you, young man." His smile was replaced with surprise. He murmured, "Mrs. Alverez?" They knew each other immediately. Carlos was grown, tall and handsome. They embraced. Carlos beamed. The second boy said, "Excuse me, you . . . you're Mrs. Alverez?" In a very serious voice he continued. "You don't know me, but I know you. Last week, Carlos and I graduated from high school. Carlos was valedictorian. In his talk he told the whole school about a teacher named Mrs. Alverez. He said he owed all his success to her. Are you *that* Mrs. Alverez?" She began to cry. Carlos embraced her again.

MOUNA-AL-UMAIRI

National Exam Day determines whether an Iraqi student may advance to the next grade. In the town of Baqubah, 1,300 students were about to be kept from taking the test. Directors of the schools refused to get the tests, and supervisors of the exam refused to come to the school to give the tests. As an excuse, they hid behind the dangers of the ongoing war between the coalition and the Iraqi forces and the al-Qaeda terrorists.

"They have a legal right to take the test," said teacher, Mouna-al-Umairi. That said, she decided to pick up the tests herself. She could not travel by the roads because they were mined. She discovered that most of them were blocked anyway. Another challenge was the Diyala River that she had to cross to get to the precious materials. She braved the dangers of traveling in a combat area where the coalition forces battled the terrorists.

She reasoned, *I don't want the students to lose their morale and think they are being left behind.*

Her second challenge was finding a way. She used any transportation she could: boat, donkey cart, car, even an ambulance. By arriving at the education offices ten minutes late, she met her third challenge—trying to pick up the tests. Bureaucrats at the office called the Center of Education in Baghdad. "She is late," someone said. "Do not give her the tests." She got on the phone with the minister of education. He said, "Tell them you are the minister of education in Diyala and I am authorizing you to take the tests. You will be my representative."

Mouna demanded the tests. She carefully placed the tests in the bag she carried. She was fearful that she might not make it back in time, or make it back at all. Stray bullets and mortar shells kept buzzing passed her all the time. As quickly as possible, she recrossed the river. When she returned she handed out the tests to eager students. She was so overwhelmed that she broke down and cried, but through her courage 1,300 students graduated.

NOTES

1. "Anne Sullivan Macy: Miracle Worker," *American Foundation for the Blind*, http://www.afb.org/annesullivan/. (Helen Selsdon.)
2. "One Courageous Teacher You Should Know," *Blackfive*, (August 15, 2007), http://www.blackfive.net/main/2007/08/one-courageous-.html. (Adapted from the story by Sergeant Armando Monroig, Fifth Mobile Public Affairs Department.)
3. Pete Reilly, "A Teacher's Story," *The Teacher'sPath* (December 20, 2006), http://preilly.wordpress.com/2006/12/20/a-teachers-story.
4. "Ancient Greece," *Ancient Civilizations*, http://ushistory.org/civ/5f.asp. (Doug Heller.)

DOCTRINES
OF MONROE

The best form of government is that which is most likely to prevent the greatest sum of evil," said James Monroe. "It is only when the people become ignorant and corrupt, when they degenerate into a populace, that they are incapable of exercising their own sovereignty." In that condition, the people are easily enslaved. Their enslavement may be by their own leaders. Yet, "Never did a government commence under such favorable circumstances, nor was ever success so complete. If we look to the history of other nations, we find no example of growth so rapid, so gigantic, of a people so prosperous."

James Monroe was born in 1758, about eighteen years before the American Revolution. His term of office was called the Era of Good Feelings. He was the last of the Virginia dynasty; that is, the presidency had been dominated by men from Virginia. By profession, he was a lawyer. By political choice he was a Democratic-Republican. He lived an honorable life as a soldier, diplomat, governor, senator, and cabinet member for previous presidents. By country, he was a patriotic American all the way.

He believed in the purpose of the Revolution. By age seventeen, he had joined the Continental army and fought in several of its battles. At Trenton, his six-foot height, broad, rugged shoulders, and massive rawboned frame made him an easy target for the Hessians he faced. A bullet lodged in one of his shoulders and punctured an auxiliary artery. He began to bleed profusely. A doctor, without adequate medical supplies, poked his finger into the wound and applied pressure to stop the bleeding.

Later, doctors searched for the bullet, but they searched in vain and could not find it. Monroe carried the memento of his fight at Trenton the rest of his life.

As a youthful politician, James Monroe joined the Anti-Federalists. He was a member of the Virginia Convention, which agreed to accept the Constitution that had been written.

He followed Thomas Jefferson's ideas, and in 1790, he was elected to the Senate. Through his efforts, the purchase of the Louisiana Territory was made final, and the vast area of land west of the Mississippi River became part of the United States. In 1836, he became the people's choice for president. For his cabinet, he chose wisely: John C. Calhoun and John Q. Adams, both with his same strong American loyalties.

His Era of Good Feelings did not last. Across the face of the nation, ugly sectional cracks opened, bringing a painful economic depression. But Monroe skillfully navigated the political challenges of his presidency, both inside the United States and outside.

Most people thought that Monroe was a master in dealing with foreign nations. Revolution in South America increased the possibility that European countries would send troops to the Americas. Monroe saw that as a threat to American sovereignty. He went before Congress in 1823 to proclaim the Monroe Doctrine. He outlined a warning for European powers to stay out of the Western Hemisphere.

Because of his strong nationalistic beliefs, he had a network of coastal forts built along the East coast to guard against any future invasions. He remembered all too well the War of 1812, just ten years earlier. His actions helped protect and unify the United States. The Monroe Doctrine, of nearly two hundred years ago, is still alive and enforced today. The most recent time they were enforced was during the Cuban Missile Crisis when President Kennedy warned Russia to stay out of Cuba.

NOTES

1. "U.S. Presidents: James Monroe," *America's Story from America's Library*, http://www americaslibrary.gov/aa/monroe/aa_monroe_subj.html.

2. http://presidents.jamesmonroe.blogspot.com.

3. "Primary Documents in American History: Monroe Doctrine," *The Library of Congress*, http://www.loc.gov/rr/program/bib/ourdocs/Monroe.html.

4. "James Monroe," *The White House*, https://www.whitehouse.gov/1600/presidents /jamesmonroe.

5. Fremont P. Wirth, *The Development of America* (Boston: American Book Co., 1946).

ORDINARY HEROES

AN ICON OF THE MOVIES

Christened Marion Michael Morrison, better known as John Wayne, he was one of Hollywood's most endearing stars. At an early age, he became a movie fan and attended free movies in the building that housed his father's business. He was a good student and a football hero at his high school. He attended the University of Southern California and also played football there. His coach found summer work for him as a movie prop man, where he became lifelong friends with John Ford. In 1939, when Ford thought Wayne was ready, he arranged for him to play the Ringo Kid in what has become his signature performance in the classic *Stagecoach.* When World War II came along, he was rejected as a soldier because of football injuries and because he was married with four children. Fans loved him, although the critics were never kind to him. Not long before he died of cancer, Wayne won Best Actor for his role in *True Grit.* John Wayne, in his personal life and in the roles he played on screen, is a heroic symbol of what is right with America.

A NEW FORM OF MATTER

In high school, Carl Wieman was noted more for being a good chess player than being a good student. He lived among the trees in the woods of Oregon and had to travel miles to school. His parents encouraged him to spend time in the library, and he read many books. He was inspired to pursue his studies in math by a friend's father who was a university professor. He gives credit to a young seventh-grade science teacher who instilled in him his insatiable interest in science. Despite his poor student performance, his attention to studies was sufficient to get him into Massachusetts Institute of Technology (MIT). At MIT, Wieman became deeply involved in physics. As he was short on money, he slept in the lab at the university and showered in the gym. In the lab he did experiments with dye lasers, blasting atoms with his research team. At Stanford, he continued to make advances in atomic science. He and his group succeeded in lowering temperatures in atoms to absolute zero. Of course, behind every successful man is a woman. Wieman credits much of his success to his wife, Sarah, who worked in his lab and edited much of his writing. Dr. Carl Wieman received the Nobel Prize in physics in 2001 for his heroic work with creating Bose-Einstein condensate.

OLD BLOOD AND GUTS

He grew up in a wealthy family where the military was respected. George Patton came from a line of soldiers dating back to the American Revolution. Even though he was an intelligent person, his dyslexia made learning slow. He took five years to complete his four-year program at the United States Military Academy at West Point. He represented the United States in the first historic pentathlon in the 1912 Olympics. In 1916, Patton worked with General John Pershing, who was sent to find Pancho Villa in Mexico. While the two of them worked together in World War I, Patton demonstrated his unique skill with armored equipment. During World War I, he was nicknamed "Old Blood and Guts." He earned this nickname because of the way he threw caution to the wind and waded right into the thick of the battle. He became too innovative for his superiors. They didn't like being shown up by a subordinate. To change this, they put him behind a desk. When the invasion of Normandy was in the making, military brass knew that the man for the job was Patton. He was given command of the Third Army. He pushed his men ahead of other armies headed for Berlin. He was a brilliant military commander who earned the respect of peers and foot soldiers alike. He never lost a battle. He was truly a heroic man.

A WOMAN IN CONGRESS

Because of financial problems, Margaret Chase Smith worked at several jobs just out of high school. This gave the future politician skills in handling and working with people, both personal and political. She married a noted publisher, but he died only four years into the marriage. Prior to his death, he had won a seat in the United States Congress, but with his death, that seat was left vacant. Margaret decided to run as his replacement. She was elected to the House of Representatives in 1948; she was a successful candidate for the United States Senate. She was the only woman in there. Two years later she wrote an important document: The Declaration of Conscience. It was an appeal for fair treatment of the people who were being accused of being subversive; that is, un-American during the McCarthy hearings in the 1950s. It was a heroic stand at the time. Margaret Chase Smith was the first woman to be nominated for President of the United States.

VROOM

It takes a special kind of reckless courage to drive a car around a short oval track at more than one hundred miles per hour. Richard Petty, considered by most to be the greatest NASCAR racing driver in the world, does that. He developed his talent in race car driving after watching his father crash the family car in a stock car rally. He began to work on his father's cars and thought about becoming a mechanic. Once he got his driver's license and discovered the city streets and the dynamics of a three-hundred-horsepower engine, he changed his mind. In 1964, he was given a special Plymouth Superbird. He racked up many victories at Daytona and NASCAR races. He became an icon to other young auto enthusiasts. His trademark is a neatly trimmed mustache; large dark shades; a flashy, wide brimmed cowboy hat; and a red button-down shirt with a collar. Richard Petty holds five Winston cups and two hundred NASCAR wins. Richard was inducted into the Motorsports Hall of Fame in 1997. He's a top ten finisher most of the time, but always a finisher.

HE WAS CALLED THE GIPPER

His life was much like thousands of other kids in early-twentieth-century America. His name was Ronald Reagan. He survived an alcoholic father, which is heroic in and of itself. He was president of the student council and a decent football player. During summers, he worked as a lifeguard. In college he took an interest in acting. Upon graduation in 1932, he signed on as a radio sports announcer. At the same time, he got into the movies. His marriage to talented movie star Jane Wyman lasted from 1940 to 1948. In World War II he rose to the rank of captain.

The fact that he appeared in more than fifty movies attests to his ability as an actor and his appeal to audiences. In his stellar performance in *Knute Rockne All American,* he played the part of George Gipp, "the Great Gipper." Reagan would live with this epithet all his life. In 1952, he married actress Nancy Davis, a real asset who supported him well in his political life. His knowledge of Hollywood politics served him in his bid to be governor of California, where he served two terms. In 1980, he was elected as president of the United States. Again, he served two terms. He solved the Iran hostage crisis and brought down the Berlin Wall. He is considered to be one of the five greatest presidents.

GOLDEN BEAR

Sometimes winning gets you hated. That's what happened to Jack Nicklaus when he beat golf fans' idol, Arnold Palmer, to win the US Open in 1962. Millions of diehard Palmer fans were crushed when their hero lost. Jack's win stands today as the most unpopular golf game ever played. Jack Nicklaus was unlike the flashy Palmer, who was a handsome, dashing, golfer who played to the crowd with a powerful, lunging swing. Jack was a round-faced, pudgy blond with the nickname "Golden Bear." His swing was deliberate, smooth, and he rarely missed. Not Palmer, grandstanding with the facial grimaces accented by chain smoking. Jack was so focused that he never even smiled. He was considered boring, but his natural talent and long swing carried him to success. He won twenty golf tournaments, made seventy PGA tours, was low-score player eight times, won Player of the Year five times, shot a fifty-one for his very first game he ever played, broke a seventy at thirteen, and won countless other tournaments and titles. He is said to be golf's greatest. To cement this title, *Golf Magazine*, in 1988, named him Player of the Century. Achievements of this magnitude demand somebody with courage.

HERO OF THE TENNIS COURTS

His father was a champion boxer and tennis enthusiast in Iran and, after moving to the United States, was determined that one of his children would become a professional tennis player. That made Andre Agassi's career choice painless. He played tennis daily, and, at fourteen, was sent to the Bollettieri Tennis Academy in Florida. Two years later, Andre Agassi became a professional tennis player. At age eighteen, he was rated fourth best in world tennis. He was a dedicated athlete who practiced constantly.

It takes stubborn determination and courage to become the best in the world at something. In 1992, Agassi grew in tennis fame. He defeated two former Wimbledon champion players: Boris Becker and John McEnroe. He set a trend that began when he shaved his balding head. Today, thousands follow his example. He interrupted his tennis career to marry a famous movie star, Brooke Shields. The marriage lasted but a short time, and then he was back playing tennis. With tournament wins and sports equipment endorsements, he raised his income to over 100 million dollars. He continued to win at tennis. He founded the Andre Agassi Foundation for Education in 2001, which raised millions to help at-risk children. Andre is the only male player to win a Career Golden Slam. For this, he remains a hero to children and adults the world over.

BUILDER OF PLANES

Like Amelia Earhart, he fell in love with airplanes when he saw his first flying machine in 1909. William Edward Boeing flew in one in 1914. He was drawn into the plane-building business and joined with engineer George Westervelt to form a company. He was able to make deals with the Department of the Navy to build training aircraft during the First World War. The Boeing Company moved quickly into the new century. Following World War I, the demand for airplanes moved to the transport of mail, passengers, and cargo. People found that in an airplane they could cross the continent in hours instead of days. He obtained contracts with the military to repair military aircraft and build biplanes. Even with the economic crash that caused a depression to grip the nation in the 1930s, Boeing's airplane building business became a large collection of companies. It included many branches for manufacturing aircraft, making parts, and training pilots. The government forced him to break up his airplane building business. He left it until World War II came along when he came back to build military aircraft on a large scale. His company built the Boeing B-29, which helped end the war. Before he died in 1956, he built the B-52, the world's largest bomber.

THE GRAND DAME OF POLITICS

She is best known for her tireless work to get the Universal Declaration of Human Rights accepted by the United Nations. Eleanor Roosevelt came from a wealthy family, but one plagued by sad circumstances. Her parents and brother died when she was ten. She and two younger brothers were left in the care of a grandmother in New York. At age twenty-one, she married a distant cousin, Franklin Delano Roosevelt. Tragedy struck them in 1921 when Franklin was crippled with polio, a disease that had no cure at that time. She nursed him back to the point where he could continue his political career. He ran for governor of the state and won. This vaulted her into a life of public service working for various groups. In 1932, she became the First Lady when FDR won the election for president of the United States. She supported him by giving speeches on human rights and women's issues. She wrote newspaper columns and made radio broadcasts to help the country's poor and those needing help. At the time, the nation was in a deep depression. Millions were out of work with no way to support themselves. She returned four times as First Lady and became a widow in 1945 before the end of World War II. The new president, Harry Truman, knew a good thing when he saw it; he appointed her as the United States delegate to the United Nations. She became a leader in worldwide efforts to improve human rights. She was awarded thirty-five honorary degrees, including a Doctor of Laws. She was one of the most courageous and heroic persons of the 1930s and 1940s.

REACHING FOR THE STARS

She was to be the first teacher to go into outer space. She had grown up excited about the space program that was booming from the time she was a youngster. At a state college, Christa McAuliffe earned a degree in history and school administration. She taught in Concord where she earned the respect of her colleagues and the community. She married her high school sweetheart, Steve McAuliffe. They moved to Maryland where he planned to study law. Christa was encouraged to apply to become the first teacher in space. She competed against doctors, authors, business leaders, and scholars. In the end, Christa McAuliffe won. She was chosen because she seemed to represent the ordinary teacher. Her NASA training endeared her to the public and her colleagues alike. Sadly, just seventy-three seconds into flight, the space shuttle exploded, killing all aboard. She will remain forever, the heroic teacher who personified courage and valor.

LET THERE BE LIGHT

He was one of America's most prolific inventors, turning out dozens of new products. Thomas Edison got over one thousand patents. Whether it is true or not, he claimed he had but three months of formal schooling. His difficulties with teachers prompted his mother to remove him from public school to homeschool him instead. She had great faith in him and said, "He is a superior child." Considering his many inventions, that was probably an understatement. During the 1860s, he developed his skills by working as a telegraph operator. Following a bout with scarlet fever, he was left partially deaf. Despite this, in 1868, he rose to the rank of an independent inventor. He learned that to make money from his inventions, he had to invent something with commercial value. In 1876, at his industrial research station in Menlo Park, he invented the Quadruplex telegraph. The most famous of his early inventions was the light bulb in 1880. Edison would light the world. It was Edison who talked Henry Ford into putting the gasoline engine in his automobiles. During World War I, Edison worked on military projects, including submarine detectors—a lifesaving invention of great value. He is also credited with having invented the factory. Thomas Edison is a hero of electrifying proportions.

BIRTH OF THE CAR

He made cars affordable for everyone. Henry Ford began as a farm boy and attended a one-room schoolhouse. At sixteen, he left home to work in a machine shop in nearby Detroit. After three years, he returned home to work on the farm and part-time at the Westinghouse Electric Corporation. In 1888, he was hired by Edison Illuminating Company to work as chief engineer. In his spare hours, he experimented building cars. He had his first success in 1893. Ten years later he created Ford Motor Company to manufacture automobiles. While he did not actually invent the automobile, he did set up an assembly-line system that made car manufacturing less costly. His wage incentives for an honest day's labor increased production. He sold fifteen million Model T cars between 1908 and 1927. He did run into troubles with government regulations, unions, competition, and employees. Employee troubles stemmed from his personality because he liked to control everything and everybody. Regardless, he was an icon in the auto industry. That made him a heroic person in every sense of the word. More than one hundred years later, some of Henry's cars are still running. It's something to be said for the quality of some of the first cars ever made.

"I'M NOBODY! WHO ARE YOU?"

She was one of America's most prolific poets, writing over 1700 poems. Sadly, in her lifetime Emily Dickinson only published seven of them and never gained profit from her work. She was quite secluded, living at home most of her life. From her quiet world, she emerged only in her poems. Many of them reflect her solitude. Her work was mainly influenced by the Civil War and the deaths of friends and relatives. She had a confidant who discouraged her from publishing her poems. Only after her death did a sister edit and make public three volumes of her work. Not until 1955 did an editor publish her entire lifetime effort. One has only to read a Dickinson poem to understand why Emily Dickinson is thought to be a poet of heroic stature—a poet for all time.

MARCH KING OF AMERICA

With his contribution of marching band music, he helped form the very fabric of American society. John Philip Sousa came from a large family; he was the third of ten children. He also came from a musical family. His father, a trombonist in the United States Marine Band, made sure his son followed in music. When John Philip Sousa was in primary school, he began successful vocal lessons and moved to a violin. He was outstanding in both. He studied several musical instruments. At age eleven he was the leader of his own dance band. All the other members of the band were adult men. John became a prominent musical figure. At age twenty-five, he was chosen to be the bandmaster for the United States Marine Band, a step above what his father did before him. He had an interest in operetta and composed fifteen operettas. In 1892, Sousa resigned his Marine Band position to form his own group. They made world tours playing the marching music that he had written. Among the most famous of his marches are "Stars and Stripes Forever" and "the Washington Post March." When the phonograph was invented, owners made several recordings of Sousa's marches and played them. They became the most popular music ever recorded. Sousa trained young musicians at the Great Lakes Naval Training Station, teaching hundreds and forming bands for several navy ships. John Philip Sousa was an American institution, and he received honors all over the world. His music was dynamic and inspired patriotism for America. Sousa welded America together more than any other influence before or since. At high school graduations, his ever popular and stately "Pomp and Circumstance" always sets the tone for the importance of the occasion. Sousa holds the position as one of America's most heroic and patriotic citizens.

DIGNITY COMES TO MOVIES

When you want an actor to portray a dignified character, you telephone Morgan Freeman. Whether he's playing a chauffeur driving a cranky old southern lady or a prisoner in a maximum security prison, the character will possess dignity. Over his career, Morgan Freeman has become one of the most popular and respected actors in the business. Pushing his regular studies aside to participate in extracurricular activities, at age eight, he stepped into an acting role. From a job in a touring company, he went on to work in some off-Broadway productions. In movies, he gave stellar performances that resulted in Oscar nominations. He won an Oscar for his performance in *Million Dollar Baby*. Morgan is a hero model for youth and adults alike.

THE GOLDEN ARCHES

Ray Kroc was selling cups when he got the idea for a restaurant. In 1954, he met the McDonald brothers, who operated a restaurant. He was impressed by their limited menu, line production methods, and cheap prices. He suggested that they franchise their business through him. They agreed and he set up McDonald's in 1955 in Chicago. Eventually, he bought out the brothers in 1961 to operate the restaurant as he wished. By 1963, he had a chain of five hundred eateries. He emphasized clean restaurants and good working habits. McDonald's now operates thousands of restaurants across the nation and in 119 countries; however, the best McDonald's hamburgers are still made in America. He really changed the way America eats.

COMPUTERS TO ORDER

While attending the University of Texas, Michael Dell thought that computers could be sold directly to the consumer. With this idea in mind, he built and sold them out of his dorm room at college. He also thought that computers should be built to the consumer's needs. With only a thousand dollars, he set up Dell Computer Corporation. The company became the largest seller of computers with the youngest CEO. He revolutionized the industry and made the cost of computers within reach for regular consumers. Being young and reasonably good-looking—with a mop of curly hair—probably contributed a little to his business success. In today's world of fast communications, he's a true ordinary hero who changed the way the world communicates.

NOTES

1. *USA Hero*, last modified April 20, 2016, http://www.usa-hero.com/. (Don Jones.)

DUTY, HONOR, COUNTRY

The attack began early on October 14, 1918. Colonel Douglas MacArthur, with great courage in fierce fighting, led the American Rainbow Division up Hill 228 that crawled with enemy soldiers, and captured it before noon. Military leaders thought of troops as entirely expendable; the deaths of thousands were an acceptable loss. For the next day, MacArthur ordered a bayonet attack to avoid the flash of rifle fire that gave away troop positions; nevertheless, the men protested bitterly. He gave up the idea.

America had sent the Forty-Second to aid the French in their fight against the Germans. For years, fighting had been at a stalemate, each side bogged down in muddy trenches. Both sides had lost thousands. The Germans, in an effort to counter the fresh troops of the Forty-Second American Division, set strong fortifications in place.

The Hindenburg Line fortifications could only be described as devilish. The line was like a net four miles in depth with interlaced barbed wire hidden in thick, knee-high grass. Pillboxes made of concrete several feet thick with dome-shaped roofs were manned by trained German soldiers with machine guns. Narrow openings or windows allowed the enemy to spray the hillside with a shower of bullets.

The Americans pushing against this defense had no cover—no foxholes in which to hide. Then came a baffling maze of trenches. Crawling into them, the men did not know whether they had found one of their own or stumbled into the enemy.

Unaware of what the men were stepping into, Commanding Officer Summerall sent them into this network of tangled barbed wire. They walked into a buzz saw—a crossfire of German rifles—that stopped them cold. MacArthur's Rainbow Division found itself deep in the thick of battle. While on a scouting trip to learn about enemy positions, he walked into an invisible sea of mustard gas, which is like breathing scalding hot water.

The Germans sprayed machine gun fire down the hill on the advancing troops. They faltered and dropped in their stride. Despite the losses, the Allied commander was furious. He yelled at MacArthur, "Take the objective or die trying!"

The next day, MacArthur's men found a weak link in the German lines. He directed a massive assault that forged ahead. They cut through the tangle of barbed wire to overrun the Côte de Châtillon and capture the enemy regiment. The men performed countless acts of bravery and courage, most beyond the call of duty. This was the Rainbow Division's finest achievement in the war.

Along came World War II. Douglas MacArthur was well prepared for this time in world history. He had graduated from the Texas Military Academy and trained at West Point where he set a record for outstanding achievement. Someone once said, "You cannot shrug your shoulders at Douglas MacArthur. There is nothing bland about him, nothing passive about him, nothing dull about him. There's no question about his patriotism, no question about his courage. He lived his entire life in the United States Army. He was born into it."

Orders sent him to the Philippines. Once there, he began a lifelong love affair with the islands. While traveling through the jungles on a routine Jeep trip with his father, to review military forces, Douglas met with a near-death run-in with bandits. Leaping from the cover of the jungle grass, they fired at the motorcade. Marksmen quickly returned rifle fire to stop the attackers.

When war came in 1941, MacArthur could only watch from his command post on Corregidor as his world crumbled like a house of cards. America was totally unprepared.

Despite problems in the Pacific Islands, President Roosevelt knew he could not let America's most popular general be captured by the Japanese. He ordered MacArthur off the islands. MacArthur regretted leaving his men, but slipped away under cover of night. As he left, he promised the men and the people of the Philippines, "I shall return." These three words ring down through history as strong as "Remember the Alamo!"

In waging the war, MacArthur had to fight on two fronts to return. One was with the Japanese, the other was with the navy who felt that the Pacific was theirs. MacArthur's brilliance in battle strategy set the stage for winning the war. He led an island-hopping fight all the way to Japan. He took some islands and hopped over others. The Japanese could not last long on these islands. They were starved into surrendering.

Marines faced bitter resistance at Guadalcanal, New Guinea, Okinawa, Tarawa, and Saipan. They suffered thousands of losses. During the battle of Saipan, thirty thousand Japanese soldiers and civilians died. Most committed suicide.

The world watched in awe when MacArthur kept his promise in October 1944, as he waded ashore at Leyte, Philippines. Aboard the USS *Missouri*, on September 2, 1945, he presided over the surrender of the Japanese to bring World War II to an end. It now became his duty to oversee the rebuilding of the defeated nation. He did this by sheer force of personality.

Five years later, MacArthur was back in the thick of battle. The Forgotten War had begun. Because of what MacArthur did in Korea, his footsteps would echo across the ages. Following the June 1950 invasion of South Korea by North Korea, the United Nations got involved. Most of the troops sent to stem the invasion were Americans.

Using his military genius, MacArthur landed troops at Inchon. This cut the North Korean offensive in half. Quickly, the invading troops were driven back. MacArthur did stop at the thirty-eighth parallel. That had been the dividing line between the two countries. He fought through the rugged mountains and across swollen rivers to the Yalu River, the very border of China. The Chinese reacted immediately. They swarmed over the border, determined to destroy everything in their path. Since MacArthur had not asked the president if he could continue the fight beyond the thirty-eighth, President Harry Truman was furious. MacArthur was acting on his best military training, but it did not meet with politics in Washington DC. By leaking rumors to discredit the general, Truman began a move to recall MacArthur.

MacArthur was a Republican. Because of his popularity, he was a possible candidate as the next president. Truman, a Democrat, knew this, so he quickly gathered what support he could from the Joint Chiefs of Staff. They were secretly envious of the famous general. They would go along with the political backroom plots of the President. This was something at which Truman quietly and secretly worked. He could not fire MacArthur for no real reason.

Truman's meeting with the Joint Chiefs was a crafty move. Because their support was vital, this meeting saved him from impeachment. MacArthur's supporters had strong reason to be upset at his firing. He was a brilliant military leader. His record from World War I and World War II was a powerful statement about his worth.

His strategy in the war in the Pacific saved thousands—if not millions—of lives. His genius showed in the landing at Inchon. When MacArthur returned to the United States, the public greeted him with lavish parades from San Francisco to New York. He planned his battles as he had been taught. He didn't think much about the politics that conspired in the backrooms of Washington DC.

In recognition of his status, Congress asked him to speak. It was here that he closed his service to America with his immortal words: "Old soldiers never die. They just fade away."

NOTES

1. http://www.eca.state.gov/education/engteach/pubs/AmLnC/br58.htm.
2. William Gardner Bell, "Douglas MacArthur," *Center of Military History*, http://www.history.army.mil/faq/mac_bio.htm.
3. "Gen. Douglas MacArthur Returns to Leyte, Philippine Islands, 20 October 1944," *Olive-Drab*, http://www.olive-drab.com/gallery/description_0081.php. (Chuck Chriss.)
4. Geoffrey Perret, *Old Soldiers Never Die: The Life of Douglas MacArthur* (New York: Random House, 1996).
5. Tad Bennicoff, "The Korean War," *Spotlight Biography*, http://smithsonianeducation.org/spotlight/korean.html. (Tad Bennicoff.)

FOR THE LOVE
OF APPLES

He roamed the middle northwest of the country as a wandering nomad carrying sacks of apple seeds. In 1802, he lashed two canoes together to float sixteen bushels of apple seeds down the Ohio River. Whenever he could, he got a horse and tied the bags of seeds onto the horse. Sometimes, he carried the bags on his own back. For John Chapman, his quest was to spread the growth of apple trees. In what became the states of Ohio, Michigan, Indiana, and Illinois, John Chapman—better known as Johnny Appleseed—planted entire orchards.

He was born in Massachusetts in 1774, just a year before the American Revolution. His father became a soldier in the war. His mother died while he was a very young boy. When he grew up, he made it his life's work to plant fruit trees. He had decided that apples had much value. If he planted apple trees in the West, he thought that settlers who moved west without much food would have something to eat as they tried to survive in the stubborn land.

In 1792, eighteen-year-old John Chapman rounded up his sister, Emily, and his eleven-year-old brother, Nathaniel, and headed west—all barefoot. His intention was to find the headwaters of the Susquehanna River, where he would work as a nurseryman. He had enough good sense to charge a few pennies for the trees he grew; however, if someone could not pay, he bartered or traded for clothing or food. More often, he gave the trees away. "You can pay later," he said to the poor settlers. He used the money to buy and plant more apple trees. If he didn't simply give the money away to someone who was hungry; he used the money to buy and plant more apple trees.

Because of his generosity, he had to dress simply—nothing fancy or costly. Sometimes he cut a hole in a sack and wore it as a shirt like a Mexican *serape*. People also commented about his bare feet. Actually, by walking barefoot all the time, the bottoms of his feet became so hardened that he could walk on grain stubble as if wearing leather shoes. Once, a rattlesnake tried to bite Johnny's foot when he was asleep, not knowing that Johnny's soles were as tough as elephant hide, the snake almost bent a fang. Once in a while, he would find shoes and wear them, but as often as not, they did not match. He lived a hard, subsistence life, without many material things. He used a tin pot both for a hat and a cooking pot.

When it came to food, meat was not on the menu. If he saw an animal mistreated, he would buy the poor creature and give it to someone who would treat it better. When he learned that a horse was about to be put down, he bought the horse some grassy acres of land and turned the animal loose to get well.

Johnny was a friend to everyone he met. Settlers, Native Americans, and animals all liked him. Johnny Appleseed not only planted apple trees and protected animals, he also preached. He thought of himself as a primitive Christian. His beliefs took him on a crusade to save settlers on the frontier during the War of 1812. British and Native American groups were roaming the country, killing the settlers. Johnny traveled night and day trying to warn everyone. He went from house to house, not even stopping to eat or rest. He was a hovering angel for those in a peril.

He was twenty-seven when he transported bushels of apple seed down the Ohio River. He planted the seed on the thousand acres he bought in Ohio. Each year he traveled hundreds of miles carrying his apple seeds and planting them wherever he roamed. In 1868, new settlers to Indiana found rows and rows of his trees growing near Fort Wayne.

Johnny Appleseed died in Indiana in 1845 at age seventy. He had spent his life wandering some one hundred thousand square miles of the Midwest, planting apple seeds all across the land. Should you visit the area northeast of the Mississippi, you'll find some of his trees still alive.

NOTES

1. "Johnny Appleseed: A Pioneer and a Legend, 1774–1845," http://www.ohioapples
.com/pdf/johnny_appleseed.pdf.

2. Patsy Stevens, "John Chapman: Johnny Appleseed," *Garden of Praise*, http://gardenofpraise
.com/ibdchap.htm.

3. Karen Clemens Warrick, *John Chapman: The Legendary Johnny Appleseed* (New York:
Enslow Publishers, 2001).

FOXHOLE WAR CORRESPONDENT

I guess it doesn't make any difference once a man is gone. Medals and speeches and victories are nothing to him anymore. He died and others lived, and nobody knows why it's so. There's nothing we can do for the ones beneath the wooden crosses, except, perhaps, to pause and murmur, Thanks, pal. —Ernie Pyle.

Writing from the front lines of battle, war correspondent Ernie Pyle was the closest thing that fighting soldiers had for a friend. He wrote, "For four days and nights they have fought hard, eaten little, washed none, and slept hardly at all." In May of 1942, traveling with the American infantrymen, he said, "Their nights have been violent with attack, fright, butchery, and their days sleepless and miserable with the crash of artillery. They are young men, but the grime and whiskers and exhaustion make them look middle-aged. There is an agony in your heart and you almost feel ashamed to look at them. They are just guys from [anywhere America] but you wouldn't remember them . . . their world can never be known to you."

There was a time when the media and correspondents praised the efforts of the fighting man. Today, Department of Defense spokesmen are incensed at what they consider the anti-military bias of the reporters who came later: "There are no more Ernie Pyles." Many people, totally ignorant of what fighting men went through, find it fashionable to criticize and belittle what soldiers do for them. They are ignorant of the fact that the freedom and comfort they enjoy now was paid for by the very men they condemn. During World War II, Ernie not only shared the hardships and dangers of battle with the little guy in the foxhole, he wrote with empathy of their ordeal, so he was welcome as more than a visitor—he was one of them.

As a team player, Ernie helped win the hearts and minds of people back home by reporting some of the truth about the suffering and dying of their sons in battle. Before the war in Europe ended, Ernie transferred to the war in the Pacific. He told friends that he did not really want to go. "I have a premonition of death. I feel that I've used up all my chances, and I hate it. I don't want to be killed." Regardless, he went. He landed in Okinawa with the United States Marines. He plodded along the dusty trails with the men. Bullets swept through them with a swishing sound like water from a hose. Men dropped without uttering a word.

The high-pitched whine of a mortar shell came from overhead; the shell exploded yards away in a ravine. Smoke, earth, and fire belched into the acrid air. Everyone crouched. Exploding air slapped their faces like a fly swatter. Ernie felt the sting. It did not slow their advance. At the moment no one knew it, but Okinawa would become the largest amphibious invasion in the Pacific. The Americans would drop more bombs and launch more shells than in any other battle. Navy guns would lob more shells onto the island than they had ever done. More people would die than would perish in both atomic blasts at Hiroshima and Nagasaki. Fifty thousand American troops, seventy thousand Japanese, and one hundred thousand civilians would die on Okinawa.

Navy guns had poured tons of shells into the Japanese fortifications. The low rising hills that the Americans worked their way up looked like the aftermath of a forest fire. The United States Marines had landed and taken the northern part of the island without great loss. In the southern part, the battle raged. Into the whirlpool of bullets and grenades, jumped Ernie Pyle.

Every time a man enters a new fight, his chances of getting killed multiply. It's like flying a two-engine plane: with two engines, chances of losing an engine are twice as great. On April 18, 1945, just four months before the end of the war, Ernie was riding in a Jeep headed for the command post when he came under fire from a Japanese machine gun. Everyone dived for cover. Pyle became an immortal hero who gave courage its name when he rose up to ask, "Is everyone all right?" In that same instant a machine gun bullet struck him in the head. He died instantly.

NOTES

1. www.airdefenseartillery.com. (The Scripps Howard Foundation.)

2. Vince Crawley, "Carthage Cemetery Honors World War II Fallen," *U.S. Department of Defense*, http://www.defense.gov/news/newsarticle.aspx?id=59401.

3. "Ernie Pyle," *Indiana Historical Society*, http://www.indianahistory.org/our -collections/reference/notable-hoosiers/ernie-pyle#.V0O-sZErLIU. (Stever Haller.)

4. http://searchinghistoricalhorizons.wordpress.com.

5. http://www.cleveland.oh.us/wmy_news/jherr41.html.

6. *U.S. Air Force*, accessed May 26, 2016, http://www.af.mil/. (Indiana University Home for History about Ernie Pyle.)

ARCHITECT OF DESIRE

Having a good start, not only do I fully intend to be the greatest architect who has ever lived, but I fully intend to be the greatest architect who will ever live. Yes, I intend to be the greatest architect of all time," said Frank Lloyd Wright early in his career.

When questioned about his vanity, Wright explained, "Early in life I had to choose between honest arrogance and hypocritical humility; I chose honest arrogance." Those who knew him endured his attitude as well as they could. His son, John, declared, "I lived a lifelong struggle to avoid being destroyed." Wright did have saving graces that his son and son-in-law, Wes Peters, said offset his arrogance. "He had so much energy; it shaped everyone around him."

Spoken a hundred years ago, Frank Lloyd Wright is probably correct. If people know of any architect, they probably know about Wright. People who haven't seen a word he's written feel at ease tossing his name into their conversations. Many who know nothing about organic architecture would give a tooth to live in one of Wright's houses.

"Wright took the fashionable American house of the early nineties, with its high-pitched roof and spindly chimneys, its numerous dormer windows and its crazy turrets and towers, and brought this wild, shambling, pseudo-romantic creation, half Pegasus and half spavined ceiling plaster down to earth," said one critic. Wright spoke often of marrying his houses to the ground. His earth-hugging, low-roofed style was proof of his desire to bring house and nature together.

301

Wright started his own firm in 1893 after leaving a prestigious company. Between 1893 and 1904, about the same time that Henry Ford was making owning the automobile fashionable, Wright designed nearly fifty buildings. It was during this period that he developed his idea of the prairie house. Features of these houses included low-pitched roofs, overhanging eaves, horizontal lines, central chimneys, open floor plans, and clerestory windows. He designed these windows high in the wall to let in the natural moods of light.

The first prairie houses were plaster with wood trim and horizontal board and batten. He built later houses with concrete and brick. They hugged the earth as if they had come to its very edge, like cowering turtles in their concrete shells. He even designed furniture to match his new concept. His designs departed from high ceilings and box rooms that were dominant at the time.

People challenged him with many domestic and legal fights. He did not let these unimportant events stop him from designing and building the Imperial Hotel in Tokyo, Japan, which opened in 1923. He was inspired by the ruins of Chichen Itza in the Yucatan. As a result, he designed a building in a dizzying collage of volcanic stone in soaring space.

Some of his most famous designs include the Oak Park Studio where he lived for some time; the Robie House in Chicago, Illinois; a second Taliesin house; the Kaufmann Residence, or Fallingwater, which looks like the waterfall it's built over in Bear Run, Pennsylvania; and the refurbished Florida Southern College complex of twelve buildings. This Methodist college, thirty-five miles east of Tampa, sits in an orange grove planted near a lake. Even today many houses feature low roofs and over-hanging eaves—signs that Wright's influence is still strong in today's designs.

Occasionally, someone wanders through history who does something that elevates him above the ordinary and the masses. He becomes a figure of heroic proportions, bigger than life. Over the years, and before he died in 1959, Frank Lloyd Wright designed one thousand buildings. Contractors built more than five hundred of them. Some four hundred of them still stand as of the year 2000. His houses are still sought after.

NOTES

1. "Writers and Artists: Frank Lloyd Wright," *America's Story from America's Library*, http://www.americaslibrary.gov/aa/wright/aa_wright_subj.html.

2. Patrick Dahlen, *Frank Lloyd Wright*, unpublished paper from Carbondale Community High School.

3. architect.architecture.sk/ieoh-ming-pei-architect/ieoh-ming-pei-architect.php.

4. http://www.independent.co.uk/arts-entertainment-/architecture/architect-of-desire -frank.

5. "Frank Lloyd Wright," *Pennsylvania Center for the Book*, (2008), http://pabook .libraries.psu.edu/palitmap/bios/Wright_Frank_Lloyd.html. (Vicky Barg 2008.)

6. Mark Roesler, "Biography," *CMG Worldwide*, http://www.cmgww.com/historic/flw /bio.html.

7. William Allin Storrer, *Biography, Frank Lloyd Wright: biography,* http://www .franklloydwrightinfo.com.

8. "Frank Lloyd Wright," *United Architects—Great Architects*, http://dannmihalake .wordpress.com/wright-frank-lloyd/.

INTO THE BREACH

We're gonna die!" screamed one of the children in the teetering bus. "We're gonna go in the river!" screamed another. Fifty-two children, ages five to fourteen, were on a charter bus returning from a swimming field trip when the bridge under the bus collapsed, sending the bus and the children toward the Mississippi River. Thrown about violently inside the vehicle, the children slammed against metal seat frames and the sides of the bus. The inside of the bus looked as if a tornado had ripped through it, heaving and twisting everything and everybody.

With his heart pounding like a steam locomotive, hair standing up on the back of his neck, sweat glistening on his bronzed face, Jeremy Hernandez thought, *I have to get these kids out of here.* The twenty-year-old summer camp staff member said to the kids, "I don't want to die either. I don't want to go in the river." The exit door was jammed against the bridge railing. No exit that way. Quickly, he threaded his way through the screaming children to the back of the bus. The seldom-used exit did not yield. He tried again. Nothing happened. The rusty hinges refused to give way. Bracing himself against the backseats, he slammed his feet against the stubborn door. It broke loose suddenly. Cheering, the kids surged forward.

For now, friction between the bus and the concrete railing kept it from slipping toward the end of the broken bridge. Nearby, some cars had burst into flame, adding to the danger that their gas tanks would explode, sending burning gasoline everywhere.

Jeremy worked feverishly. *They're like my little brothers and sisters,* he was thinking. He stayed on the bus, even though the bus began to skid toward the open space that fell away to the river. He could easily go into the river with the bus.

One of the first rescuers to appear at the back of the bus was twenty-year-old Gary Babineau. He saw cars vanish before him. He heard a rumbling "like a jackhammer," he said. The ground under his car gave way sending him into a free fall thirty feet straight down. Then the sky rained large chunks of concrete that crashed about him, barely missing him. He climbed out of his mangled pickup and heard kids shrieking above. He saw the teetering bus hanging off the guardrail. He jumped onto the rocks under the bridge, climbed up onto the broken section, and ran to the bus. When he got there, Jeremy was already lifting kids out the back. Gary scooped up two at a time and carried them to safety. He returned time and time again. The kids were screaming; some were in shock.

By now, others, recognizing the danger to the children, climbed onto the crumbling bridge. Jeremy had the children lined up in the aisle. One by one he gathered them up and handed them out to eager arms. Some of the children were stiff with fear and clinging to Gary like toy teddy bears with their arms and legs tightly wrapped around him.

The reality of what they did finally set in many hours later. "I guess I was an idiot for running under a bridge that was falling," Gary confessed. "But I did what any man should have done."

As for Jeremy, he said, "If it would have been a second sooner, we'd have been in the river." He shudders just thinking about it. "I looked over at the river, and my heart started beating faster." So into the breach Jeremy Hernandez leaped. For Gary Babineau, climbing under a falling bridge to save kids wasn't much different. Without regard to their own safety or their lives, they became angels of mercy.

NOTES

1. "I-35 Mississippi River Bridge," *Wikipedia*, http://en.wikipedia.org/wiki/I-35 _Mississippi_River_bridge.
2. http://www.monstersandcritics.com. (Steve Ragan.)
3. http://www.tcdailyplanet.net/article/2007-08-02-hope-and-heroism-bridge.html. (Mary Turck.)

AGAINST ALL ODDS

Millennia ago, a nation of people called the Philistines decided to war against the Israelites. They stood on a mountain across a green valley from the mountain where the Israelites camped. They sent out one of their soldiers whose name was Goliath. He was a giant of a man. He wore armor that weighed 150 pounds. Brass plates protected his legs. The tip of his spear weighed twenty pounds. Only a very large, very strong man could carry such armor. Because he was so much larger than any of the Israelite men, he stood like a huge oak tree, feet spread apart and planted like roots, a frightening mass.

In the forty days that the armies had been camped on the mountains, Goliath cried out every day, "Why are you here to do battle? I am a Philistine, and you are but servants to Saul. Choose a man and let him come to do battle with me. If he kills me, we will be your servants. If I kill him, you will be our servants."

King Saul and his army were scared to do battle with Goliath. Honor decreed that only one man fight, but no man by himself would fight the giant. What were they going to do?

Among the Israelites was a man named Jesse who had eight sons; three were already in Saul's army. His youngest was David, who stood about five feet tall and weighed less than a sack of potatoes. His eyes sparkled in his tan face, and his dark hair glistened and made soft curls about his forehead. He looked after his father's sheep. One day Jesse said, "David, run to the army camp where your brothers are and give them some roasted corn and loaves of bread. Take some cheese and dates too. Find out how your brothers are doing, and bring me word of the battle."

David arose early the next morning and left the sheep with another herder. He arrived at the Israelite camp as the armies were about to fight each other. David found his brothers and gave them the food that he had brought. Suddenly came the roar of the giant. Again, he challenged the Israelites to send out a man. "I defy the armies of Israel this day; give me a man that we may fight together." As they had done every time before, the soldiers trembled and ran away. When they had overcome their fear, they said to David, "Did you see that giant defy Israel?"

In the Israelite camp, David asked, "Who is he that should defy the living God? What shall be done to the man who kills the Philistine and takes away the reproach to Israel?"

The men answered, "If any man kills the giant, King Saul will give him great riches and make that man's family free."

When one of David's brothers heard this he was angry that David might seek riches for himself. "Why did you come here and with whom have you left the few sheep that our father owns? I know your pride and your heart. You left the sheep to come down to watch the battle."

David replied, "What have I done now? Is there not cause?"

When Saul heard this, he sent for David. The youth said to the king, "Let no man's heart fail because of this giant of a man. I will go and fight this Philistine."

"You are not able to go against this Philistine. You're just a youth. He is a man of war and has trained to be a warrior all his life."

"I am keeper of my father's sheep. A lion came and took one out of the flock. I went after the lion and killed him and saved the lamb. A bear came to take another sheep. I delivered the sheep from the paw of the bear. This Philistine is no different. He will be as one of them, seeing that he has defied the armies of the living God."

Saul attempted to speak but David was not finished. He continued, saying, "The Lord that delivered me out of the paw of the lion and paw of the bear, he too will deliver me out of the hand of this boastful Philistine."

Saul called for his personal armor and shield and sword. The servants placed it on David—a coat of heavy mail; body armor made of small, overlapping metal rings; a brass helmet. It, too, was heavy. In his hand they placed the iron sword, weighing ten pounds. On Goliath, all this heavy body armor would be an easy load. On David, it was cumbersome, clumsy, and too much weight. It got in the way of his ability to move. He looked like an over-loaded pack animal. "I cannot go with all this armor. I have never used it before." So, he took it off.

Instead, he took his staff and searched in the stream for some smooth stones. He chose five. These he placed in his shepherd's bag. He also carried a sling.

He approached Goliath. The giant looked at his opponent, a tanned youth with fair complexion and small build. On the hill, the two looked like an aged and gnarled tree and a young sapling. The giant roared, "Am I a dog that you come to beat me with sticks and stones?" He cursed David and called on his pagan gods. "Come to me, and I will feed your flesh to the birds."

"You come against me with sword and spear and shield. I come in the name of the Lord of hosts, the God of the armies of Israel, whom you have defied," David said. "This day will the Lord deliver you into my hands. Not you, but I will feed you to the birds. I will take your head from your shoulders and give it to the hosts of the Philistines. All the world will know that there is a God in Israel."

This made Goliath furious. He came at David, but the lad was ready and ran straight toward the giant. He pulled a stone from his bag and fitted it into the sling. He twirled the sling over his head as smoothly as a spinning top and let the stone go. It landed against Goliath's forehead and sank into his head. The stunned giant gasped and crashed to the ground like a lumbering elephant. David had no sword, so he ran forward and pulled the giant's weapon from his hand. He swung the sword down hard to slay the enemy. The men cheered loudly. The Philistines fled in fear. David's courage had won the day.

NOTES

1. *The Holy Bible Containing the Old and New Testaments* (Philadelphia: National Bible Press, 1963).

2. Patsy Stevens, "David and Goliath," *Garden of Praise*, http://gardenofpraise.com/bibl14s.htm.

THE DEMISE OF POLIOMYELITIS

There are few things as horrifying as seeing an innocent child hobbled with metal braces, or a child confined in an iron lung—a large metal tank that looks like a huge incubator, in which the body is encased and only the head sticks out. Breathing is possible only by artificial mechanics. Parents or nurses hover nearby, ready to help the crippled child do anything. These scenes were all too present in the 1940s and earlier and up into the 1950s. Up to this time nearly every family lost a child to some childhood disease.

Summertime was cause for alarm. It frightened parents and with good cause: during the summer, a common childhood disease raged, paralyzing or killing their children. Public swimming pools were suspect, so parents did not allow their children in them. The cause for alarm: poliomyelitis, or polio.

Nothing was more feared at the time. It struck down too many thousands of children and young people. Even presidents were not immune. At age twenty-eight, Franklin D. Roosevelt became a victim. He used crutches or a wheelchair when he was elected president of the United States in 1933.

Everyone hoped for a cure. Scientists and doctors had searched for a remedy long before this time, driven by the disease that reached its highest peak in the 1950s. Polio held the nation in absolute terror. This common fear brought the people together more than any other time in its history. Millions of Americans donated money, held fundraisers, and

309

established the March of Dimes. Through these efforts, people raised millions of dollars for research and treatments.

Jonas Salk was born in the middle of World War I. At a very young age, he showed exceptional promise and was an unusually bright student. He graduated from high school when he was fifteen. He had wanted to be a lawyer, but luckily for the world, he changed his mind to become a doctor.

He immediately began research on influenza. Remembering the millions who died after World War I of influenza, many doctors worked tirelessly to find a cure. The nation avoided another epidemic when doctors invented a flu vaccine. Salk transferred to the University of Pittsburgh, where he began researching a cure for polio. For eight years he tried one experiment after another. In 1952, he and his team created the first vaccine that worked. Two years later, Salk felt it was time to try the discovery on a wide scale. Almost two million school children took part. They lined up, rolled up their sleeves, and bravely endured the jab of the vaccine needle.

Newspaper headlines announced the finding of a cure on April 12, 1955. They shouted their praises: "Polio Routed! Vaccine Safe! Parents Need Fear No More!" Shopkeepers painted messages on their windows to express the nation's gratitude: "Thank you, Jonas Salk."

Salk had made the vaccine by killing the polio virus. The only drawback to Salk's vaccine was having to administer it by needle. Countries that have used Salk's vaccine are disease-free. Jonas Salk's polio cure was one of the lifesaving medical discoveries of the twentieth century. Many people recall the fear and crippling caused by the disease, and realize how far we've come. Thanks to Dr. Salk, the United States was declared to be polio free in 1979. Someone asked who owns the vaccine. Deflecting the praise he received, Dr. Salk said, "The people! Could you patent the sun?"

NOTES

1. "Testimony," *HHS.gov* (Washington, DC: November 13, 2003), http://www.hhs.gov/asl/testify/t031113.html.
2. "'A Calculated Risk': The Salk Polio Vaccine Field Trials of 1954," *NCBI*, http://www.ncbi.nlm.nih.gov/pmc/articles/PMC1114166/.
3. "Polio Disease—Questions and Answers," *Centers for Disease Control and Prevention*, http://www.cdc.gov/vaccines/vpd-vac/polio/dis-faqs.htm.

FALLEN PEACE CORPS HEROES

JEREMIAH MACK

His mom describes him as funny, charming, loving, genuine, loyal, but intense. Certainly, the word courageous needs to be included. Any untried, innocent, young person who marches off to do battle with a hostile world in a foreign land must arm himself with courage.

Jeremiah Mack was born in Portland, Maine, to Donna and Michael, who raised him mostly in Stoughton and Raynham, Massachusetts. He, however, chose a life of travel, new vistas, and challenges, thus putting himself in Africa with the Peace Corps. He was a tall Adonis with a pleasant smile who joined the American Peace Corps in 1995. He ended up in Niger, Africa, where he lived nearly two years, teaching the local masons to construct *maisons sans bois,* houses without wood. He loved what he was doing.

Prior to going to Niger, Jeremiah had graduated from Boston College High School in 1989 and Tulane University in 1993. From Tulane, he migrated to Breckenridge, Colorado, for two more years where he worked as a busboy, lift operator, and learned the trade of stonemason. It was this skill that he took to Niger. All this time, he was training, building on, and planning for a tour with the Peace Corps.

On Mother's Day, 1997, he phoned home to talk with his loving mom and beautiful sister. He was happy and excited about the trip he was going to make in July to visit them. He spoke of plans for the future and a new love. He spent the evening with friends in Niamey. Next morning he climbed into his open bush vehicle and started for a friend's village to install some windows.

A pedestrian walked into the roadway. Jeremiah swerved to miss the man and was thrown from his truck. He landed against some boulders and died instantly. To have known Jeremiah is to love him. Because of his courage, he is still an inspiration to everyone.

JESSE THYNE

Ask any student. There are teachers, then there are teachers who make a difference in the lives of their students. One of those teachers who made a difference was Jesse Thyne. While he tutored only briefly in the United States, he made a contribution in Guinea. What he did impressed students there. They speak of him in glowing terms. "He wanted to help teach children," they said.

Jesse, who made friends easily, touched the hearts of those he met. He always made a strong impression. In Guinea, tribalism is a way of life. Each tribe wanted Jesse to commit to one or the other. While taking an African name, he would not be drawn into the trap. Instead, he fused the two names into one—*El Hadji Abdoulaye Diallo-Bah*. Thus he was able to fulfill his dream of teaching, but to both tribes. Regretfully, Jesse's dream came to a sudden and tragic end.

On January 7, 2000, because of terrible and neglected road conditions, twenty-four-year-old Jesse perished in a bush taxi crash on a narrow dirt road outside Pita. At the time, he was a second-year Pasadena City College math student. He loved cooking, playing harmonica, tutoring elementary kids, and making everyone laugh. While in Guinea, he wrote hundreds of letters to friends at home. Because of the close connections he had, his death hit hard those left behind. His legacy continues in the village library that the Peace Corps constructed and dedicated to honor his memory and the impact that he made on so many in such a brief time.

His death cut short his plans to continue public service. When his Peace Corps time was up, he was going to teach math to inner-city kids in Washington, DC. Friends and his former students say, "He was a light to all who knew him. We will always remember the joy and the love he brought to his work, and to us." Locals built a memorial in Pita, Guinea, and named a school for him. He remains vibrantly alive to those who knew and loved Jesse Thyne.

BETH BOWERS

Like all other Peace Corps Volunteers, Beth Bowers was someone who thought the world should be a better place for everyone. Like all other Peace Corps volunteers, she was active with a purpose. Since childhood, Beth had fly-fished with her dad, studied piano, attended karate classes to earn a black belt, and attended every summer Ashland Shakespeare production staged. She was on the dance team, was co-captain of the cheerleaders, sang in the school music productions, and achieved the honor of valedictorian of her graduating class.

Beth grew up in a pastoral setting near Salem, Oregon. She marveled at the peacocks that roamed the neighborhood. Her white pony was a unicorn even if no one else could see the horn.

When it came time for college, she chose Earlham in Indiana because it had a Japanese Studies program, emphasized peace, and because no one else whom she knew was going there. She took up skydiving, rode horses, and spent her junior year at the University of Tokyo. On a trip to Southeast Asia, she decided she needed more exposure to underdeveloped countries to gain a true global picture. She knew that the Peace Corps was the ideal place to learn.

Armed with a knowledge of fish and of fishing with her father, Beth chose the fish-farming program in Zambia. The place was remote, far from the nearest village. She learned that being assigned to the outer regions of Zambia was one of the most hazardous Peace Corps jobs. Hikes with family in the rugged mountains of Oregon had prepared her for the task. She was already familiar with the rhythm of rural life. She took to the fish-farming program in a wink.

On March 6, 2002, Beth was riding her bike to a meeting. Details of what happened on the way are sketchy, but she was tossed from her bike and suffered serious injuries and died. Beth is described as a child of light, an adventurer of the spirit, and a seeker of world peace. Her dream lives on in the memorial library built to honor her and through her warmth and light.

JOHN PARROTT

He belongs to that group of visionaries, activists, and scholars who see the world as a place in need of change. John Parrott was a person of unending curiosity. As an adolescent, he chose the education channels on television and watched *Mr. Science* instead of brain-numbing sitcoms. He loved the chemistry set he received for Christmas one year. He attended Boys State where he was a National Merit Finalist—all the while working full time to help support the family.

Like 50 percent of the population, he doubted the rhetoric about security, justice, and equality. His parents said, "He lived without delusions."

In college, he majored in mathematics and investigated the new emerging science of computers. He also studied German, Chinese, Latin, and Swahili. While at Florida State University, John became involved in the Congress of Racial Equality. This brought him hate mail and arrests for marches and sit-ins.

At war with the conditions in America in 1965, John joined the Peace Corps. During the interview, the interviewer said, "John is not a bland applicant." They sent him to Kenya, where he ended up at Lake Turkana. Here he helped build a fish and crocodile meat factory. The place, like many Peace Corps assignments, was far from a city. There, he lived a harsh and cruel life.

He lived among the political changes taking place in Africa and America. In Los Angeles, blacks burned south Los Angeles in race riots. In Kenya, nationalism was taking over the country. Unrest, danger, and threats to the lives of everyone were common. Despite it all, John enjoyed the natural beauty of East Africa and the visits to Lake Nakuru.

John vanished. They found the remains of his body on the shores of the lake. At just twenty-two, another Peace Corps volunteer had seen his last sunset in Africa.

NOTES

1. "Heroes of War and Peace," *Fallen Peace Corps Volunteers: Memorial Project*, http:// fpcv.org/heroes-of-war-and-peace. (Permission to use *FPCV* sites given by Donna Mack, a mother of a fallen Peace Corps volunteer.)

2. "Elizabeth Bowers," *Fallen Peace Corps Volunteers: Memorial Project*, http://fpcv.org /volunteers/elizabeth-bowers/.

3. "Jeremiah Mack," *Fallen Peace Corps Volunteers: Memorial Project*, http://fpcv.org /volunteers/jeremiah-mack/.

4. "Jesse Patrick Thyne," *Fallen Peace Corps Volunteers: Memorial Project*, http://fpcv .org /volunteers/jesse-patrick-thyne/.

5. "John Parrott," *Fallen Peace Corps Volunteers: Memorial Project*, http://fpcv.org /volunteers/john-parrott/.

TRACKS ACROSS
THE CONTINENT

The vision of one man led to the building of the transcontinental railroad. While the rest of the nation was still doubtful, Theodore Judah dreamed of a railroad that would connect the East with the West. He had graduated from Rensselaer Polytechnic Institute. With diploma in hand, he set about to build two railroads—the Niagara Gorge followed by the Troy and Schenectady.

He helped build the Erie Canal, a common mode of transportation at the time, yet he still dreamed of building railroads. In 1854, he left for the West to lay out a railroad near Sacramento, California. Obsessed with his dream of a transcontinental railroad, he talked some men into supporting the plan. The Central Pacific Railroad sprang to life.

Becoming dissatisfied with these men, Theodore looked for financial support elsewhere. While railroads were spreading like large rooting systems east of the Mississippi, they hadn't taken root in the West. He was so eager to build the railroad that people called him "Crazy Judah." In the face of smiles, snickers, outright disbelief, and hurtful ridicule, he defied the naysayers when he built the Sacramento railroad line. It connected San Francisco to the gold country via Sacramento to become the first railroad built in the West.

Ever possessed with his dream, Judah traveled to Washington, DC to lobby Congress for support where he planted the seed of a transcontinental railroad. He came home convinced that the line had to be built by businessmen, not by the craftiness of politicians or the slower-than-molasses-in-January workings of the government.

To this end he continued to search for a route through the High Sierras. One of his biggest problems was finding financial backing. He was eager when he received an invitation from Doc Strong, a storekeeper at Dutch Flat in the Donner Pass. In July 1860, the two of them climbed the easy, continuous rise that a steam engine needed to climb to get through the Sierras. He came home happy, as excited as a boy on his first date, to push his dream even further. He had found a way!

Once Judah had done his groundwork, found a route, drawn plans, and presented his plan in Sacramento, investors appeared as if sprung from the earth. Collis Huntington attended one of Judah's meetings. He invited the engineer to meet secretly, at which time he offered 1,500 dollars for the countryside. As his fortune grew, he bought a grocery store that brought in money he could invest.

Fed up with being a lawyer, Leland Stanford joined the mad rush to California. Unlike some of the others, he did not come for gold, but arrived later in 1852. Like his future partners, he became a part owner in a wholesale grocery. By 1860, the store was booming with business, and Judah had become the sole owner. He formed a mutual admiration with Huntington, Hopkins, and Crocker. Through his energy, success, and sheer presence, he would eventually be nominated for governor.

If a mountain could be a man, Charles Crocker was one. Besides Judah, he was the only board member, who had traveled any part of the road. In 1849, he left Indiana leading a team of emigrants across the Platte Valley, heading straight for Sacramento. Actually, he traveled the future route of the Pacific Railroad. He tried mining but failed. Like his future partners, he opted for a less strenuous job as a dry goods merchant. In 1860, they offered him a piece of the railroad, and he jumped aboard. The Big Four, as they came to be known, was now formed.

Although Judah had great dreams and skills in planning the railroad, he had little cash. He was promised an equal share of the company plus a position on the board that eventually included Doc Strong. In 1861, Judah and Strong traveled to the Sierras to map the route for the railroad. He was excited to see his dream turning into something solid. For many years, the South had been the force that blocked the building of a railroad. With the coming of the Civil War, that block vanished. Congress quickly passed a railroad act to aid in the construction.

"We have drawn the elephant, now let us see if we can harness him up," Judah telegraphed to his partners. His enthusiasm did not last long.

By 1863, the others steadily alienated him. More and more they kept Judah in the dark about plans. As construction moved along, he saw that the quality was not being maintained. Since Congress had placed a condition that the railroad be completed by 1876, speed became the motive. Also, the Central Pacific Company and the Union Pacific building from the East were paid by the mile. They would receive 16,000 dollars per mile for level land, 36,000 dollars per mile for hilly land, and 48,000 dollars per mile for building through mountains. The more miles they built, the more money they made. They also received 6,400 acres of land per mile. Judah's partners were concerned only with profits, not the engineer's vision.

Owners of the Central Pacific were unhappy with how slowly work progressed on the railroad. At the end of the first twenty-three miles stood the High Sierras, some ten to fourteen thousand feet high. Someone suggested that they use Chinese labor, but others thought the Chinese to be too small. Charles Crocker retorted, "The Chinese built the Great Wall of China, didn't they?" In 1865, the owners hired Chinese to lay ties and set dynamite for the dangerous work of blasting.

To conquer the many sheer cliffs, foremen lowered the workers in baskets, and while hanging there, the Chinese hammered away at the solid granite and then planted explosives. In building the tunnels, they pounded the holes and set explosives and ran for their lives. Some did not make it. They worked for about twenty-eight dollars a month, lived in mud huts, cooked their own food, consisting of fish, dried oysters, mushrooms, and seaweed. Once in a while they could find some fruit.

In addition to the mountain barriers, the Central Pacific faced harsh winters that also took lives. The Big Four, however, did not have to deal with the trickery of the mobile credit that drained millions of dollars away from the Union Pacific. Nor did they have to deal with hostile tribes who resented the laying of tracks across their land. The Central Pacific owners bought them with passes for free rides on the line. When the Union had made it through the Rockies, and the Central had made it through the Sierras, they began a race. Whoever could lay more track, received more money. Workers of each railroad raced to lay the most track in a day. The Central won when the workers laid ten miles of track one day. A sign still stands at the spot.

Eventually, construction crews ignored each other and continued to build side-by-side but in opposite directions, hoping to be paid for the track they laid. Congress stopped this and, on May 10, 1869, the rails met at Promontory Point, Utah. Judah had tied East and West. The whole nation cheered. Sadly, Theodore Judah did not celebrate what he had begun. Sometime earlier, on a trek through Panama, he had been bitten by malaria mosquitoes, contracted yellow fever, and died.

NOTES

1. John Debo Galloway, *The First Transcontinental Railroad* (New York: Simmons -Boardman, 1950), 52–93.
2. Helen Hinckley, *Rails from the West: A Biography of Theodore D. Judah* (San Marino, California: Golden West Books, 1969).
3. Deborah Blake, "The Driving of the Golden Spike, Utah," *OnlineUtah.com*, http:// www.onlineutah.com/golden_spike_history_05.shtml.
4. Robert E. Riegel, *America Moves West* (New York: Henry Holt & Company, 1931).
5. J. David Rogers, *Theodore Judah and the Blazing of the First Transcontinental Railroad over the Sierra Nevadas* (Berkeley, California: University of California Department of Civil and Environmental Engineering, unpublished), http://web.mst.edu/-rogersda /american&military_history/theodore%20judah%20and%20the%20blazing%20 of%20the%20first%20transcontinental%20railroad-Sierra%20Nevada-Rogers.pdf.
6. "Driving the Last Spike," *The Virtual Museum of the City of San Francisco*, www .sfmuseum.org/hist1/rail.html.
7. Robert M. Utley and Francis A. Ketterson Jr., *Golden Spike* (Washington, DC: National Park Service, 1969).

PIRATE PATRIOT

On September 23, 1779, John Paul Jones lashed his ship, the USS *Bonhomme Richard*, to the British HMS *Serapis*. He was about to engage in battle. The British ship of forty-four guns and the *Countess of Scarborough* of twenty-eight guns were leading a convoy back from the Baltic. Jones met the British convoy at Flamborough Head in the North Sea. The Flamborough Head is an eight-mile promontory of chalk cliffs on the Yorkshire coast of England. The waters are always in turmoil with winds blistering ship and sailor alike. Seals play in the choppy surf, and the temperatures sometimes rise to 60 degrees in the summer.

Captain Jones had been sailing these waters since late 1777. He raided the English shipping, looking for ways to distress the British. On several occasions he had seized their ships, made a raid on land against Whitehaven, England, and captured the British twenty-gun warship, *Drake*. In all these adventures he was successful. The British called him a pirate. The Americans called him a hero and a patriot.

It was seven in the evening when Jones closed with the *Serapis*. They were like two floating mountains buffeted by an unforgiving storm. His ship was blasted in the first exchange of cannon fire. Much of his firepower was destroyed. The blast killed many of his gunners. Richard Pearson, captain of the British ship, called above the noise of battle, "Do you surrender?" It was at this moment Jones called back with his now-immortal reply, "I have not yet begun to fight!"

What followed was bloody and fierce. With the two ships literally locked together, they could not escape or make a run for it. With the blood rushing through their veins like a rumble of thunder in their ears, sharpshooting United States Marines and sailors in Jones's top ranks raked the *Serapis* with gunfire. They swept its decks from bow to stern. John Paul felt the surge of blood through his veins and the hair on his arms bristle as he wielded his sword and waded into the heart of battle. As his crew continued the fight, they could feel the heat at their backs from fires that burned their ship. The *Bonhomme Richard* was taking water into the holds and sinking under them.

One of Jones's men finally threw a grenade down the hatchway of the *Serapis*. The explosion blew the innards of the ship apart like a bursting watermelon. The lower deck splintered into matchwood and crumbled like fallen timbers. Both ships looked like Swiss cheese with holes blown in their sides and rigging sprawled across the decks. The Americans repelled one final attack before Captain Pearson decided he'd had enough. He hauled down the British flag.

Jones and the remains of his crew climbed aboard the *Serapis* at half past ten, four hours after the battle began, to watch their gallant *Bonhomme* sink into the icy waters of the North Sea.

Courageous John Paul Jones died in France in 1792. Royalty buried him in a lead coffin in St. Louis Cemetery, which belonged to the French Royal Family. Four years later, France's new revolutionary government sold the cemetery and promptly forgot about his grave.

In 1854, an American colonel tried to bring Jones's body home. Since he had been born in Scotland before coming to America, Scottish relatives did not allow it, burying him in an abandoned cemetery. In 1905, the American ambassador began a thorough search. Jones was found. Immediately, no nonsense President Teddy Roosevelt said, "Speak softly, but carry a big stick," and sent four cruisers to bring Jones home. Needless to say, John Paul Jones came home to rest in the Naval Academy Chapel.

Friends and fellow navy men remember him for his strong will and refusal to surrender when the slightest hope of victory was still in sight. "He gave our navy its earliest traditions of heroism and victory with honor."